Praise for *When Jesu*

'An absolutely engrossing read from the vɛ ... ...drew takes us into the psychedelic fabric of the Jesus People Movement, offering a candid, insider perspective of the messiness, colour, and spirituality of a unique moment in both Church history ... and pop culture.

I was struck not so much by the big names – the Wimbers, the Kendricks and the Greens – but by the impact on regular men and women at a time when the traditional church did not seem to have much traction. Andrew demonstrates that the Jesus People did not simply fight decay in the Church, but brought something fresh, a movement that revitalised the faith across many nations, with echoes reverberating to this day.

The book weaves together story after story from multitudes of angles. The result is one consistent narrative of what God was doing behind the scenes – transforming lives, breaking addictions, restoring brokenness and connecting the lonely into his family. The depth of colour and richness of detail was astounding – I wholeheartedly recommend this book!'

Revd Andy du Feu, Principal, Moorlands College

'Andrew Whitman's *When Jesus Met Hippies* has done yeoman work in highlighting the heretofore underrated impact of the 1970s Jesus People Movement upon the evolution of the British religious scene. Far from being merely an American import, Whitman demonstrates that the Jesus People in their UK manifestations developed distinctive adaptations of the movement within a British context that have had profound knock-on effects down into the present-day. *When Jesus Met Hippies* is a must-read for those interested in both the international dimensions of the Jesus People Movement, and the forces that have shaped contemporary evangelicalism in the UK.'

***Larry Eskridge, Author of* God's Forever Family:
The Jesus People Movement in America**

'I welcome this well-researched account of the many diverse and lasting impacts of the Jesus Movement in the British Church. It is a work of double value: recording much that might otherwise be forgotten but also raising vital and relevant issues of how the Church responds when God's Spirit works.'

J.John, Evangelist, Speaker and Author

'Every old Jesus Freak should read this, as well as everyone who has inherited the spoils of this mighty move of God.

This is our story of revival from 1967-74. It is hard to encompass all the varying strains of this vast movement, yet Andrew has masterfully encapsulated the whole messy miracle-laden time when God's presence was thick like a blanket.

Representing hours of exhaustive research and interviews with those who lived the life, Andrew has conveyed the breadth of a modern-day great awakening, crisscrossing ministries, and continents, culminating in a UK story that has never been told.

Weaving an intricate, multi-layered narrative, the reader gets an overview of a generation outside the establishment rocked to its core – exhausted dropouts who finally gave in to Jesus. From barefooted, longhaired hippies entering sacred sanctuaries to raw new converts baptising and discipling their peers, Andrew interlaces that unwieldy, multi-faceted time of salvation with astute cultural analysis.

There is reassurance here when wondering whether all those scrappy, burned-out times sleeping on floors in overcrowded communes and church pews, living on peanut butter and jelly sandwiches, setting up bands on street corners to get the word out, were all worth it. Andrew has documented the answer.

Yes, it was.'

Susan Palosaari Cowper, Jesus Family Co-founder, Archivist and Writer

'I love to hear stories of "heaven touching earth", known by some as revivals, by others as awakenings. Andrew Whitman's book is more than a mere "history of" – it's a personal insight into a "spiritual awakening" amongst a generation of youth, initially in the USA that spread like wildfire to the UK, Europe, and even as far as Australia. Andrew himself was impacted. His book therefore is full of relevant context and cultural reflections and considerations of the consequences.

Though coming from a Christian family and a different church tradition in my own spiritual journey, his writings awakened memories that I share about names, music and places that were central to our story. This book, more than anything else, defines what a sovereign move of God looks, sounds, and feels like. My heart response, as ever, is "Sovereign Lord, do it again" and in our times "May Jesus Christ be made known."'

Revd Canon Chris Bowater OSL, GRSM, LRAM, ARCM, DipEd
Worship Leader, Songwriter, Author and Pastor

'I am most grateful to Andrew for this scholarly and insightful book. I trust that through it, God would inform your mind, stir your spirit and raise your faith for another great move of his Spirit!'

Gareth Lloyd-Jones, Senior Pastor Ridgeway Community
Church and Team Leader of Kinetic Network

'What an interesting and stimulating read! Andrew writes extensively and engagingly about the Jesus People Movement, a movement splattered with revival. Before reading *When Jesus Met Hippies*, although having a strong interest in Church history, I was unaware of how Jesus People had inspired the Greenbelt Festival and, in turn, the plethora of festivals we enjoy today. There is much to glean from the marks of the Jesus People Movement. I am particularly inspired by the observation that the Jesus People had "well-thumbed Bibles". Knowing Andrew personally, this is true for him, and what I pray will be true for the next generation.

Andrew sheds light on the precious legacy that we now enjoy the fruit from. This book certainly builds faith and expectancy for what God can do, particularly through young people. Oh, how I long to see youth as the forerunners of evangelism, so "Do it again, Lord!"'

Samantha Pink, Youth and Children's Pastor, GodFirst Church, Christchurch, Dorset

'I really enjoyed Andrew's overview of the Jesus People Movement. I found it both inspiring and instructive. It encourages us to look to the Lord to "do it again" while at the same time being aware of some of the pitfalls and excesses in any such movement.

Andrew shows that the 1970s – a time of social, economic, and political upheaval – was no barrier to the Lord working in a powerful way; in fact in many ways, it precipitated it. This encouraged me to pray that we might see a new move of God in this generation that would bring many to Jesus.

It is easy to think that history is linear – we can assume that things are either getting steadily better (as some secular progressives would suggest) or continually worse (as some conservative Christians fear). In reality, the history of the Church has been cyclical with times of decline eventually replaced with seasons of growth.

Perhaps we will see the tide of God's blessing come in again during our lifetime – Andrew's book will certainly cause us to long and pray for that to be the case.'

Michael Ots, Evangelist, Author and Field Director of the Fellowship of Evangelists in the Universities of Europe (FEUER)

When Jesus Met Hippies

The story and legacy of the
Jesus People Movement in the UK

ANDREW WHITMAN

malcolm down
PUBLISHING

First published in 2023 by

malcolm down
PUBLISHING

www.malcolmdown.co.uk

27 26 25 24 23   7 6 5 4 3 2 1

The right of Andrew Whitman to be identified as the author of this work has been asserted by him in accordance with the Copyright, Designs and Patents Act 1988.

British Library Cataloguing in Publication Data
A catalogue record for this book is available from the British Library.

ISBN 978-1-915046-72-7

Unless otherwise indicated, Scripture quotations are taken from
New International Version (Anglicised edition)
Copyright ©1979, 1984, 2011 by Biblica (formerly International Bible Society).
Used by permission of Hodder & Stoughton Publishers, an Hachette UK company.
All rights reserved.
'NIV' is a registered trademark of Biblica (formerly International Bible Society).
UK trademark number 1448790.

Cover design by Esther Kotecha
Art direction by Sarah Grace

Printed in the UK

Typeset using Atomik ePublisher from Easypress Technologies.

On the seventieth anniversary of my natural birth, and the fiftieth of my new birth in Christ, I thank my God: Father, Son and Holy Spirit.

I gladly dedicate this book to my Whitman family. To my parents, Michael (d. 2004) and Nan and my siblings, Richard and Claire. To my wife Rosie, and our two sons and their families: Philip and Naomi, Riley, Emelia and Cleo, and Thomas and Sophie with Judah, Abel, Isaac and Boaz. And to the future generations to come...

Additionally, I want to thank my Jesus Family, who brought me to faith in the summer of 1973. To benefactors, Kenneth and Pauline Frampton (d. 1988 and 2007 respectively). To pioneer leaders, Jim (d. 2011) and Susan Palosaari Cowper. To the disciple-makers, Christian and Sabine Beese, and the prayerful encouragers, Dave and Ginny Hoyt. Finally, to Jesus Family members across the UK and USA today... this is for *you*.

Contents

Part 3: The Jesus People Predictions

PART 1

The Jesus People Beginnings

1.

When Jesus Strides In, the Echoes Sound Out

Echoes bounced around the four walls.

It was coffee time. People gathered in the church welcome area after the service. There was no soundproofing installed, so conversation was hampered.

I'd just met Josh for the first time and, as good Brits do, we asked each other what we did for a living. He was in his third year reading History. I was a retired pastor writing a book.

'What's your book about then?' Josh asked.

'Oh, you'd never have heard of it in a million years!' I replied.

'Try me,' he said.

'I'm writing about the Jesus People revival of the 1970s.'

'Actually, I've heard of it. Perhaps in a talk, or maybe a Q and A session, from either Todd White or Michael Koulianos.'

We began to chat some more about the Jesus People, the early connections to the Vineyard movement and Lonnie Frisbee's renowned Mothers' Day Service of 1980.

The names Josh had mentioned intrigued me. Two current leaders picking up on the echoes of a revival that stretched back to the hippy counterculture of the well-publicised 'Summer of Love' in 1967.

The longest recorded echo of all time lasted seventy-five seconds.

It was produced and measured by two men in Scotland on 3 June 2012 in a tunnel twice the length of a football pitch. The first man, Trevor Cox, was Professor of Acoustic Engineering at Salford University. The second, Allan Kilpatrick, looked after historical Scottish monuments for a living. He was an expert at the Inchindown test site, an abandoned fuel bunker built before the Second World War in the Scottish Highlands.

On that momentous day, Kilpatrick fired a pistol loaded with blanks, while Professor Cox recorded the response through microphones situated at the far end of the tunnel. Using a standard technique borrowed from concert hall acoustics, Cox had never experienced such a sound before. At the start, he played around by shouting out loud and found that the noise just kept going. But when he fired the pistol, he could not believe it. He instantly knew it was a world record. It made it into the *Guinness Book of Records*, having confidently beaten the previous record by sixty seconds.

It is now more than fifty years since the birth of the Jesus People Movement (JPM).

Is it time to consider the enduring echoes of a movement often considered a revival? And explore how it has significantly impacted the culture of the UK and how it might refresh our faith today?

Before trying to answer these vital questions, it's important to understand what the Jesus People Movement was all about.

In essence, the JPM was a season where God saved and moved in the hearts of hippies in the USA. The movement is often said to have begun in California, but this is only partially true. There were breakouts of what God was doing right across North America. It didn't seem as though these occurrences were coordinated. However, as the movement grew, Jesus People soon began to swap notes and exchange ideas.

The movement began against the backdrop of enormous social upheaval in post-war America with a church seemingly unable to connect with the youth and counterculture of the day. Hippies who had met Jesus would have felt like 'fish out of water'. It lasted for about seven years from 1967-74, particularly grabbing the headlines of the watching media and the fascinated public in 1971.

Initially, converted hippies reached people like themselves. Often called 'street people', they chatted about Jesus on the pavements and invited people into their communes. Discipling of new believers, many from dysfunctional families, took place and everything happened so quickly it was difficult to pause for breath. A few established churches were supportive, but the majority were not.

Later, existing Christian youth jumped on the bandwagon too as they'd become disillusioned with the dinosaur-like faith of their parents' generation.

In the early seventies, the news spread far and wide in an age without social media. It quickly crossed the Atlantic over to Europe, right down to Australasia and was embraced by many young people. Homegrown Jesus People ministries were initiated, with the USA being the lead inspirators. This didn't mean, however, that Jesus People ministries weren't adapted for their own cultural contexts.

There was a flurry of books, articles, and debates in the USA. Some were positive, others less so, but there was no doubt that people were starting to reflect. What on earth was going on?

Towards the tail-end of the JPM, the counterculture movement was also disappearing. However, the spiritual traction of the Jesus People hadn't stopped. Rather, it had morphed and dispersed. Many new believers married and started families, participated in training or tied down regular jobs, and they soon became responsible for mortgage or rent payments. They were faced with a challenge. How can they face the pressure of adult life without losing their newfound zeal for Jesus? And out in the community, new churches were emerging and youth mission agencies benefitted from an influx of impassioned workers.

The impact of the JPM is still felt today, particularly now that its fifty-year jubilee has come and gone. Many leaders are announcing the advent of an imminent 'new Jesus People revival'.

Asbury College in Kentucky, previously touched by the JPM, had a further awakening in February 2023, which was livestreamed globally. Greg Laurie's *Jesus Revolution*[1] was released the same month, with unexpected box-office success. Back in the UK, Chroma Church in Leicester saw 150 new Jesus followers added to their ranks in 2022. They are encouraging Christians and churches to seek God for revival today.

*

But was the JPM a revival? How can we describe what God graciously did in transforming hippies into Jesus People during that season?

Many people do use overtly biblical terms such as revival or awakening.

Jesus People historian David Di Sabatino identifies the themes and influences of the movement as 'a classic Christian revival' that displays 'elements of conservative Christian revivalism'.[2]

He especially highlights this revival as displaying a spiritual experience that is geared towards warm feelings rather than cold thinking. In December 2013, the UK's Jesus Liberation Front leader Geoff Bone also described the movement as a revival.[3]

One early participant, Baptist Pastor Kent Philpott, identifies the JPM as an 'awakening', probably the fourth great awakening in America's history. For him, it clearly has 'the marks of a genuine spiritual revival or awakening', further explained by his reference to three historians of awakenings, including the renowned Jonathan Edwards and his five signs of awakenings. Philpott shrewdly concludes though, that 'like every genuine revival or awakening, the ending of the sovereign moving of God may open the door to human efforts to exploit or continue the awakening'.[4]

Others prefer to use non-biblical language to identify the Jesus People as a revolution, movement, or revitalisation.

On a popular level, the word 'revolution' is used by Californian pastor and evangelist Greg Laurie, who came to know Jesus during the movement. Even though he also describes it as surfing in the wake of eighteenth-century American 'revivals'. Despite this, in his popularly written book and 2023 film of the same name, Laurie labels it the *Jesus Revolution*. Laurie prefers the word 'revolution' for two reasons: first, it marks the spiritual revolution of people from the inside-out, described by Jesus as a new birth; second, it signifies a historical revolution that brings people's focus back to Jesus.[5] In 1973, UK Anglican clergyman Geoffrey Corry used precisely the same term in his booklet *Jesus Bubble or Jesus Revolution*.[6]

From a historical angle, 'movement' is used by leading scholar Larry Eskridge in the introduction to his excellent book *God's Forever Family*.

Fully recognising that many viewed the Jesus People as the promise of something bigger to come, Eskridge himself chooses the description of a 'religious movement' that was 'one of the most significant American religious phenomena of the postwar period'.[7] Interestingly, Larry was a participant in the movement. As a senior high school student in the Chicago area in the 1970s, he engaged with its Jesus rallies, coffeehouses, 'One Way' signs and street papers.

What about a 'revitalisation'? A sociological perspective comes front and centre in this concept.

Kevin John Smith was an Australian JPM leader and biker-minister, renowned in the UK for roaring into Greenbelt Festivals at full-throttle. He discusses the potential descriptions of the JPM as a revival or a revitalisation in the first chapter of his book *The Origins, Nature, and Significance of the Jesus Movement*.

Smith perceives revival as 'usually associated with sizeable gatherings, highly emotional evangelistic meetings, and mass conversions to the faith'.[8] He proceeds to argue they emphasise personal salvation rather than cultural transformation. Conversely, Smith speaks of a revitalisation movement as God breathing fresh life into lifeless churches and youth ministries during a time of cultural decay.

In this book, I have chosen to use the term 'movement' about the Jesus People Movement (JPM), whilst personally holding the view that it was a revival of sorts. As 'revival' is commonly used vaguely, I offer my own working definition:

'An awe-inspiring work of God within a large group of people where he restores godly faith to believers and births saving faith in Jesus in the hearts of those who don't yet believe. From there, the Holy Spirit usually impacts their local communities and wider societies.'

Across a broad spectrum, some 'revivals' focus more on existing believers coming to fresh spiritual life. Whereas others concentrate on new believers first receiving eternal life. My contention is that the American JPM was the latter. It zoned in on the lost during the 1960s counterculture years. This led to a vast tranche of young people being converted and discipled and, as a result, uplifted a generation who were searching for hope.

However, why am I choosing to use the word 'movement' in this book? I have three reasons.

Firstly, 'a revival' sounds like a single entity or a cohesive occurrence. However, the Holy Spirit was working through the JPM in many places and diverse ways, both in the USA and the UK.

Secondly, even if we describe the American movement as a full-blown 'revival', it was not quite so prolific in the UK. It would probably be more accurate to say 'pockets of revival'. Writing from the UK perspective, then, movement is more appropriate.

Finally, it could be misleading to lump together authoritarian cults and their off-beat theology with 'a revival', particularly when its source is regularly ascribed to 'the Spirit of truth' (John 16:13).

Although we hear a clear echo of the movement from across the Atlantic in the UK, this echo was complemented by other homegrown sounds too. How? Let's do two things: look through a zoom lens at how my own story was largely part of this movement before then focusing a wide-angle lens on the larger American story of 1967-74.

2.

This is Your Life, But Not on Television

My Story[1]

I was born on 1 May 1953 into the Baby Boomer generation.

Raised by parents who owned a mixed farm producing milk and corn, I lived outside a town called Enfield, tucked just inside the M25 which circles around London. My parents met not long after the Second World War ended. My mum was my dad's nurse in hospital, love blossomed and after marrying, they both became hard-working farmers. They were nominally Christian in their moral values, but not yet followers of Jesus.

During my primary school years, they packed me off to the nearby village Sunday School where we played a game called Draw Your Swords – a race to flick to different Bible verses. There were also sweets for learning memory verses. Apart from this, my only other exposure to the gospel was being dragged along to the Bible group Crusaders by my school friend, Graham.

The roots of this early exposure to the gospel did not yet go down deep. In 1971, I went to Leeds University to study Economics, hoping to become a Chartered Accountant. Not long after, I was protesting on the city's streets against 'Maggie Thatcher, Milk Snatcher'. When it came to studying, I'd say I learnt more about music, beer, dope, and women than economics. I was drawn into the hippy movement as an inquisitive but cautious participant. Smoking my fair share of cannabis with housemates

9

and friends, I did the usual rounds of gigs and festivals. Many people I knew were tripping on acid and taking speed. It perhaps goes without saying that my first two years of university were highly experimental but nothing ever satisfied me.

It was in this same year of 1971 that I was surprised to find that my younger sister Claire had become a Christian after receiving a Gideon New Testament at school. The next year, my brother Richard followed her, and I distinctly remember giving them a hard time for their new-found faith. I was involved in the enlightened hippy culture with its curious mixture of high ideals and wild experimentation and they were going in a different direction. They pressed on though. Attending a local Open Brethren church, they quickly began using their musical skills by serving alongside local evangelists like Doug Barnett.

Summer 1973 was a formative season for me.

I was spending the summer at home before embarking on my final year of study in Leeds. I worked on the farm during the harvest, carting corn from the fields to the barn and later stacking bales onto the trailers. Over the August Bank Holiday weekend, Richard and Claire invited me to a Christian rock musical called *Lonesome Stone*. Staged at the iconic Rainbow Theatre in Finsbury Park, it was not far from Highbury football ground where my much-loved Arsenal Football Club played. At the time, it was a famous rock music venue, hosting the likes of Van Morrison, Lou Reed and Genesis. The presentation was put on by the Jesus Family community, hailing originally from Milwaukee, but now based in south London.

Looking back, I can see God was drawing me to go, seemingly 'against my own will'.

I went two nights running and was mesmerised by a story that featured a 'lonesome' hippy-type coming to know Jesus. God particularly spoke to me through the song 'Goin' Back'. These lyrics seemed to strike a chord (excuse the pun).

'I think I'm going back to the Lord I once knew in my youth; I think I'm returning to the days when I was young enough to know the truth.'[2]

The simplicity of my Sunday School days quickly resurfaced.

On the first night of the show, I wandered around afterwards hoping a cast member would approach me for a chat. Nothing happened, so I went up to a member of the Jesus Family who played the 'second drunk' in the cast. He was a young German man called Christian Beese. He patiently listened to my story and then prayed for real peace to surround us and for Jesus to make himself known to me. I can't remember praying any kind of 'sinner's prayer', but in that moment, I knew I wholly trusted Jesus and felt a profound sense of being clean inside.

The image of Jesus on the cross especially captivated me, positively 'ruining' me for anything else for the rest of my life. I duly returned to the show the next night, the final Saturday of *Lonesome Stone*. I linked up with Christian again, joining cast members onstage as they exuberantly celebrated at the end of the show's two-month run.

A few days later, I went out and bought a brown leather Bible[3] and began to hungrily devour it. It was utterly alive! I started going to church with Claire and Richard on Sunday mornings, despite feeling like a cultural fish out of water. A man named Charles Marsh, a retired missionary to Muslims, took my family and me under his spiritual wing. In the manner that Open Brethren churches encouraged, I would occasionally contribute by reading out Scriptures during the meetings.

After my conversion, I returned to university in late September as a new creation in Christ, dreading my final year of studies in economics. My earlier interest had waned immensely, partly because of the profound awakening I had experienced. During the first few weeks, the Christian Union unsuccessfully tried to recruit me. I refused to sign a doctrinal belief statement that was a requirement for membership; that was too structured for a hip believer like me.

Subsequently, I got involved with the Anglican chaplaincy where I was befriended by the curate Stuart Burns, now an Anglican Benedictine abbot. The vicar there surprised me; he agreed to baptise me by full immersion at the local Baptist Church even though I'd been 'christened' as a baby in the Anglican Church. I remember coming up from the water and a candle was placed in my hands. I was now following Jesus, 'the light of the world' (John 8:12).

Around this time, I had a variety of formative influences on my growing faith. In early 1974, I met two couples who had arrived to evangelise and disciple students through Campus Crusade for Christ.[4] I was well-nurtured by one of the couples, Nigel Spencer and his wife Helen. I still remember going out to witness with Nigel in the halls of residence and being thrown in at the deep end.

'Andy, why don't you tell these guys how you became a Jesus follower?'

Meanwhile, Christian, from the Jesus Family in London, was keeping in touch via letter and was always assuring me of his prayers. He also sent me literature that warned me off the cults, stressing that Jesus was the only way to God, and he also encouraged me to receive the baptism in the Holy Spirit.

On Thursday 2 May 1974, the day after my twenty-first birthday, I was instrumental in putting on a gig for the Jesus Family band, The Sheep. This was held in the Union Refectory at Leeds University, and my spiritual mentor, Nigel, helped me organise things. As part of their UK-wide tour, the event was also a promotional gig for the *Lonesome Stone* run at St George's Hall in Bradford later that month. Shortly afterwards, I visited the Jesus Family house at Beulah Hill in Upper Norwood. I can vividly remember Phil Booth from Radio Worldwide leading an eye-opening Bible study on Romans 6 and 'our position in Christ'.

After scraping through university, I became the lead vocalist in a Christian rock band called Sirius. Our aim was to 'hit the road' with Jesus' message. However, most of us were spiritually immature and that plan was quickly shelved. Gifted lead guitarist, Jules Hardwick, went on to be known for playing at the Greenbelt Festival with Steve Fairnie's innovative bands Fish Co. and Writz. Greenbelt was a happy home to the Jesus People Movement in the UK. I attended in 1975 where I reconnected with Jesus Family friends.

Inspired by the Jesus People Movement, I then worked for Campus Crusade for Christ. Through them, I evangelised and discipled students in various universities across the UK. After seven years, I attended London Bible College[5] before getting involved in various local church ministries. In an unfortunate twist of events, I lost touch with Christian a year or so after coming to know Jesus. Happily, though, we reconnected around nine years ago during a sabbatical from church ministry in the summer of 2014.

I flew to Hamburg to visit Christian and his family. The following summer, I returned and had the honour of conducting the wedding service for his daughter Maris and her fiancé Julian.

It had been a long road from spiritual indifference to a radical conversion and on to impacting a future generation. The rest, as they say, is history. Or is it?

Our Story

Subsequently, it took me decades to realise that I had come to know Jesus through a genuine spiritual awakening. This led to the beginning of a long research journey about ten years ago. I wanted to chart the story of the JPM in the UK, not just to retell it, but to also explore its impact and inspire a new generation.

Yet the inescapable fact remains that the Jesus People Movement was first and foremost a phenomenon birthed in the USA.

The Jesus Family, whose *Lonesome Stone* musical was so influential to my conversion, were from Milwaukee in the States. In the well-rehearsed story of 1960s America, 1967 is a pivotal year. Students protesting the Vietnam War became more organised, the use of LSD and marijuana doubled in a year, and San Francisco hosted the 'Summer of Love'. It was in that same city and year that the initial Jesus People are thought to have emerged. They were hippies evangelising to their peers and included Ted and Liz Wise.

Ted was a beatnik, an arty nonconformist predating the hippies. Liz, alongside her dope lifestyle, was a regular at the conservative First Baptist Church of Mill Valley.

Reading the New Testament, Ted said, 'Jesus knocked me off my metaphysical ass!'[6]

After a bad trip on LSD, he had responded to a gospel invitation at Liz's church. Later, they pioneered the Living Room, a storefront outreach centre in the renowned Haight-Ashbury area of San Francisco. They offered food, rest and chat and they saw twenty people coming to Jesus weekly.

Others in San Francisco were Dave Hoyt, a new believer from a Hare

Krishna background, and his friend and Baptist seminarian, Kent Philpott. They would go out and preach on the streets, inviting people back to the Living Room during the day. At different stages, both ministries gained financial support from a group of local Baptist pastors calling themselves 'Evangelical Concerns'.

With such a surge in growth, these ministries began to form communes where inhabitants shared possessions in the early church style as recorded in Acts. In nearby Novato, Ted and Liz Wise started the appropriately named House of Acts. Its impulse towards community living was a blend of both hippy and Christian ideals. The community enjoyed a fruitful time of welcoming newcomers, such as Lonnie Frisbee and his wife Connie. The House of Acts dispersed after eighteen months.

The rapid growth saw similar mission initiatives start and stop, along with the speedy movement of people between groups in various locations. Such quick changes often meant increasingly cult-like groups went unchecked. However, groups like the Children of God and the Way International, both of which were started in 1967, did eventually become recognised as dangerous cults.

The years between 1968 and 1970 were a long hangover from the 'Summer of Love' as social unrest continued to feature. Student protests against the Vietnam War intensified, not helped by President Nixon's promise to withdraw, while secretly initiating the bombing of North Vietnam. Martin Luther King was assassinated in April 1968, followed by race riots in more than a hundred cities. Then there was 1969, the year when cult leader Charles Manson provoked the Manson Family murders. Things were exploding across society and the fallout was unsettling American citizens.

At the same time, God's Spirit was powerfully at work.

'Disillusioned student activists, hippie seekers, drug burnouts, and Christian teenagers looking to put their faith into action were all caught up in a wave of excitement, believing that God's Spirit had brought them all together.'[7]

Many came to faith in Jesus, and despite their tumultuous nature, these years proved to be the most formative for the JPM.

It was in Los Angeles, the same city where the tragic Manson Family murders occurred, that flamboyant Southern Baptist pastor Arthur Blessitt launched his ministry on Sunset Strip.

Next door to a topless club, he opened 'His Place' as a twenty-four-hour ministry for young people. Some neighbours weren't pleased with its influence. After they put pressure on the police, Blessitt was hit with the threat of his lease being terminated. But he wouldn't let that stop him. Blessitt chained himself to a twelve-foot cross and fasted. The ministry continued. This experience became Blessitt's inspiration, along with a word from God, to carry his cross 3,500 miles from Los Angeles to Washington DC in 1970.

One of the most significant meetings in the history of the JPM was between Lonnie Frisbee and Pastor Chuck Smith in 1968.

The hippy evangelist and pastor-teacher played to each other's strengths, and together they facilitated change in countercultural converts and the existing congregation of Calvary Chapel. During Lonnie's time there, 4,000 were converted and half were baptised in the Pacific Ocean nearby. Whilst serving, he and Connie initially ministered alongside another couple called John and Jackie Higgins who were also converted hippies. They worked together to establish communal houses before the Frisbees focused on evangelism and the Higgins placed a heavier emphasis on discipleship and moved on to Oregon, eventually establishing 178 Shiloh House communities nationwide.

This era of growth for the movement saw many leaders and groups emerge. Many were not hippy converts but they sought to use their gifts to evangelise to the prevailing youth culture. In 1969, the Christian World Liberation Front was launched by Dr Jack Sparks. Creatively evangelistic, they published the underground paper *Right On!*, as well as promoting a drama troupe and translating the Bible into hip language. Their Jesus Christ 'Wanted' poster wryly highlighted him 'practising medicine, wine-making and food distribution without a licence'.[8]

Then there was Linda Meissner, who through her experience of working with New York gangs in the early 1960s, initiated the Jesus People Army in Seattle and the Pacific Northwest in 1969. They evangelised to 2,000 people weekly through the Catacombs coffeehouse, launched their *Agape* newspaper, and established communal houses.

One of the most prominent Christian voices of the time was Hal Lindsey, who published *The Late Great Planet Earth*[9] in 1970. His book strongly argued we were living in the end times. Based on the Bible and daily news, it sold twenty million copies and was a must-read for any self-respecting Jesus Freak. The movement was now gathering momentum alongside a growing expectation of Jesus' soon return.

By 1971, what had been a fringe movement became a story for the mainstream media as the Jesus Movement made the front cover of *Time* magazine.

In the same year, Linda Meissner ignored the advice of others by joining the radical Children of God. Before her Jesus People Army dissolved, though, trainee couple Jim and Sue Palosaari started what became the Jesus Family in Milwaukee in 1971. They grew rapidly before heading to Scandinavia, then London, where I was converted through their *Lonesome Stone* musical.

The increased media attention only propelled the use of music and media as evangelistic tools. It also seemed to put the name of Jesus on the pens of popular songwriters and playwrights. What became Contemporary Christian Music (CCM) had its raw, modest beginnings here too. New believers expressed their faith in song, Jesus Festivals emerged, Christian music magazines were launched, and mail-order companies sold cassettes by post. Underground papers also hit the streets, such as Duane Pederson's *The Hollywood Free Paper*, which printed 500,000 copies at its peak.

Finally, in June 1972, the largest event of the JPM was organised.

Explo '72 gathered 80,000 young people intending to train them on how to evangelise across the States. There were morning seminars and afternoon outreach as well as evening meetings where Billy Graham spoke. Performances were given by the most popular Jesus Rocker of the day, Larry Norman, with country musicians Johnny Cash and recent convert, Kris Kristofferson playing too.

Yet this peak was also the beginning of the end.

From 1973 onwards, the hippy counterculture began to fizzle out. There was no need for Vietnam protests as Richard Nixon was committed to pulling troops out. Public discussion and openness to spirituality had marked the era but that was fading too. Ultimately, the travelling evangelism and end-times declarations were replaced by family, vocational and financial responsibilities.

And where was the imminent second coming?

Some people integrated into historic Church denominations that had more intellectual rigour, while others opted for the fresh 'New Paradigm Churches'[10] like Calvary Chapel and the Vineyard Christian Fellowship. In October 1973, sociologist Richard Enroth posed the poignant question, 'Where Have All the Jesus People Gone?'[11]

While the revival years were over, the Jesus People had grown up and dispersed into different and new ventures.

For all those who found a home in evangelical churches, there were others still caught up in the dangerous environment of fringe groups. The media, parents and disaffected Christians wanted to expose abuse like the reputed mind-control of the Children of God. Some members were deprogrammed from the groups' teachings by anti-cult experts like Ted Patrick. As a result, false messiahs and offbeat communities were hot news.

Di Sabatino helpfully concludes that 'by 1974 the Jesus People Movement was not as readily identifiable as it had been only three years previously'. He goes on to talk about the responsibilities of regular life and comments that 'the once highly visible ocean side baptismal services … had been replaced by more mundane endeavours'.[12]

So, how did the JPM play out in the UK? Don't worry, we'll get there soon, but to truly understand the movement, we must first explore what made it so different.

3.

The Jesus People Make Their Colourful Marks in Life

In the previous chapter, we painted a picture of the Jesus People. We explored my own story in the UK as well as the broader tale in America. So, what vivid colours defined the JPM? Let's have a look at ten distinguishing marks of the movement, all of which are important for us going forward in this book.

Hippy Background

'I have become all things to all people so that by all possible means I might save some' (1 Corinthians 9:22).

A 'hippy' is someone, most likely in the 1960s, who rejected conventional values which impacted their behaviour, dress, and drug use. Other common traits are long hair, campaigning for love and peace and living communally. Many of the early American Jesus People were from a hippy background and were heavily involved with the counterculture of the 1967 'Summer of Love' in San Francisco. Those who ministered to them, such as Arthur Blessitt in Los Angeles, often adopted hippy dress and language to reach individuals in this context. He regularly used phrases like 'turned on to Jesus',[1] and so he reflected Paul's missionary strategy as the apostle to 'outsider' Gentiles. Blessitt adapted his lifestyle to theirs to evangelise to them.

Later, existing church youth, tired of the churches' traditionalism, got on board and identified with the Jesus People lifestyle. However, integrating the converted hippies into established churches was tricky on both sides of the Atlantic. Yet another parallel to the New Testament. Integrating Gentile Jesus followers into the predominantly Jewish church couldn't have been easy.

Those ministering to young people didn't always have to adopt their style though. In the UK, someone as conservative as Mrs Boxall, the recognised 'mother' of the Jesus Liberation Front, discipled people simply by loving them well, rather than through transforming her identity.

Jesus-focused

'For I resolved to know nothing while I was with you except Jesus Christ and him crucified' (1 Corinthians 2:2).

Hippy believers in the late 1960s and early 1970s were often dubbed 'Jesus People' or 'Jesus Freaks'. Unsurprisingly, some converts felt Jesus was something of a first-century subversive hippy – an assumption shared by many in the wider counterculture. Some biblical language, such as Christians being followers of 'The Way' (Acts 9:2; 24:14), affirming Jesus as the only route to the Father (John 14:6), had a familiar ring to a journeying generation of spiritual seekers.

Scholar Larry Eskridge, commenting on the Living Room storefront outreach, said, 'Inside, casual conversations "were always steered to talking about Jesus."'[2]

With many Eastern gurus on offer in the late sixties, Jesus was the unique divine-human rabbi. Across the 'pond' in the UK, some groups named themselves appropriately: the Jesus Family, the Jesus Liberation Front, and the Jesus Army.

In terms of becoming Christians, people were strongly encouraged to 'accept Jesus as their personal Lord and Saviour' – a popular and much-discussed evangelical phrase to this day.

As to recognising Jesus' full identity, some observers expected new believers to instantly adopt a full-blown doctrine of the Trinity. This would come with time.

Bible-centred

'And beginning with Moses and all the Prophets, he [Jesus] explained to them what was said in all the Scriptures concerning himself' (Luke 24:27).

Jesus People had very well-thumbed Bibles. They were carried around, studied in the community, quoted on the streets, memorised in their hearts, and read out in worship. Conversely, it was the cults, such as the Children of God, who eventually exalted their founder's words above Scripture, distorting the Bible's message in the process.

Bible translations written in contemporary English, such as *Good News for Modern Man* (1966) and *The Living Bible* (1970) paraphrase were popular amongst Jesus Freaks. At Calvary Chapel, Pastor Chuck Smith was famed for preaching through the entire Bible verse-by-verse. Few people got bored and Smith's approach continues in the forty-odd Calvary Chapels in the UK today.

Primitively printed Bible study sheets were given to new believers to nurture their understanding of the faith and find their way around Scripture. The Jesus People were gradually weaned off the baby's 'milk' and onto 'solid food' (Hebrews 5:11-14).

Despite being accused of being overly experiential, and having unusual interpretations about the end times, the Jesus People treasured the written Word of God greatly. It was a firm and objective anchor for their faith.

Contemporary Music

'Do not get drunk on wine, which leads to debauchery. Instead, be filled with the Spirit. Speak to one another with psalms, hymns and spiritual songs. Sing and make music in your heart to the Lord' (Ephesians 5:18-19).

Spiritual awakenings are often accompanied by the composition of fresh music and this one was no exception.

Back in the 1700s, revivalist John Wesley's brother, Charles, wrote innovative hymns to teach new believers Christian truths. Amongst the Jesus People, there was lots of evidence for original music. A good number of professional musicians had been saved too, such as Calvary Chapel's group Love Song. Musical styles were pulled heavily from that era, including folk, country, pop and blues. However, rock 'n' roll took the crown in terms of popularity when songwriters put Scripture or testimony to music.

Initially, contemporary music was used to share Jesus with lost people, as in the Jesus Family's *Lonesome Stone* musical. New acts were often showcased at the annual Greenbelt Festival in the UK. Later, especially from the 1980s onwards, there was a greater emphasis on contemporary worship music. For example, the intimate songs of the Vineyard Christian Fellowship. Their momentum touched the UK, where the 1999 album *Hungry* was produced, becoming the best-selling Vineyard album on both sides of the Atlantic.

In the 1970s, serious 'worship wars' broke out. Some claimed that rock's origins were Satanic, while others like Larry Norman retorted, as demonstrated in the title of his famous song, 'Why Should the Devil Have All the Good Music?'

Regardless, the Jesus People colourfully expressed their newfound faith through music and were daringly evangelistic in doing so. In time, the roots of this creative outburst would spawn the rapidly commercialised Christian Contemporary Music (CCM) industry.

Communal Living

'All the believers were together and had everything in common … They broke bread in their homes' (Acts 2:44,46).

Communal living, inspired by a return to the practices of the Jerusalem church, featured heavily in the early years of the Jesus People.

Communes already existed in the counterculture. They were launched as an antidote to society's individualism and consumerism. It was pretty 'hip' to share a house and made good sense economically. This made it an easy transition for the Jesus People to disciple new Christians in community houses as many had come from dysfunctional families.

Two Bible passages in Acts were often quoted as inspiration for communal living by the Jesus People. These were about the early Jerusalem church in Acts 2:42-47 and 4:32-35. These houses would take in new believers, seekers, or those in need to evangelise and disciple them as they shared food, life, and Scripture. Mike MacIntosh of Calvary Chapel described them as a 'spiritual seminary for the hippies'.[3]

Living in community was usually voluntary and temporary and was not preached as the sole biblical way to live.

In the UK, the Jesus Army, despite their tragic failings, had the longest-lasting Christian community in Europe. The Jesus Family had three houses in south London and four throughout Greater Manchester. The Gospel Outreach group, originally from Eureka in northern California, rented a seventy-bed residential centre owned by the famous Cadbury family. There, they would disciple new believers in the Birmingham area.

End-times Orientation

'… we wait for the blessed hope – the glorious appearing of our great God and Saviour, Jesus Christ' (Titus 2:13).

The hope of Jesus' second coming was utterly central to new believers. In studying the Scriptures and watching contemporary events unfold, his return was expected any minute. Based largely on Matthew 24:36-41, one notable JPM anthem was Larry Norman's lament, 'I Wish We'd All Been Ready'.

The call to get ready was strongly underlined by prominent Bible teacher and author Hal Lindsey, renowned for his best-selling book, *The Late Great Planet Earth*.[4]

At Calvary Chapel, pastor Chuck Smith added fuel to this fire through his systematic teaching. The atmosphere was apocalyptic and electric.

At its root, the received view was known as 'premillennialism', one that taught Jesus would physically return to earth before his thousand-year reign.[5] Before this event, his Church would be supernaturally whisked up to heaven in 'the rapture', believers escaping 'the great tribulation' (Revelation 7:14). Looking back today, many Jesus People realise this isn't the only possible understanding of the end-times. There were many alternative views. Some believed Jesus' physical return would occur after he had reigned invisibly on earth for a thousand years while others argued that the thousand years were only John's literary symbol for reigning.[6] However, questions were subsequently raised, such as: 'Did Jesus teach the "rapture"?' and 'How can we correctly link contemporary events in Israel to the Bible?'

The Jesus Liberation Front certainly pushed this premillennial perspective, especially through selling multiple audio cassettes. Ironically, this was an end-times emphasis that originally had its historic origin in the UK, from early leaders of the Plymouth Brethren church such as the highly influential J.N. Darby. His teaching eventually found its way across the Atlantic, featuring widely in the Scofield Reference Bible.

The popular focus on the end times led to the following motivation: Get as many people saved before time quickly runs out ...

Street Evangelism

'Then the master told his servant, "Go out to the roads and country lanes and make them come in, so that my house will be full"' (Luke 14:23).

Jesus was a hot topic of conversation on the streets. Good news flew out with a real sense of ease, aided and abetted by the outdoor culture of sunny Southern California. Arthur Blessitt even ran his own 'Street University' evangelism course every summer.[7] For Jesus People, street evangelism referred more to their overall mentality than a geographical feature. They went where people were already gathering, such as the way the Christian World Liberation Front witnessed to campus activists at the University of California in Berkeley.

Street evangelism was combined with storefront outreaches where people were invited to drop in for a chat, plus communes were open to those needing a 'crash pad' for the night. The Jesus People's community lifestyle was magnetically evangelistic.

In the UK, the Jesus Liberation Front regularly shared Jesus on the streets of Hemel Hempstead, inviting people back to their Sunnyhill Road base. Sometimes, they baptised converts in the rivers in town. Noel Stanton's Jesus Army reached out to the public, adorned in their camouflaged combat jackets. Meanwhile, Arthur Blessitt trekked across the UK with his sizeable cross, witnessing as he went. Gone were the days of inviting people to church to 'sit under the sound of the gospel' on a Sunday evening!

It was time to exit the ghetto of the church and touch the marketplace in the local community.

Church Ambivalence

'Neither do men pour new wine into old wineskins. If they do, the skins will burst, the wine will run out and the wineskins will be ruined' (Matthew 9:17).

The Jesus People often had a dim view of churches they perceived as too traditional; culturally, they were fish out of water. For a season, their various Houses were effectively their 'church'.

Church services were still important though. Some leaders initiated what author Donald Miller calls 'New Paradigm Churches' – congregations such as the informal Calvary Chapel and Vineyard Christian Fellowship. Other leaders, like Duane Pederson and Jack Sparks, pioneered the liturgical Evangelical Orthodox Church. They rejected innovation of belief and opted for an old and historically rooted tradition. Thus, a wide range of new 'wineskins' were created. Perhaps ironically, though, early outreach to hippies was heavily financed by a group of Baptist pastors who called themselves 'Evangelical Concerns'.

Meanwhile, in the UK, the context was quite different. In the heyday of the 1970s charismatic renewal movement, some radical young believers were spawning 'house churches'. From the following decade onwards, Calvary Chapel and the Vineyard Christian Fellowship planted forty churches and 140 fellowships respectively. Also, when Vineyard leader John Wimber began serving the UK church in the early 1980s, he was far from church-ambivalent. He actively wanted every branch of church life represented in his training conferences. Others though, such as influential musician Larry Norman, sat extremely lightly to the local church.

Overall, though, hip new converts in the UK were encouraged to join a regular, local, Bible-believing church. Conversely, cults like the Children of God and the Twelve Tribes[8] were exclusive and opposed to any church that wasn't their own.

Charismatic Experience

'This salvation, which was first announced by the Lord, was confirmed to us by those who heard him. God also testified to it by signs, wonders and various miracles, and gifts of the Holy Spirit' (Hebrews 2:3-4).

From the very start, the JPM had a decidedly charismatic tone to it: new believers were quickly filled with the Spirit; many regularly worshipped in a supernatural language called the 'gift of tongues', and tangible miracles occurred, often involving material provision. Given the dark backgrounds of individuals, many new Jesus People required prayer for release from strongholds in their lives. The details aside, the Holy Spirit was actively honoured and welcomed.

There was one man who was prolific in this charismatic arena across the USA. Lonnie Frisbee, the enigmatic, miracle-working evangelist, successively worked alongside Chuck Smith and John Wimber. Smith, with his Pentecostal roots, had a strong emphasis on biblical teaching but was cautious of what he felt were charismatic extremes. Conversely, Wimber argued that signs and wonders should accompany evangelism, and both he and Frisbee had a significant influence on the introduction of charismatic practice and theology at Holy Trinity Brompton in London, home of the 'Alpha' course. Their influence also inspired the genesis of the Soul Survivor youth church and its annual festivals in the UK.

For the UK church, existing renewal fires were further stoked by Jimmy and Carol Owens' popular musical *Come Together* with its Jesus People inspiration. For example, in the middle section of the performance, a 'pew-sitting in rows' mentality was replaced by believers encouraging one another in smaller groups. This was later termed 'body ministry'.

However, on both sides of the Atlantic, there were pitched battles about the gift of tongues. Some said this spiritual gift was 'of the devil' while others argued you were a second-class Christian without it.

The living experience of the Holy Spirit was the heartbeat of the Jesus People's discipleship and ministry. They were truly charismatic believers.

Literature Production

'But these [miraculous signs] are written that you may believe that Jesus is the Christ, the Son of God, and that by believing you may have life in his name' (John 20:31).

John's Gospel is God-given Scripture, intended to convince people of the truth of Jesus. While not divinely inspired, the Jesus People literature was published with a similar purpose. Naturally, such publications included Bible passages, but were also inclined to take a leaf out of the apostle Paul's book who used philosophical and poetic literature when preaching to literate intellectuals in Athens.[9]

Street papers were prominent in the wider counterculture, so Jesus People got in on the act; they developed material for non-believers. For example, *Right On!* was produced by the Christian World Liberation Front for campus-based academics. Targeted broadly to street people, the Milwaukee Jesus People also launched their more populist *Street Level* paper. A gifted art student, converted locally, helped to produce its vivid graphics. Additionally, cartoonist Jack Chick (not a Jesus Person himself) produced the widely used *Chick Tracts*, measuring just three by five inches and often anti-Catholic in content.

Meanwhile, the Children of God, soon to be recognised as a cult, produced their own papers too. Soon, they were openly selling *Mo Letters* on the streets, which contained founder 'Moses' Berg's skewed new revelations, many of which became highly immoral in content.

Across the Atlantic in the UK, the later twentieth century welcomed the prevalence of underground papers like the infamously obscene *Oz* and the *International Times* (*It*), whose premises were often raided by the police.

So, what wholesome alternatives were offered by Christians?

Despite being a music-orientated magazine for young Jesus followers, *Buzz* published special editions geared towards non-Christians, featuring thorough articles on apologetics and issues such as Jesus' identity. A drug rehabilitation ministry, led by Vic Ramsey, also developed a more colourful street paper called *VIBRATIONS* which had an overtly countercultural audience.

In an age before the internet and social media, using the printed page was crucial and it had a positive impact in making Jesus known.

So, there we go. Now we have a good understanding of the defining traits of the Jesus People Movement, we can dig deeper into the 1960s culture of the United Kingdom. Its various upheavals provided the crucial backdrop for what God was about to do as the seventies dawned.

4.

Welcome to the Swinging Sixties or the Permissive Society

The strongest memory of my teens is the vast generation gap.

As a north Londoner, I was on the geographical fringe of the city's 'Swinging Sixties', typified by Soho's music scene. My parents, conversely, were anxious about the amoral 'Permissive Society' we were growing up in. Life was a mixed bag for me. I remember watching Winston Churchill's funeral in black and white with my grandma in 1965 and feeling incredibly morose. Quite the contrast came the following year when England won the football World Cup and I was ecstatic. In a quick scan of the decade, I went from a Year 2 pupil in a village primary school at the beginning to a student preparing to win a coveted place at university at the end.

Before looking at the Jesus People Movement of the early 1970s in the UK, it's worth us getting a bird's-eye view of the preceding years...

During the 1950s, young people continued to mirror their parents' lifestyles. However, the distinct concept of being a 'teenager' emerged in the 1960s. As a social group, they were individuals on a journey, not people who were static. They feared moving on from this life phase too quickly, so they liked to linger in it.

In their helpful book *God and the Generations*, David Hilborn and Matt Bird contend, 'It may not have been until 1967 that a thoroughgoing, alternative "youth culture" emerged in the West along with the coming of the term "generation gap."'[1]

They argue the reason was as much to do with marketing strategy as youthful idealism. Meanwhile, a March 1967 article in the Christian magazine *Crusade* spoke of 'The Drifting Generation'.[2] This highlighted how much young people were estranged from their elders and their traditional institutions. Just like Paul McCartney's fictional 'Eleanor Rigby', it seemed Father McKenzie was crafting a sermon no one wanted to listen to.

So, our generation was drifting aimlessly. Like a huge ship, we were anchorless in terms of stability and rudderless in terms of direction. And the harbour was nowhere to be found.

It would be wrong to imply that every young person was countercultural in the 1960s. Some remained pro-establishment and stood up for long-standing values. However, many did 'drop out', embracing 'My Generation' with Pete Townshend of The Who. Those who stayed put, though, were patronisingly called 'straights' by their more radical contemporaries.

Surveying the sixties, I have chosen to highlight three things that young people wanted: a satisfaction that lasted, a spirituality which enlightened, and a society that worked.

Mick Jagger belted out that we ain't got none as we were still looking for the *satisfaction that lasted*. It proved frustratingly elusive. Were we even looking in the right places?

'If you remember the 1960s, you really weren't there!'

This anonymous quote is usually attributed to the American comedian Charlie Fleischer. Whoever came up with this line, it poignantly highlighted the increasing use of intoxicating drugs during this decade of upheaval. According to the hit 1977 single of punk-rocker Ian Dury, it was the era of 'Sex and Drugs and Rock and Roll'.

'Free love' and 'Make love, not war' were telling slogans of the time. There were few restraints on sexual experience. Contraception was widely available; 'the pill' was published on the recommended list of the British Family Planning Association in October 1961. Fashion guru Mary Quant spoke about getting pregnant as a continuing anxiety, but claimed the pill was a genuine revolution in female health. If women did fall pregnant, they could hunt down unhygienic, backstreet abortion clinics. Subsequently, The Abortion Act 1967 made terminations legal up to twenty-eight weeks of the foetus' life.

For homosexuals, their reluctantly closeted lifestyle was remedied. Homosexual acts between consenting adults over the age of twenty-one were declared legal in the amended Sexual Offences Act of 1967.

The door to free and safe sex was swinging wide open. Many of us walked through it, sadly disconnected from any commitment to our sexual partners.

While no such legal freedoms were introduced regarding the use of drugs, the practice certainly increased. LSD guru Timothy Leary's famed mantra, 'Turn on, tune in, drop out', was first publicly vocalised to a gathering of 30,000 hippies in San Francisco in January 1967. Here in the UK, young people were exposed to a variety of illegal drugs. Many got high smoking a cannabis joint, dropped amphetamine pills such as speed, and tried out the psychedelic reality-altering LSD, popularly known as 'acid'.

From 1964-66, three pieces of legislation were passed to hinder the use and availability of such drugs. A year later, Mick Jagger and Keith Richards of the Rolling Stones turned a blind eye to the new laws, both ending up in Chichester Magistrates Court for minor drug offences. The pair were momentarily behind bars, later released on appeal, and subsequently viewed by fans as celebrity scapegoats. Two years on, Home Secretary James Callaghan tried to halt the tide of permissiveness by dismissing the Wootton Committee's recommendation to legalise cannabis. Drug use had become a huge issue as some wrestled with addiction and rehab admissions were increasingly common.

Meanwhile, outspoken Beatle John Lennon was busy stirring up controversy about the relative merits of rock 'n' roll and Jesus. Interviewed in March 1966, he boldly stated, 'Christianity will go. It will vanish and shrink … We're more popular than Jesus now. I don't know which will go first, rock 'n' roll or Christianity.'[3] Five years later, he was alone on the LP cover of *Imagine*, dreaming of a religion-free utopia.

It seemed the sixties were characterised by an almost religious devotion to the decade's music, which was sometimes quite spiritual in content. In 1969, Norman Greenbaum sang about a mystical 'Spirit in the Sky', while The Byrds vocalised the fact that 'Jesus Is Just Alright'. Styles were extremely varied, including R&B (rhythm and blues), folk, pop and even psychedelic rock. However, the 'hard rock' genre often mirrored youthful rebellion. Our cold-hearted parents' generation was always trying to put us down, so we warmly embraced 'our generation'. Musically, the establishment's BBC Radio was hardly trendsetting, but offshore pirate stations like Radio Caroline and Radio London were.

Sadly, after three years, both were callously put off-air by the 1967 Marine Offences Act.

It is hard to overestimate, or ignore, the impact of The Beatles and their accompanying 'Beatlemania'. The band performed for almost the entire decade, selling eighty million records by August 1964. A year before their final live and impromptu performance on the roof of Apple Records in central London, they released the anti-Vietnam song 'Revolution'. Almost prophetically, its anti-authority theme was followed by the 'Winter of Discontent' when widespread strikes occurred between November 1968 and February 1969.

On 26 May 1967, though, the ground-breaking album *Sergeant Pepper's Lonely Hearts Club Band* was released. One Saturday morning, when I was just fourteen, my younger brother Richard and I bought a vinyl copy from Woolies[4] in Enfield town. It cost a whopping thirty shillings and blew our young minds. Its lyrics were a barometer of our times. The album, perhaps with some hyperbole, was according to *Times* theatre critic Kenneth Tynan, 'a decisive moment in the history of western civilization'.[5]

Was it really getting better all the time, or were we just trying to fix a hole in our lives with things that ultimately didn't satisfy us? It seemed The Beatles didn't know, and neither did we. Sex, drugs and rock 'n' roll hadn't delivered. Jimi Hendrix experienced plenty of all three yet died choking on his vomit at the age of twenty-seven, not long after the close of the 1960s.

Even though we viewed religion and church as 'old hat', there was a huge search for a *spirituality that enlightened* us. We would take that for a test drive. There were masses on offer in our pick-and-mix world. Would our faith go West for Christianity, East for gurus, or 'underground' for alternatives?

Post-war church attendance had been dwindling, despite many having an intuitive allegiance that was merely cultural. Some Christians, trying to combat the malaise, began to start fellowships in their living rooms which were quickly termed 'house churches'.

The publication of *Honest to God*[6] by the Anglican Bishop of Southwark, Dr John Robinson in March 1963 caused some confusion. Attempting to communicate the divine to a secular audience, the bishop caused a real storm with his beliefs. First, a personal Creator-God does not exist, just an impersonal 'ground of our being'. Second, for something to be morally right, only love needs to be its motivation, however vaguely defined. The ordinary person was all at sea.

'East is east, and west is west, and never the twain shall meet' said Rudyard Kipling in 1889. Seven decades on, this was proved untrue as Eastern religions gained popularity. For example, Westernised brands of Hinduism were freely available: The Beatles had their short-lived guru, the Maharishi Mahesh Yogi, founder of Transcendental Meditation. Lead guitarist George Harrison sang, 'My Sweet Lord' in praise of the Hindu deity Krishna. Many of these Eastern spiritual influences blossomed during the following decade; the New Age Movement[7] loomed over the horizon, promising spiritual awakening by gazing deeply within yourself.

Christianity still got a look-in though. Not long after the curtain came down on the decade, the West End theatre musicals *Godspell* and *Jesus Christ Superstar* hit our stages in 1971 and 1972 respectively. However, as the 1960s had worn on, the options in the spiritual supermarket increased – no choice was better than any other. The basic mantra was, 'If it's true for you, it's true!'

It may sound odd to add the term 'underground' into the mix with church and spirituality. Historically, it emerged following rivalry wars between scooter-borne 'mods' and leather-jacketed 'rockers' in the first half of the decade. The 'underground' was not another name for the London Tube line, but the equivalent of the American hippy scene. This movement, in the second half of the sixties, had its implied creed in anarchy. Geographically, the most iconic go-to place was Eel Pie Island, in the centre of the River Thames near Twickenham. Bands played rock and R&B (rhythm and blues) in its hotel ballroom,[8] including The Rolling Stones, The Who, The Yardbirds, Pink Floyd and Deep Purple. By 1970, the island, accessible only by boat, housed the largest hippy commune in the UK.

However, the Met Police gave the underground tribe a good run for their money. For example, *Oz* was launched in 1967 by two Australians, but became infamous in June 1971 for a well-publicised obscenity trial. A fifteen-year-old schoolboy, invited to be a guest editor, added a highly sexualised parody of Rupert Bear to an edition, which many found offensive.

Creativity was key to the underground; there was psychedelic art everywhere you looked, one example being the artwork produced by Hipgnosis for Pink Floyd's album covers. Fashion was part of the scene too. Carnaby Street in Soho was all the rage for hip clothing, pictured on the front cover of *Time* magazine on 15 April 1966. The famed King's Road in Chelsea also had its trendy boutiques, responsible for replacing long, floaty dresses for women with suggestive miniskirts.

In short, the values of the underground were another option for the wild child of the 1960s. Its approach paralleled the USA's hippy culture where the stance was anti-establishment, yearning for *a society that worked* more like an authentic community.

As it stood, politically, both the right- and left-wing successively appeared unfit for purpose. Westminster led us into boom and bust respectively. On 20 July 1957, future Conservative prime minister, Harold McMillan, famously stated that most Brits have never had such a good lifestyle, convincing the electorate to move him into Number 10 in 1959. The post-war economic 'boom' gathered steam, fuelled by the production of steel, cars and coal, resulting in people earning more and spending more.

Five years on, the Labour Party's pipe-smoking Yorkshireman, Harold Wilson, became the youngest prime minister for 150 years. In a post-industrial age, his vision was to promote high-tech jobs forged in the 'white heat' of the scientific revolution. The futuristic *Tomorrow's World* was a must-watch on TV. Much later that decade, though, things went 'bust'. Spending more than they had, the country's sterling was devalued by a massive fourteen per cent. Harold Wilson bizarrely tried to convince the populace that the pound in their pockets would not lose its value. They were not convinced and so Labour was voted out of office.

The sixties was the era when young people began to seriously lose trust in politicians, accelerated by the John Profumo scandal of 1963. The Secretary of War was discovered to have had a two-year affair with a model and call girl, Christine Keeler, who was also dangerously and sexually involved with a Russian spy. Whatever trust the public had was further weakened by the development of political satire in the early 1960s. *Private Eye* magazine was launched in 1961 by Richard Ingrams, with the late-night TV show *That Was The Week That Was* hot on its heels in November 1962. Both the satirical press and television lampooned politicians regularly. How could we trust our leaders anymore?

Some politicians' policies caused deep mistrust too, especially those of Roy Jenkins, Labour's Home Secretary from 1965-67. His liberalising tendencies brought wide-ranging progressive social reforms in the late 1960s, all in the name of Jenkins' 'civilised society'. They included, for instance, liberalising the laws on abortion, divorce, and the death penalty; together with those on theatre censorship, homosexuality, and betting. Some loved it, others such as moral campaigner Mary Whitehouse hated this 'permissive society'. The moral goalposts were being swiftly moved, while religiously based ethics were left on the bench.

Philosophically, a big change of thinking was germinating in the 1960s. It has been rightly observed that what happens in the hallowed corridors of academia quickly finds its way onto the streets. 'Modernity' had reigned since the late seventeenth-century Enlightenment. It was long assumed that we all fit into over-arching big stories in life, whether religious or political and that we should have immense confidence in the progress of scientific research. Our moral values were to be analysed rationally and logically. In this decade, though, the new worldview of 'postmodernity' pulled the rug from under these ideas. The day of universal big stories we all fit into (like Christianity, Islam, or Marxism) had disappeared; all we were left with was a random collection of our little, individual stories. Few people could put this sea change into words, but the atmosphere was momentously changing, especially after 1970. In its wake was a radical demolition of people's approaches to life.[9]

For society at large, optimism and pessimism co-existed in the 1960s.

The burgeoning technology industry was very upbeat; seventy-five per cent of homes had television by 1961, and BBC2 were the first to broadcast in colour six years later. Meanwhile, the revolutionary new aeroplane Concorde had its test flight on 9 April 1969. The sleek plane operated commercially seven years later. Then, of course, the first man walked on the moon in 1969. Things were looking up.

It wasn't all fun and games though. The nuclear age hung over us like a cloud. In the early-mid 1960s, there were CND peace marches prompted by this calamitous threat. For example, in 1963, seventy thousand demonstrators marched from the Atomic Weapons Research Establishment in Aldermaston to protest in London. Ecologically, there were signs we were harming the planet. The Torrey Canyon oil tanker off the coast of Cornwall spilt thirty-two million tons of oil into the pristine blue sea in 1967. It was the first globally televised eco-disaster. Meanwhile, Northern Ireland became a powder keg. 'The Troubles' kicked off in 1968 and British troops were deployed in the province the following year. Racially too, immigration levels from Europe dismayed some people, their concerns stoked by Enoch Powell's 'Rivers of Blood' speech of 20 April 1968. Tensions were high, and racism was a present danger. Issues like these brought us down to earth with a bump.

With apologies to Dickens' *A Tale of Two Cities*, 'It was the best of times, it was the worst of times.'[10]

Our sixties generation seemed to live a life dominated by three questions:

Assuming being fulfilled in life is good, how can we gain it for the long term?

Can it be bought on the shelves of the religious supermarket somewhere?

What kind of a society do we and our children want to live in?

There was a lady in the first-century Middle East, as recorded in John 4:1-42, asking precisely the same questions. This unchaperoned woman from 'up north' met Jesus at a historic well in the blazing midday sun. Having unsuccessfully tried to find satisfaction in relationships, her latest man was the sixth in a long line of partners, a few of whom would probably have discarded her. Being a Samaritan, of mixed-race origin, she's muddled and confused by two competing spiritualities on offer. Psychologically isolated from her frosty neighbours in Sychar, she yearns for a new experience of being included in her town's community life. We don't know her name. It could hardly have been 'Ms Well-Woman'.

Whatever her identity, those brought up in the UK during the sixties can certainly identify with her.

The answer to her heart's cry was an encounter with the Jesus of the New Testament. Read the passage for yourself. You will discover how he revealed himself as God's liberating 'Christ' and spoke of the 'time' of his imminent death. The woman responds by declaring Jesus as her 'Saviour'.[11]

The woman's 'water' of *satisfaction* had run out – six successive partners hadn't brought her what she was looking for. In its place, Jesus offered her a long-term solution – 'a spring of water welling up to eternal life' (v.14).

Her new *spirituality* wouldn't depend on where she worshipped.[12] Jesus' rapidly approaching death would wipe her moral slate clean. A door was swinging open to access God as her Father. His Spirit would make her a worshipper from the inside out: 'God is spirit, and his worshippers must worship in spirit and in truth' (v.24).

The woman is previously pictured as being isolated from *society*, living on the lonely margins of her town's life. Now she belongs to Sychar Community Church, indeed she is its founder. Subsequent members tell her, 'We no longer believe just because of what you have said; now we have heard for ourselves, and we know that this man really is the Saviour of the world' (v.42).

There was God-given hope for a woman drifting from one relationship to the next in first-century Samaria. So, what about the generation of drifters in the sixties?

PART 2

The Jesus People Seasons

Winter 1970-71

5.

Liberation is Front and Centre of
This Jesus Community

British couple Geoff and Lyn Bone sensed a call to cross-cultural mission and so went to Sydney, Australia for training. Predictably, New Tribes Mission taught apprentice missionaries how to reach tribes. It was a good year 'down under', with their first child Ruth being born and spending Christmas on the beach. They imbibed helpful church-planting principles with anthropology thrown into the mix. Who knew where God would send them next? It would be made clear on their arrival home in Hemel Hempstead.

There, Lyn's brother Chris Boxall and sister-in-law Kimmy were at full stretch. Drug-taking hippies had been saved in town. They were not your average church types, but maybe a different 'tribe'? It was time Geoff and Lyn shared their missionary principles and put them to work on their home turf. A highly responsive community was on their doorstep; no need to fly thousands of miles to reach them. The two couples joined together in discipling this hippy tribe. The men grew their hair and dispensed with collar and tie; their wives dressed down too – this was the embryonic Jesus Liberation Front.

There was a decade-long run up to the founding of the Jesus Liberation Front (JLF). It began in a home on Sunnyhill Road, Hemel Hempstead. Edgar and Mabel Boxall were the parents of Lyn Bone and Chris Boxall. In 1960, the couple decided to reach children for Christ, so initiated a neighbourhood Sunday School in their living room. It quickly snow-balled, spreading into the front room, then filling the bedrooms. Mrs B, as she was fondly called, taught old hymns on a traditional pedal organ. Scripture was taught, exams were set, and prizes were given. By 1966, Mabel recalls, 'There came the suggestion of a wooden hut or large summer house being built in the garden.'[1] It ended up being a brick-built structure with a bitumen felt roof and was named 'Sunnyhill Christian Fellowship'.

People-wise, Mr Boxall was a conservative Baptist and an intriguing character, prone to disappearing for weeks at a time. Mrs Boxall was a mixture of the strait-laced and a forward-thinking radical. Later, as JLF's 'mum', she would relate lovingly and authentically to the hippy community.

By 1970, Chris Boxall was married to Kimmy. As part of Sunnyhill Christian Fellowship, the couple engaged in door-to-door evangelism and street witnessing, seeing hippies come to faith one by one. In the summer of 1971, renowned evangelist Dick Saunders brought his week-long 'Way to Life' crusade to Hemel Hempstead. He left behind a nucleus of forty young believers who needed nurturing and strong leadership. For these two reasons, the Boxalls were struggling with a bulging living room as they discipled baby Christians. In God's purpose, Geoff and Lyn Bone returned from their training 'down under' later that summer. They were instantly recruited.

The following year, the Jesus Liberation Front kicked off in earnest. Its title may have been inspired by the JPM's Christian World Liberation Front, or through encountering freedom-fighting communists one night, or possibly suggested by early member Sally Monahan during a brain-storm. However, Geoff thinks that he first floated the name in a casual conversation during a JLF minibus trip.

Whatever the case, he recalls: 'In October 1971 we decided to invite other young Christians from all over the country to unite with us in an all-out, end-time battle against Satan. Our aim was to mobilise Christians everywhere into a spiritual revolution for Jesus Christ.'[2] The invitation in *Buzz* magazine yielded a massive 600 replies. JLF's membership quickly and steeply climbed to a peak of 3,000.

Initially, JLF and Sunnyhill Christian Fellowship were one entity and on 21 November 1971, Geoff and Chris were formally ordained as pastors to the fellowship's forty-strong members. As their youth ministry received greater attention, the name JLF stuck better. It was thought the younger generation would find it more accessible. Seven core members were baptised in the River Bulbourne on 14 May 1972 as a public witness to the town. Ten weeks later, though, a life-shattering event shook the community. On 26 July, Geoff was involved in a tragic accident.

Previously, Arthur Blessitt, the cross-carrying evangelist from California, had seen 3,000 young people saved in Northern Ireland over six weeks of walking. Invited by the Belfast YMCA to discuss follow-up, Geoff saw an opportunity for growth, only three JLF members being from Ulster. He promptly jumped on a plane, surprising one Belfast member by knocking on his door at 6.00 a.m. Tornado-like Geoff made personal connections, visited conflict-torn Shankill Road, met the local YMCA leaders, and placed a newspaper advert for a Jesus People rally the following Saturday. He flew home that same day, promising to return the Wednesday after the rally. However, this subsequent flight was scuppered by a Heathrow air traffic controllers' strike. It took two hours of phone calls to garner tickets to fly from Gatwick the following day. Geoff, travelling with Lyn's Irish friend Breda, arrived at Watford Junction station at 5.30 a.m. Snoozing in the waiting room, their train began to move off, and the pair dashed onto the platform, sprinting alongside the carriage. As the locomotive gathered speed, Geoff hung onto the carriage door handle. Abruptly jolted off his feet, he fell between the platform and the train, damaging both legs. Breda comforted him on the track. Geoff, losing blood, repeated 'Jesus… Jesus…' and two railway staff protected his left leg while applying a tourniquet to the other.

Within nine minutes, a siren-blaring ambulance drove Geoff to hospital; he wasn't expected to survive. After three hours of surgery, with five doctors in attendance, he was still alive. Recovery was slow, but more than three weeks later, on Sunday 20th August, he was carried into the crammed hall on Sunnyside Road. One hundred and fifty young worshippers, plus an overflow outside, welcomed him home. One JLF member, Richard Hogarth, said, 'I can only describe the atmosphere as being pervaded by the manifest presence of God. It was awesome.'[3]

Six days later, a nurse ordered Geoff to go home and have a quiet weekend. Instead, that Saturday evening he attended London's Festival for Jesus. Spotted by leaders, he was carried on stage and quizzed by Peter Hill about God's keeping power.

'I'd just fallen under a train, but I'm alive,' he replied.

A month later, Geoff was fully discharged from the hospital before eventually having artificial legs fitted, but still he continued ministering.

From summer 1972 to 1977, Geoff's family and fellow leaders experienced a season of frantic growth amidst logistical challenges. That first year, Chris Boxall bought a red London bus transformed into a 'Jesus Bus' to transport the thirty-one-strong JLF contingent to the Munich Olympics' outreach. In April 1973, reporter John Percival and crew arrived for a week to shoot a documentary for the BBC *Time For a Change* series. An entire episode was devoted to the Hemel-based ministry. JLF participated in outreach training at Spre-e 73 in late August, before going on to host a full dress rehearsal of *Come Together* at Hemel Hempstead Pavilion Theatre in September. In March 1974, Geoff began writing a monthly column for the national *Buzz* magazine. There was tangible unity among local fellowships, largely fostered by JLF's 'Gathered for Power' meetings in the Pavilion. The pace was unrelenting. That's often the case when God is moving powerfully.

In 1977, though, things finally fell apart at the seams: the Bones' marital difficulties and subsequent adultery was exposed. A meeting was called to talk about church discipline. The issue was discussed over the following seven days. Despite thinking the situation had been mishandled, Geoff stepped down from leadership immediately, handing JLF over to the four home group leaders. It marked the group's demise after six whirlwind years. In Geoff's words, it had been 'a fairly short-lived phenomenon which helped young people identify with the gospel'.[4]

Over those six years, there was a cross-fertilisation of people and influences within the extended Jesus People community.

Larry Norman performed at Gathered for Power in early 1972, drawing a massive crowd of 1,100 people to the Pavilion. Much later, Barry McGuire of 'Eve of Destruction' fame performed there too. Attending events like these was de rigueur for young Christians at the time.

Additionally, Geoff highlights a 1973 meeting with the American leader of London's Jesus Family:

> I did meet with Jim Palosaari once. He suggested getting together, and [he] would bring his newspaper *Everyman* over. It was quite an attractive idea, but I still had a suspicion: I didn't know these people, a bunch of Americans that looked somewhat cult-like in style. They might be OK, but maybe not. So, if I throw my lot in with them, I am ditching the whole thing. So, I thought, 'No, I prefer a bit of caution here. We'll stay friends, keep an eye on them, but I'll stay a bit distant. Meanwhile, we'll carry on as normal ourselves.'[5]

Later, speaking to me in 2013, Geoff regretted this decision, wishing they had joined forces to be stronger together.

In 1975, Geoff flew across the Atlantic to meet Chuck Smith, ending up sharing his testimony at Calvary Chapel. It was an eye-opener for him to see how Americans did things.

Geoff reflected, 'It's a slightly parallel situation to mine at JLF, a formerly traditional evangelical pastor [Smith] reaching hippy-types.'[6] Chuck subsequently spoke at another Gathered for Power event in Hemel Hempstead.

For all these reasons, Bone wasn't now describing himself as a pastor but as 'a leader in the Jesus Movement that was sweeping across America and the world'.[7]

So, were the Jesus People the sole influence on JLF? There are three ways to address that question.

PhD student Roger Curl was researching three Christian communities, but not JLF. However, he had discovered Geoff's conviction that the Front's origins were 'in the Neo-Pentecostal and "house church" movements, which were gaining considerable interest in England when it [JLF] began'.[8] The former term is an alternative for the 1960s and 1970s 'charismatic movement'; the latter describes people exiting established churches to restore New Testament Church life in homes.

Secondly, though, Curl also contended that, 'The Jesus Liberation Front was the only British organisation of any significance which resembled the American movement', his evidence being that, 'it supplied tapes, posters and teaching materials, and arranged extensive witnessing.'[9] This was further confirmed by 1970s Christian journalist, Michael Jacob, who claimed JLF was 'one of the closest English parallels to the American Jesus movement'.[10]

Thirdly, in 2013 I asked Geoff personally, 'Did JLF come from the charismatic movement, the American Jesus People, or was it indigenous to the UK?' His speedy and forthright reply was, 'Definitely indigenous!'[11]

Homegrown in the UK, yes, but a hybrid of sorts.

So, to what extent did JLF mirror the ten marks of the Jesus People?

Positively, they fruitfully evangelised hippies and adopted hippy culture. Mrs Boxall loved them without becoming like them. One Sunday morning, JLF members went to Chesham to hear the famous Dr Martyn Lloyd-Jones preach. Local member Richard Hogarth recalls, 'They arrived in their hippy bus, many of them in hippy clothes and barefoot. There was a kerfuffle at the door as they arrived late, with the doorman unhappy to let such "undesirables" in. Dr Martyn overruled and insisted that they had pride of place seated on the floor at the front of the church.'[12]

In terms of further similarities to the JPM, JLF were as Jesus-centred as the words are throughout a stick of Brighton rock. They were overtly charismatic in their theology and lifestyle and distributed masses of cassette tapes about the end-times. While Bible-centred, some members felt there was not enough teaching about whole-life discipleship. From the very outset, the group were involved in street outreach, subsequently training others more widely. Musically, their group, 11:59, developed homegrown songs too.

For JLF, communal living and literature production had a brief shelf-life: 'Hendlylake' was a five-bed house owned by the Department of the Environment, leased for a peppercorn rent of £2 per week. Communal living was experimented with, but Geoff closed it down after a year, arguing that salty Christians should be scattered in the community, not ghettoised. In hindsight, he wished he had roomed there and run it as a longer-term commune.[13] The group also attempted to produce their own paper on a primitive tabletop printer that rarely worked. Graphic artist Brian Boggis relocated to get it off the ground, but it never did. Entrepreneurial Geoff felt he was too slow. He reflected, 'I found things needed to be done fast. I had an idea one day, done the next day, and on to the next idea.'[14] However, Chris Boxall's Liberation Recordings did get the spoken word out effectively.

The only mark of the JPM that was absent in JLF was church ambivalence. Locally, they built church unity, especially through their Gathered for Power events at the Pavilion. Geoff commented that crumbling barriers signify that, 'We are now beginning to discern the Body as a unit within the locality rather than a number of individual units within the locality.'[15]

Denominationally, the group's support came from Baptists, Methodists, and Pentecostals. Geoff wrote pieces for their respective papers, plus the *Church of England Newspaper*. Even though JLF members joined one of their contemporary, action-orientated groups, they were still encouraged to be part of home churches, as were new converts.

* * *

So, what legacy did JLF leave behind?

The first was using principles of cross-cultural mission in their own UK backyard;[16] they were not merely for pioneering overseas, but for the local early seventies' hippy 'tribe'. People say that today's Generation Z is unlikely to be religious but are incredibly open to all brands of spirituality. I can hear clear resonances here from the Hemel Hempstead days. One question remains though: how can we target specific demographics whilst simultaneously growing inter-generational churches?

Secondly, the indigenous JLF was described by Roger Curl as 'a British organisation'.[17] The special relationship between America and the UK may be a good one. However, it doesn't mean we needed to precisely copy what Californian Jesus People did. For example, they baptised new believers in the ocean, whereas the landlocked JLF baptised them in the local rivers. We can learn from others' principles but be intelligent in how we apply them according to our own culture and circumstances.

Finally, we often learn more from failures than successes.

During revivals, there is often minimal Bible teaching to disciple young people for the long-term. The slick JLF answer to most questions was, 'Do more evangelism!' We need a lifelong, disciple-making culture in today's UK Church, especially for family life. While revival fires blazed, the marriages of both leadership couples in the JLF sadly ended in divorce.[18] Without being judgmental, or unduly wise after the event, home-life discipleship is crucial.

Winter 1970-71

6.

Meet the Army Marching on its Spiritual Stomach

It was a regular Sunday at 10.30 a.m. at the little Baptist chapel. The time late winter in February 1971. The place the small village of Bugbrooke, Northamptonshire. Deacons were welcoming people at the door with a handshake. Inside, hymns melodiously wafted out from the organ. The choir was warming up their voices to lead worship. The table was pristinely set to celebrate communion. Pastor Noel had entered the sanctuary to lead the service. It felt like just another Sunday, but a surprise visitor was about to arrive.

That previous week, Pastor Noel and his deacons had agreed to allow members to contribute openly during the Lord's Supper – a high-risk strategy! When the time came, a man called John burst out with the gift of tongues, an unknown language supernaturally given to praise God. His voice reached the rafters. A second person translated it into English for everyone's benefit, using the gift of the interpretation of tongues. A spontaneous message from God, or prophecy, followed immediately afterwards. The invading wind of the Holy Spirit had blown in through an open door.

Soon this fellowship, turned upside down by the Holy Spirit's immediate presence, would be viewed as part of the JPM in the UK. Historically, the chapel began life in 1805, growing so vigorously that it kick-started new churches locally. Meanwhile, Noel Stanton came to know Jesus on the streets of Sydney, Australia during his navy service. Following training for ministry in the UK, he became Bugbrooke's part-time pastor in 1957. Although he led as a traditional Baptist, there was a strong hunger for a more nourishing community life.

Following a decade of hard graft, Stanton felt minimal power in his ministry. This was exacerbated after he had read David Wilkerson's account of reaching New York gang members in his book *The Cross and the Switchblade*.[1] A dozen or so people began meeting on Saturday evenings to study Luke's book of Acts. They were desperate to discover the keys to the early church's success. Praying in the manse a few months later, their pastor was overwhelmed by the Holy Spirit for hour upon hour... His congregation felt he had become like a hundred-watt light bulb. Not long afterwards, on that February morning, the gust of the Spirit blew into the church.

Ahead lay five stages of the church's journey, with lots of twists and turns on the road, but a tragic car crash at the end...

From 1968 to 1973, revival reigned. Prayer moved up the agenda quickly. Two hundred people were converted in a village of eight hundred; they were 'bikers, drug users, glue sniffers, New Agers and others who had emerged from the hippie culture'.[2] Even the *Daily Mail* viewed the religious fervour as unprecedented, explicitly likening the Bugbrooke believers to 'Jesus Freaks'. Thames Television filmed a documentary entitled *The Lord Took Hold of Bugbrooke*[3] that premiered the following year. Not every Christian was delighted though, as forty-three members resigned to worship elsewhere.

Between 1974-78, the church moved from a rather stiff traditional Baptist stance to putting a higher value on community, hence their new name, 'The Jesus Fellowship Church'. Their vision was directly inspired by the Old Testament teaching about Jerusalem being God's dwelling place, 'Zion'. The church viewed itself as a visible 'city on a hill'.[4] Bugbrooke Hall was bought at auction for £67,000, followed by a farm and other houses. Three hundred and fifty people were living in this 'New Creation Christian Community' by 1979.

However, a rocky patch was emerging from the fertile soil of the community. For the following seven years, there was flak from outsiders – these Christians were breaking the mould of 1980s individualism and were viewed as being too radical, especially in sharing their property. To many, it looked like a cult. Anxious parents complained and anti-cult bodies investigated. The church had been an active part of two Christian umbrella groups but was ousted from the Evangelical Alliance in 1986 and the Baptist Union the following year. They defensively pulled up the drawbridge.

On 18 April 1987, an important turning point was the launch of the evangelistic Jesus Army, attired in their multi-coloured combat jackets. For the next twenty-two years, the community worked hard to identify with the wider society and broader church. Engaging more fully with non-believers' culture, they launched a ministry amongst 'thrash metal' musicians. The fellowship also attempted to visibly blend into the charismatic house-church branch of the Church, relating to leaders like John Noble of the Team Spirit group. Wider unity came through welcoming all believers to their high-profile 'Wembley Praise Days' led by mainstream worship leaders. The Jesus Fellowship Church/Jesus Army had permanently let down its drawbridge.

The final period, from 2009 to 2019, precipitated the community's implosion. A metaphorical car crash was looming, caused by dangerous driving. The seeds of destruction go back to Noel Stanton's death in 2009. Soon afterwards, leaders admitted allegations of abuse had been levelled at Stanton. Four years later, they openly invited people to whistle-blow about wider incidents of bullying and abuse. Many came forward. *Operation Lifeboat* was initiated by Northamptonshire Police and more than two hundred complaints were logged including misogynistic behaviour towards women. Membership plummeted to under a thousand. The journey's terminus was on Sunday 26 May 2019. Constitutionally, the Jesus Fellowship Church was no more. The vehicle was a 'write-off', but does the God of compassion still care for it's many bruised passengers? Currently, as I write, solicitors are still working hard to unravel complex property and financial issues, serving the Trust in making some redress to those tragically affected before the end of 2023.[5]

So, what about the relationship between the Jesus Fellowship and the JPM? There were two specific occasions where the Jesus Fellowship were viewed as part of the JPM.

Predictably, the first was in the early 1970s, when the American movement was at its peak. It was hot news internationally. The Bugbrooke church was receiving breathless phone calls and getting inspiring letters about God moving. This resulted in wannabe young Jesus Freaks in the village giving raucous, 'Give us a J!' shouts while wearing their hair long and pointing their 'One Way' fingers heavenwards. In July 1971, the *Northampton Chronicle and Echo* paper carried an article on the local Jesus People revolutionaries, clearly inspired by and a parallel to the American movement.[6] Further traction came three months later when the Fellowship welcomed a visit from the evangelist, Arthur Blessitt.

Conversions were regularly happening in Northamptonshire. Let me introduce you to the 'larger than life' Rufus. He had taken the Glastonbury hippy trail, lived in London's drug scene, was into Zen masters, and dealt in acid locally. First meeting Noel Stanton outside the Black Lion in Northampton, Rufus consequentially experienced first-hand the magnetic 'extra' of the community. One day, while pruning his cannabis plants, Rufus had a visit from Noel. He felt distinctly unclean in his presence. Sometime later, the sensitive side of his conscience felt incredibly guilty; he had disobeyed his rigorous, macrobiotic diet by 'sinning' with a Swiss roll. Quickly ringing Noel, Rufus said he was a sinner needing Jesus. He was lent Nicky Cruz's book *Run Baby Run* and, despite disliking the blood and guts, found personal forgiveness while reading about the gang leader turned Jesus follower.

The second touchpoint was in the late 1980s and early 1990s. Jesus Army soldiers were now reaching young adults born to the previous 'wild child' generation. Cooper and Farrant poignantly reflected, 'The 60s Jesus Movement had barely touched this country but now a new wave was on its way.'[7] 1989 saw a whopping 75,000 copies of their multi-coloured *Jesus Revolution Streetpapers* distributed in towns, villages, beach resorts and music festivals. The Army's fresh 'Jesus Revolution' emphasis was launched in the summer of 1991, marked in August by a positive demonstration in Trafalgar Square, the group's band playing between the two bronze lions. Enthusiastic young believers swarmed the streets celebrating Jesus as the nineties' hero. It was high time Generation J (for Jesus) replaced Generation X.

Noel Stanton's editorial for *Jesus Life* magazine in early 1997 spoke of 'a fledgling … grassroots Jesus movement'.[8] With 1970s' resonances, it was Holy Spirit directed and appeared raw and wild, with belief in Jesus being rife.

Meet Mary, who encountered the Jesus Army during this time. She had been assaulted at the age of seventeen, and subsequently tried to numb the pain in fantasies like Teddy Boys, Goths, New Age, and the theatre. Later, she graduated in Philosophy and began acting professionally. She found middle-class Christianity incredibly boring. Living in Oxford in 1992, Mary discovered Palm Tree Cottage, a Jesus Fellowship house just outside the city. This inclusive community gathered people like hippies, skinheads, a doctor, and a zany housewife. It was alluring; she gave it a try and found Jesus. Sadly, her marriage later disintegrated, resulting in her moving to Bugbrooke with her two-year-old son. Mary found her real identity and a little haven of security amongst the colourful characters there.

So, what were the varied JPM influences upon the Jesus Fellowship Church and Jesus Army?

There were four.

In 1962, Teen Challenge founder, David Wilkerson, wrote *The Cross and the Switchblade*, recounting his work amongst gang members in New York City's Brooklyn and Harlem. The Pentecostal pastor high-lighted baptism in the Spirit and the gift of tongues as aids to helping teenagers renounce drugs and violence. Reading this book accelerated Stanton's longings for Holy Spirit revival and helped him resolve his theological qualms about tongues. Another book was written by a Teen Challenge convert, former Mau Maus gang leader, Nicky Cruz. First meeting Wilkerson, the Puerto Rican thug had threatened to kill him. *Run Baby Run* was the narrative of Cruz's conversion, published in 1968.[9]

A second influence was the energetic JPM evangelist Arthur Blessitt, whose story is recounted in his 1971 book *Turned on to Jesus*.[10] That same year, Blessitt had experienced a flurry of media interest when he landed in the UK. On Saturday 11 September, the gospel preacher gathered crowds in Trafalgar Square to celebrate his team as they began the long witnessing trek to Scotland. One pit stop was the county town of Northampton. Typically, Arthur hit the streets locally, proving a contagious inspiration to the Bugbrooke believers and leaving behind bags of enthusiasm and trails of Jesus stickers.

The Atlantic Ocean didn't stop JPM stories from rippling across to our shores. The Jesus Fellowship, busily developing their community, were especially stirred by news of American discipleship Houses, drawn by their earthy display of undiscriminating brotherly love. Stephen Hunt notes, 'While the Jesus Fellowship had no direct links with the Californian Jesus People, it did provide a similar model in terms of communal living and the adoption of counter-cultural themes.'[11]

News items were also transmitted to Bugbrooke through music and film. Calvary Chapel's band Love Song, who had a Beatles-type sound, performed at the church. Messianic Jewish duo, Lamb,[12] reputedly like Simon and Garfunkel, played at one community house too. Film-wise, Jesus Fellowship historians Cooper and Farrant recall rather vaguely, 'We watched a film on the Jesus Revolution.'[13] This was most likely the primitive and raw 1971 mini-documentary, *The Son Worshippers*. If so, it prominently featured troubadour Larry Norman, another agent of change, who performed in nearby Northampton during the spring of 1972.

Lastly, there are some more random influences upon the Jesus Army. The Jesus Family's *Lonesome Stone* led to converts who joined the Army, and the JPM-inspired Nationwide Festival of Light in 1971 generated 'a sense of spiritual excitement [that] inspired people to try to move into the village to be near the thriving chapel'.[14]

So far, we have seen the sizeable influence of the JPM upon a little village Baptist chapel renewed by the Holy Spirit. Clearly though, the Jesus People did not directly generate Bugbrooke's life. Instead, UK charismatic renewal was probably the more immediate source. How can we best articulate its relationship with the American JPM?

Steam railway enthusiasts travel far and wide to see historic locomotives moving on closely parallel tracks. These two respective rails are not the same entity, but distinct ones, yet they work together in partnership. Lying side-by-side, they cause God's purposes to get up a head of steam in speeding towards the final buffers.

* * *

The ever-present Holy Spirit fell in February 1971. He blew into a little church tucked away in Bugbrooke. Over the past half-century, what legacies have this fellowship gifted to the UK Church?

One key distinctive they modelled, ironically, is being one of the longest-lasting Christian communities in Europe. Fifty years is a huge lifespan compared to America's Shiloh Houses which disbanded after eighteen years. The only real parallel is Jesus People USA, whose intentional community in the Uptown area of Chicago has lasted since 1972. This historic longevity makes the Jesus Fellowship's demise more tragic for its members, especially those still burned by its cataclysmic fallout.

Another area that demands attention is their theology of the end times, which goes against the grain of classic JPM teaching. On balance, the Jesus People were 'tomorrow' people, looking for the King to imminently establish his future kingdom on earth, coupled with an urgency to rescue people before he returned. The Jesus Fellowship and Army shared this burden, but in contrast were 'today' people, experiencing kingdom life together in the here and now. Ensconced in rural Bugbrooke Hall and its surrounding homes, they were Zion today, not Zion tomorrow.

Innovatively, in many areas, the community 'widened the net' compared to the JPM. Evangelistically, they touched university students and local villagers as well as hippy types, integrating them as one. Musically, too, they composed homegrown new songs but were also famed for singing multiple verses of the old hymns of Wesley and Watts.

Their ambivalence about being part of the wider Church was dangerous. Such a lack of accountability contributed strongly to their downfall. Internally, Noel Stanton had a robust theology of submitting to authority (especially for women). Over-dependence on him as a charismatic leader led to an unquestioning submission and a consequent lack of God-given liberty. Abuse can go unchecked in this kind of climate. Its exposure teaches us a lasting lesson: churches must value external accountability while living with an internal freedom.

Despite deeply painful and culpable errors, God powerfully used the Jesus Fellowship to shake up the rest of the UK Church. They encouraged a radical 24/7 lifestyle which more powerfully reflected the outreach of the early church in the book of Acts.

Spring 1971

7.

Throw This Frisbee and He Will Fly Back Quickly

It was the last day of Spring 1971; the printing presses were rolling in New York, five hours behind London. Another weekly edition of *Time* magazine was being produced, soon to be flown over to UK newsagents. The front cover boldly proclaimed, 'The Jesus Revolution'. In the centre was a Jesus lookalike figure. The brightly coloured reds, yellows, blues and purples complemented the headline story, 'The Alternative Jesus: Psychedelic Christ'.

A young, long-haired, bearded hippy had his photo inside the magazine; he resembled the stereotypical white Jesus of the Western world. Thousands had come to Christ through him in southern California. His image was going viral. Afterwards, people recognised his face on the streets of Europe. Three months later, the evangelist would attempt to speak to social campaigners in Trafalgar Square – that is, until the male 'nuns' turned up…

So, who was this enigmatic figure?

The young man was Lonnie Frisbee.

Lonnie Frisbee was born in Santa Ana, California on 6 June 1949. He came from a dysfunctional family and was abused at eight years old by a male babysitter. During high school, he danced on the TV show *Shebang* and apparently 'looked like a little teenage Jesus'.[1] Dancing and art were his two great loves, and Lonnie left home in late 1966 to attend the Academy of Art College in San Francisco.

He had a keen Christian grandmother, plus experience of Christian summer camps, but Lonnie's conversion eventually came in 1967. By then, he was a nudist, vegetarian, and gay hippy. Spiritually, Lonnie was involved in a drug cult dabbling in mysticism, often reading his Bible whilst dropping acid. One day, in the remote Tahquitz Canyon, Lonnie was on an acid trip minus clothes, when he had a theophany of Jesus as the unique route to the Father. Lonnie was told he would bear this truth to thousands of lost individuals and baptise them in the ocean.

That autumn, the Living Room team encountered Lonnie on the streets, bizarrely preaching Jesus in tandem with flying saucers. The mentally confused young man came home and joined their community. New believer Connie Bremer also moved in. She was a young woman Lonnie often purchased drugs from at the Brotherhood commune. Their friendship was rekindled, and early in 1968, they married. Both were damaged goods but were slowly stabilised and grew in Christ.

As we will explore in Chapter 24, in January 1968 Lonnie was introduced to Chuck and Kay Smith. For the 'straight' pair, he was a novelty hippy and very welcome to stay for dinner. Lonnie drove to pick Connie up from their current home and the couple stayed with the Smiths for two days. Before too long, he was recruited to Chuck's staff as a youth evangelist.

On the first Sunday that Lonnie and Connie worshipped at Calvary Chapel together, Kay Smith had a prophetic message for them. Having shared their stories and prayed together at the altar, she declared to them, 'Because of your praise and adoration before my throne tonight I'm going to bless the whole coast of California.'

With hearing this message, and having further visions, Lonnie said, 'The Lord continued to say it [the blessing] would move across the United States and go to the different parts of the world.'[2]

Essentially, as a team, Chuck had the Word and Lonnie had the Spirit. Lonnie led Wednesday nights, where hippies were invited in, and they experienced spiritual outpourings. 'Afterglows', when the Spirit's power was imparted immediately after Sunday meetings in a separate room, caused huge friction between Smith and Frisbee.

On 17 May 1968, Lonnie and Connie started to co-lead the 'House of

Miracles' commune, speedily gaining thirty-five new converts. The Frisbees lived in abject poverty as Lonnie was unpaid. However, he somehow earnt a crust through his oil paintings.

The following year, Greg Laurie, Californian co-producer of the 2023 film *Jesus Revolution*,[3] was blessed in becoming a Jesus follower through Lonnie. As for Lonnie himself, he received attention for these multiple conversions, featuring in editions of three renowned magazines in 1971.[4] The promised worldwide blessing was coming to fruition and would soon hit UK shores.

Time flew by and Lonnie ended up in the UK at three important junctures – in the early part of the 1970s, 1980s and 1990s respectively. The Spirit-filled evangelist certainly left his mark behind.

Lonnie's first European ministry trip was to Denmark during the Easter of 1970, accompanying Kenn Gulliksen, who was soon to become the early Vineyard's founder.[5] It was the following year, though, that he and Connie first arrived on UK soil. Lonnie had been invited to address successive launch events for the Nationwide Festival of Light – a campaign speaking out against society's moral decay and promoting a return to Christian values.

Thursday 9 September 1971 marked the inaugural meeting at Westminster Central Hall, London, with a sell-out crowd of 3,700 people. 'Operation Rupert Bear' protestors, contesting for gay and women's rights, were present; six men provocatively dressed as 'nuns' stormed the stage unsuccessfully and were swiftly shown the exit. Afterwards, Lonnie sat on a question-and-answer panel with Cliff Richard, the former being the first Jesus Freak most people had ever seen. Declaring the last days had arrived, and God was sweeping across the nation, he was warmly applauded. Lonnie's friends near the press desk gave him a nod and an amen.

Meanwhile, on Saturday 25 September, the launch in Trafalgar Square kicked off before a concert in Hyde Park. Lonnie stood to speak but he was again shouted down by the heckling 'nuns'. Connie failed to catch his eye so they could pray together. Eventually, Lonnie left the stage, symbolically 'shaking the dust off his feet' (Luke 10:10-11). This was one of the only occasions when the couple faced a hostile reception; they stepped forward to much warmer welcomes in the future.

The second Frisbee visit loomed across the horizon in 1981-2.

For historical context, since leaving Calvary Chapel in late 1971, he and Connie had unsuccessfully tried to mend their marriage in Florida; Lonnie then returned to California alone, for a second, unobtrusive phase at Calvary Chapel. However, by 1980, Lonnie was ministering independently. He had just returned from an overseas trip. When home, he often worshipped at the Wimbers' church, so they naturally wanted to get to know him. Following a pleasant dinner together, John later felt a nudge to invite Lonnie to speak at church, which happened on Mother's Day 1980. The Vineyard Christian Fellowship was meeting in the prestigious Canyon High School in Anaheim, California. That night, Lonnie gave his personal testimony before reading Isaiah 60:1-3 about God's glory appearing over people. He finished by encouraging those under twenty-five to receive the Holy Spirit's anointing. From his piano stool John saw how 'The place looked like a battlefield. Bodies were everywhere, falling, shaking, weeping, wailing, speaking in tongues.'[6]

According to Carol Wimber, it was, 'the watershed experience that launched us into what is today called power evangelism'.[7]

This profound experience snowballed into cross-cultural missions to the UK. Lonnie was soon used by God in two Anglican settings the first year and in Baptist and Anglican contexts the next.

In June 1981, a thirty-strong Vineyard team arrived in leafy Chorleywood, Hertfordshire for St Andrew's Church Pentecost weekend. John Wimber preached a simple message, 'Jesus wants his Church back', and immediately afterwards all of heaven was let loose. John's wife Carol recalls 'Lonnie praying for a line of young people, holding hands, and the Holy Spirit going from one to the other right down the line of them...'[8]

Next, it was Lonnie's turn to preach. He called upon reticent team member Debbie to testify about her healing from asthma as a demonstration to the UK church of the healing power of God. Vicar David Pytches remembers how 'There was "holy chaos" as many fell down in the pews when hippy evangelist and Jesus People veteran Lonnie Frisbee (part of Wimber's team) invoked the Spirit.'[9]

York was the next stop. The rector of St Michael le Belfrey, David Watson, had previously met John Wimber in Anaheim whilst lecturing on church renewal at the nearby Fuller Seminary. The two of them, alongside Lonnie, ministered together over a weekend where a prostitute called Libby, who was troubled by more than thirty demons, found freedom in a back room. Lonnie interceded so powerfully that it became deeply ingrained in the Anglican clergyman's memory.

The following year, in June 1982, Lonnie was part of the Vineyard team for a second time. They served Baptist fellowships, not only Anglican churches. Their host, Pastor Douglas McBain, had grasped the fact that Lonnie was playing a key role in the Vineyard ministry, especially during each session's 'Clinic' time where 'the presence and reality of the Spirit was sought through the ministry of Frisbee'.[10]

In the north-west, one key occasion was a renewal weekend on 'Power Evangelism'. It took place at the Baptist Church in Lytham St Annes in June. Wimber didn't feel especially sparkling teaching-wise, so cut his session short. Pastor Nigel Wright tells the story: 'He had even brought along his personal fun-maker, in the guise of an aging hippy called Lonnie Frisbee. Lonnie encouraged us to sing "Majesty" twice and, after praying, simply invited the Holy Spirit to come. What then happened is exceedingly difficult to describe. Within seconds, the inside of our attractive, Edwardian Baptist chapel was transformed into something resembling a battlefield. Holy carnage reigned.'[11] Nigel Wright himself was resting on the deck shaking and praying hard, his church members following suit. It was an unprecedented visitation for the Lancashire Baptists.

Meanwhile, from 28-29 June, the Vineyard team visited what would become the famous 'Alpha' church, Holy Trinity Brompton in London. Across the road from the iconic Harrods, its curate was future vicar, Sandy Millar. Four years on, Nicky Gumbel would be Sandy's curate. Knowing Lonnie's scary reputation, the church leaders were apprehensive about him speaking publicly. Expressing strong concern to Wimber, Lonnie reluctantly caved into their wishes and stayed quiet during the service. He had to go and cool off outside, but his hour soon came...

After Wimber's message and altar call, team members Blaine and Becky Cook recall the following account of events: 'From the very top of the stairs he just walked down, putting his hands straight out in front of him … and started *yelling* in tongues at the top of his voice.'[12] As Lonnie walked through the crowd, people parted like the Red Sea. Everybody fell to the ground as if a huge lightning bolt had hit them. Lonnie disappeared up the stairs again. Nicky Gumbel was perturbed by the fact that 'The prayers of Frisbee were especially alarming, leading to physical manifestations such as shaking, crying and hyper-ventilating.'[13] The following night, though, Nicky himself experienced a 10,000 volts phenomenon, which led to a prophetic commissioning for evangelism from Wimber.

By 1983, though, Lonnie had parted company with John Wimber's Vineyard after the former's six-month gay affair had come to light. He spent the following decade in obscurity but travelled to places like South Africa and South America, and reputedly visited England again in 1986.[14] Four years later, many Frisbee family members came to know Jesus at Lonnie's new church home; Set Free Church in Anaheim, California was run by biker-pastor, Phil Aguilar. Whilst in Anaheim and planning a trip to Egypt with Palestinian friend Marwan Bahu, Lonnie felt God redirecting him in prayer. They were to attend the Vineyard's Docklands conference in London in October 1990.[15] On his third significant UK visit, Lonnie and Marwan were paying ticketholders, just like the 8,000 others.

It was a controversial conference. A prophecy that revival would happen at the conference had come from the established Kansas City Prophet,[16] Paul Cain. However, it appeared unfulfilled. Twenty-two years earlier, in late 1968, Cain had prophesied over the early JPM's Frisbee. During the conference, though, the pair passed like ships in the night. Eventually, they met up, attending a post-conference meeting in Kensington Temple where John Wimber spoke. Cain recalls, 'Lonnie, I remember, sat in the balcony on the left side of this church, and at one point he got up and gave a prophecy that just rang out all through the meeting without a microphone or anything. It made the hair on my neck stand up.'[17] Sadly, given their previous partnership, Wimber didn't recognise or acknowledge Lonnie.

Lonnie was not walking with God from the mid-1980s but gradually came back to him. Around late November 1991, Lonnie found out he was HIV positive. He began losing weight the following year and sadly died from AIDS on 12 March 1993. Lonnie's funeral service took place in Robert Schuller's Crystal Cathedral in California five days later. Unsurprisingly, perhaps, he was compared to an anointed, but immoral, biblical judge. Chuck Smith highlighted the parallels with the Spirit-empowered Samson who, he mused out loud, probably never fulfilled his ultimate potential in God. What might have transpired had he done so? Ex-wife Connie viewed Smith's comments as hurtful and one last knock-out blow for Lonnie. His body was buried in the cemetery campus afterwards, his headstone identifying him as 'Minister – Missionary – Evangelist' with a quote by the apostle Paul about God's kingdom entailing 'righteousness, peace and joy in the Holy Spirit' (Romans 14:17).

* * *

What main legacies, then, did Lonnie bequeath to the UK Church today?

Frisbee's greatest influence was experiencing the Holy Spirit and his anointing and how he modelled this personally in his UK mission trips. Lonnie demonstrated a 'naturally supernatural' lifestyle, despite sometimes appearing whacky. Legitimate questions were prompted though. Firstly, Baptist pastor, Nigel Wright, wondered if Lonnie's power was divinely generated or if he was 'one of those human beings who is naturally gifted with great psychic energy'.[18] Secondly, Wright asked in light of the subsequent mid-1990s 'Toronto Blessing', whether concrete manifestations are biblically authentic, or might they merely be human responses to God's presence?

Then there was Lonnie's wrestling with homosexual tendencies and behaviour. Of course, similar issues exist in the UK today as proposed legislation about 'conversion therapy' is currently on the table. Worship-leader Vicky Beeching shared her painful story of 'coming out' in 2014 in her book *Undivided*. Sam Allberry, the founder of Living Out, is a British vicar now ministering in Nashville, Tennessee. He believes, conversely, in God's help in countering homosexual temptation and therefore remaining celibate. The debate is very live right now.

A wider issue emerging here is Lonnie's 'fathering'. While Lonnie was a person of independent spirit, Lonnie's natural father and stepfather, and later spiritual fathers – Chuck Smith and John Wimber – did cut him adrift. Certainly, Chuck Smith Junior, Chuck's son, candidly felt these two father-figures had turned away from Lonnie, causing him immeasurable pain. In the UK, we need spiritual fathers and mothers to help younger leaders fly through turbulent conditions as a constructive legacy from Lonnie's difficult life.

Finally, some argue that Lonnie has been written out of published histories due to embarrassment over his sexuality. In his book *Hipster Christianity,* cultural commentator Brett McCracken suggests the youth revivalist 'was ultimately disposable, because he was … never valued in and of himself. He was a utility; a gimmick that worked.'[19] Surely, the Bible's legacy teaches us that people can come with their warts 'n' all, yet still be recipients of an amazing grace that makes us both valued and godly.

Summer 1971

8.

Blessitt as He Carries the Cross Through Your Town

It was midday on Thursday 2 September 1971. A group of thirty journalists gathered eagerly in Arrivals at Heathrow Airport; they had received a tip-off from a colleague on the *Daily Mirror*. The reporters were expecting a Hollywood celebrity of sorts; he walked in pushing his own trolley – the 'Minister of Sunset Strip'. His hippy-like extended family followed him into the concourse, all looking like they needed a good freshen-up. Before too long the BBC had whisked them off to Lime Grove Studios for a live 6 p.m. broadcast of the popular news programme *Nationwide*.

Nine days afterwards, the minister would start pacing out the length and breadth of the UK with his wooden cross. Even later that month, London's Hyde Park would be his venue. Instead of debating at Speakers' Corner, a rally of 5,000 people would be addressed, leading them to pray the Lord's Prayer together and cry out for a God-given revival. This was the first visit of the flamboyant Revd Arthur Blessitt.

Arthur Owen Blessitt was born in Greenville, Mississippi on 27 October 1940. He became a Christian at a meeting in a tent when he was just seven years old, and he started to preach in his mid-teens. Training at San Francisco's Golden Gate Seminary in 1965, he found the lecturers and fellow students cold in spirit and liberal in theology. So, Arthur left. He then preached in nightclubs and casinos in Nevada before returning to southern California to minister unsuccessfully on fairgrounds.

'It was at this point that Blessitt claimed a direct call from God to minister to the down-and-out.'[1]

He and his wife, Sherry, started distributing tracts and sandwiches on the streets. On Memorial Day 1967, seventeen youngsters joined their outreach team at the hippy Love-In at Griffith Park, Los Angeles. The organiser gave Arthur five minutes onstage between the bands. This was the first time he had ever used hip-talk, such as by contrasting the experience of 'coming down from a trip' to knowing Jesus as the everlasting trip. He went on to ask those who wanted to receive Jesus to meet him under a tree. A hundred or more did and fourteen came to faith.

'Word went out over the wires that hippies were getting religion,' said Christian journalist Ed Plowman. 'Even European newsmen reported the phenomenon.'[2]

Given the countercultural climate, Arthur began to dress differently. He ditched the suit and tie and, as he says, 'Switched to turtlenecks and psychedelically patterned slacks or bell bottoms and sandals. Then came the beads.'[3] He also plastered 'Reds'[4] everywhere: circular stickers with mottos like 'Turn on to Jesus' and 'Real peace is Jesus', accompanied by a combined cross and dove symbol.

Leading Jesus People scholar David Di Sabatino comments, 'Though his circus-barker, evangelistic style made many uncomfortable, Blessitt is an important cog in the story of the Jesus people.'[5] Subsequently, Arthur's team began to reach people on Sunset Strip in Los Angeles. In March 1968, he started renting a storefront for $600 per month. 'His Place', open 24/7, was a 'cross between an old-style skid row mission and a psychedelic coffeehouse'.[6] The gospel, food and drink were all free – an irresistible fare to junkies, bikers, and runaways in the city. Arthur then recruited addiction counsellors, formed a band called Eternal Rush, and became known as the 'Minister of Sunset Strip'. New converts would do 'toilet service' – flushing their redundant drugs down the loos. Arthur claimed more than 10,000 conversions by 1969. Daytime discipleship classes were put on for new believers.

Soon, pavement congestion drew strong opposition from the police and neighbouring bar owners. The solution? Get rid of the hippy Christians by abruptly terminating the lease of His Place. In protest, Arthur placed a cross on the pavement, chained himself to it, and started a four-week fast. Press attention resulted in Arthur being offered an alternative place by Jewish businessman, William Penzner. With God's help, greed's dominance had been broken. Arthur Blessitt had made quite a name for himself, subsequently being asked to speak more widely at Jesus concerts and rallies. Unusually, he celebrated Christmas Day 1969 by starting to lug his twelve-foot by six-foot cross to Washington DC. Arthur was calling America to repent and turn to Jesus. The edition of *Time* magazine on 3 August 1970 featured a photo of him in Manhattan carrying the cross; it speedily became his most identifiable symbol. Arthur, however, was about to go global. David Di Sabatino, probably alluding to his obvious showmanship, claimed, 'His notoriety as a prominent Jesus People leader compelled him overseas.'[7] Arthur, though, saw the Jesus Movement steaming ahead in the USA. He had completed his mission at home and would now shift overseas to carry the cross the length and breadth of Britain.

A few days before flying out from New York, Arthur was interviewed by *Daily Mirror* reporter John Smith.[8] The journalist cannily asked Blessitt for his flight number and London arrival time; the UK press were thus on standby. Arthur and the team took off on 1 September and, after a frustrating four-hour lay-off, arrived at Heathrow the next day. There was a sea of inquisitive journalists and camera-flashing photographers awaiting them.

Having navigated customs, the next stop was the *Nationwide* television studio, where the team sang, 'God Is Not Dead' and son, Joel Blessitt, led a Jesus cheer. Speaking about Brits, Arthur's avowed ambition was to move them out of their respectable ancient buildings and into people's roads and homes to both share Jesus' good news and serve the needy. The papers regularly described his rugged-looking team as 'Jesus Freaks', preaching a hip gospel about being turned on by Jesus.

Meanwhile, Arthur's previous wooden cross was irretrievably broken, but given its steel reinforcing, it was too heavy to walk with anyway. The evangelist quickly located a London timberyard, purchasing four-by-four wood to construct a new one and adding a wheel to stop the pavement from wearing it down.

Nine days after arriving, crowds gathered in Trafalgar Square to catapult the team towards beautiful Scotland. Many members of the press were there, labelling Arthur the Jesus Movement leader, but he corrected them by stating, 'This is not a revolution that is soon to pass, just as it is not a revolution that has just begun. Our leader is Jesus Christ. He is Lord.'[9]

Arriving in Birmingham, Arthur publicly outlined five ideals of the JPM: happy worship, the biblical Jesus, compassion for fellow humans, zeal for gospel sharing, and a victorious Church.[10] The team pressed on to Nottingham, through the steel capital of Sheffield, and then to a smoke-filled Leeds, preaching both to crowds and individuals on the road. Arthur was particularly distraught about seeing church buildings boarded-up or converted into barns or nightclubs. Two muscular friends, Jim McPheeters and Dale Larsen, walked with Arthur and helped him carry the cross.

On one occasion, Arthur, Jim, and Dale were accosted by a reporter and a photographer for an interview and photoshoot. Arthur recounts that 'After the interview, the photographer wanted to take a photograph.

'He said, "Would you please stand with your cross and two disciples on either side?"

'"Oh, they aren't my disciples," I said. "They are the Lord's."

'"Oh, pardon me," he said with his British accent. "Would you have your two lords stand beside you?"'[11]

The A1 then beckoned towards Edinburgh. His maternal grandmother was a Campbell, so Scotland was in Arthur's genes. Reporters had recommended the group locate themselves at the Mound[12] on arrival. A runaway teenage girl requested help, having previously seen them on TV, then gave her life to Jesus. The next day, a Friday, a widely publicised meeting was planned at midday; it only drew two people – this new Christian girl and future evangelist, Ian Leitch.[13] By Sunday, though, an enthusiastic crowd of a thousand had gathered in the freezing rain. This particular visit to Edinburgh gave a template for future outreach in the team's Jesus Movement; it involved both personal witnessing and holding larger crusades, often in the open air.

The trek continued west to the urban sprawl of Glasgow. Meetings sprung up in parks, universities, and on the streets. Church-wise, Arthur preached at Tent Hall, the church inspired by the visit of American evangelist D.L. Moody in February 1837. The team were also welcomed by Revd George

Duncan[14] at The Tron Church. Ray Husthwaite, an eighteen-year-old sixth former, was invited by the attractive daughter of a Church of Scotland minister to hear Arthur preach. He remembers:

> We listened, we believed, we were loaded up with bright red 'Jesus Saves' stickers, we were turned loose on the slightly staid C of S [Church of Scotland] congregation. We roamed the streets, we went into the pubs, we witnessed to addicts, we started a youth Bible study and prayer meeting, we evangelised the school. The enthusiasm was boundless, the catch was great. We sang the choruses. The music was dreadful, but we loved it. Who cares if it was three-chord jingles like 'Happy, happy, happy, yes we're happy; Happy are the people whose God is the Looorrrrrddddd'?

Reminiscing in 2017, Ray said, 'I was, in fact, one of the legendary Jesus People in Scotland of all places. I suppose today I am just older, slower, fatter, and filled with a lot more theology.'[15]

Afterwards, a quick-fire visit to Ireland beckoned, before heading back to London for the Nationwide Festival of Light. Arthur ministered in Belfast, before he set off with his wife Sherry and their four kids, to walk the one hundred miles to Dublin. It was uncomfortably cold, windy, and rainy. People would open their doors to the Jesus People and many were led to Christ on their doorsteps. His Place team members Dale and Sandy Larsen accompanied them but, committed to discipling people long-term, they subsequently settled down in Northern Ireland. Making their home in Warrenpoint, County Down, they later networked with similar groups of believers.

On Saturday 25 September 1971, Arthur played a hugely significant part in the Nationwide Festival of Light afternoon rally in Hyde Park, as fully described in Chapter 9. He preached about deciding for Jesus, challenged believers to expect UK revival, and led the kneeling crowd in song and prayer. It was a truly unforgettable day.

In 1972, Blessitt made a return visit from April to June, organised by Northern Irish businessman Graham Lacey who had arranged the visit largely through his Nationwide Festival of Light contacts. This created tangible unease for Arthur, as he wanted to be viewed as neutral and not linked to any organisation or, indeed, church denomination. One rare exception that slipped through the net, was his appearance on the front page of the *Methodist Recorder* in April of that year.

In England, he revisited Trafalgar Square for an afternoon meeting and later that evening, he filled three-quarters of the 8,000-seater Empire Pool in Wembley.

Meanwhile, back in Northern Ireland, there were 3,000 young people saved. This was the backdrop to Geoff Bone's aborted trip to Belfast in July 1972 (as recounted in Chapter 5): YMCA leaders in the city had asked for Geoff's advice in following up with these new believers. One of the most high-profile events was when Arthur invited Billy Graham into Belfast's most troubled area. He took the well-known evangelist into a pub, after which the pair crossed over to the other side of the 'peace line'. When a bomb went off, they walked to the site to show care. The event was picked up by the news media, with its implicit message spreading globally. Arthur also preached down in the Republic of Ireland too, memorably at two universities, including the world-renowned Trinity College.

Speaking in 1972, Michael Jacob critiques Blessitt twice over. Firstly, for failing in his forecast of revival in 1971 and secondly, for 'planting' Christian supporters as pretend gospel-responders, aimed at drawing nonbelievers to come forward at the invitation.[16] Conversely, Arthur was encouraged that thousands had professed faith in Jesus and reflected, 'I could imagine what true awakening could be. It was an unforgettable feeling.'[17] He did subsequently claim the Jesus Movement revival had indeed swept through the UK at that time. Arthur was back once more in 1973.

How, then, did Arthur Blessitt's ministry reflect the JPM?

Arthur himself was not from a hippy background; neither did his family live in a communal setting. Whilst Spirit-filled himself, Arthur did not over-emphasise this in his ministry. He loved the Bible deeply but was an anecdotal, rather than expository, teacher. The two most prominent similarities to the JPM are his focus on Jesus and street outreach. Firstly, Arthur's simple message was exemplary in shining the spotlight on the

person of Jesus, with a clear view to introducing everyone to the crucified, risen Son of God. This was the Jesus at the very core of the New
Testament. Secondly, Arthur knew nothing of ghettoised Christians who
didn't leave their church buildings to be witnesses. Hiding away was not
an option; the gospel was public truth. Arthur was at his happiest out
on the highways and byways. To quote American Christian journalist Ed
Plowman, 'In his heart, Arthur Blessitt is a street Christian.'[18]

* * *

Some people leave a legacy of long-term succession for their ministries
but not in the case of eighty-three-year-old Arthur and his second
wife Denise. To quote onetime Australian JPM leader John Smith,
'Incendiary orators such as Blessitt did not intend to leave a legacy of
organised movements, but they saw their role as apostolic and catalytic
within the culture, hoping to set an example that would be voluntarily
taken up by the culture and the existing institutions.'[19] Arthur certainly
sparked things off in the UK. Like me, some readers may be slightly
older and maybe wiser now, but are we still stirred by his example to
keep gossiping the gospel?

Additionally, two UK evangelists' lives were dramatically impacted
by Arthur.[20] Bradford-based Jim King and friends were already involved
in growing street outreach when, in 1973, he was personally invited by
Arthur to train at his Street University in Santa Monica. Jim ended up
participating five summers in a row. Inspired by this, he and his wife Sue
planted the first UK Calvary Chapel in their living room in 1978. Jim
still trains evangelists today through his 'Gospel Vision' project.[21] North
of the border, in Edinburgh, Ian Leitch was a singer with the 1960s group
The Heralds. It was at the start of the seventies that he met Arthur first-
hand. Ian subsequently became a fruitful evangelist with The Heralds
Trust for fifty-three years until his death on 19 June 2022.[22] Maybe the
UK Church needs to 'ordain' evangelists more often…

Finally, Arthur modelled the use of visual creativity in grabbing people's
attention, including his cross-carrying and mastering the media of the
day. As a critical observer, in 1973 Geoffrey Corry positively argued that

his 'importance will probably lie in his contribution towards creating a climate of opinion in which Jesus is news…'[23]

Some have viewed this as narcissistic attention-seeking; others see it as publicising Jesus to outsiders to the faith. Whatever the case, one can hardly ignore a man walking through a town with a cross in tow!

Autumn 1971

9.

A Festival Hits the Capital Before Going Nationwide

Free music festivals at Hyde Park in London were commonplace in the 1970s. I had attended an open-air gig there myself, featuring Eric Clapton's short-lived band, Blind Faith. This one was different though. Nationwide beacons had 'advertised' it beforehand. Prince Charles, the future King of England, sent a telegram. Mother Teresa ensured her audio cassette message arrived on time. Cliff Richard drove onto the grass in his Rolls-Royce. Participants joyfully marched over from Trafalgar Square. It wasn't all sweetness and light though: the 'Angry Brigade' threw stink bombs and food fragments at participants and some gave Nazi 'Sieg Heil' salutes. Afterwards, though, the park was cleaner than before the festival.

It was late afternoon on Saturday 25 September 1971. A rally for 80,000 young people had begun. Banners paraded with 'Jesus Christ is the solution' to our moral pollution; 'J-E-S-U-S!' shouts rang out everywhere. Even the newly converted sixty-eight-year-old journalist Malcolm Muggeridge engaged in the famed index-finger pointing to heaven. It was the second event of the day to launch the Nationwide Festival of Light. Moral campaigning was going public.

So, how did things begin for this body that still influences our society for Christ?

Peter and Janet Hill had been engaged in mission work in India for four years. Two of those were with youth organisation Operation Mobilisation.

Travelling their way home overland in November 1970, the couple returned to the UK and the ready availability of pornography in ordinary newsagents startled them. During a week of prayer and fasting, Peter had an unexpected but clear vision. Positively, tens of thousands of young people were marching for Christ and righteousness in London. Negatively, a form of dark opposition arrived, trying to invade the march.

Peter promptly asked God for three confirmations. They came.

Firstly, he read a magazine article about Christians uniting. Secondly, at a prayer and Bible week, the guests heard of a ten-thousand-strong march in Blackburn, calling for both higher morality and vigorous witnessing. Thirdly, one of the week's leaders, Campbell McAlpine, had mused, 'Why don't we rally in Trafalgar Square or Hyde Park?' An unexpected fourth confirmation also came when he heard American missionary Jean Darnell's vision: 'It was a bird's-eye view of a kind of haze over the whole British Isles, like a green fog. And then little pinpricks of lights began to appear, from the top of Scotland to Land's End, likes fires breaking out all over the nation.'[1]

Peter then floated his idea with clergy contacts. He also met with journalist and satirist Malcolm Muggeridge and controversial National Viewers and Listeners' Association campaigner Mary Whitehouse. Other influencers threw their lot in after an Evangelical Alliance meeting in Chelsea, London. These included war veteran Lieutenant General Sir William Dobbie as Chairman. The festival's twin aims were to address 'sexploitation' and moral pollution and to present the claims of Jesus. This led to the idea of two distinct gatherings, linked by a march of witness from one to the other. In discussion with Peter Hill, regarding becoming a Council member, Muggeridge vocalised, 'It's a festival of light', and the name stuck. Adopted in early June at a meeting of fourteen people at Spitalfields rectory, the word 'nationwide' was quickly added. There would be three events stretching over two distinct days: an inaugural rally in Westminster Central Hall on Thursday 16 September 1971, followed by a Saturday afternoon outdoor launch in Trafalgar Square ten days later, before marching on to Hyde Park where 100,000 people were expected to attend.

Regarding Jesus People involvement, hip minister Lonnie Frisbee was on a Q&A panel at the inaugural event and unsuccessfully attempted to speak in Trafalgar Square.[2]

Two more JPM personnel were involved in Saturday's launch.

Country Faith were one of many groups emerging from Calvary Chapel. Another, Love Song led by Chuck Girard, was touring the States at the time. A festival organiser had phoned Maranatha! Music, asking, 'Can Love Song play at the London Festival?' However, they were promptly told they were otherwise engaged. The second question was, 'Might you suggest another band to represent the Californian Jesus People?' Secretary Carol Butler was quite embarrassed; Country Faith was her husband Chuck's band so, being naturally biased, was it appropriate for her to promote them? However, it was an expenses-paid trip and their first international gig, so, the airport was the next stop ...

Guitarist Butler had a beautiful voice, singing alongside three other guitarists and a drummer, in what British journalist John Capon described as 'one of the best Jesus People groups'.[3] Backing singer, Debby Retino, was later the creative genius behind the innovative *Psalty the Singing Songbook* for kids.[4] Butler recalls, 'At Trafalgar Square, we did most of our music, but just one or two songs in Hyde Park ... In 1972 we were re-invited back for the "Festival for Jesus."'[5] A song performed at Hyde Park, remembered by Colonel Dobbie's wife Flo, started with the lyrics: 'Feel the warmth around you. Hear the music in the air. Feel the peace surround you. Smiling faces everywhere. Listen closely to the words we share. Our Lord Jesus wants to take you there.'[6]

Arthur Blessitt's full story appears in Chapter 8. Regarding the Nationwide Festival of Light, though, this flamboyant character was prominent at the 4 p.m. rally in Hyde Park. How did the Sunset Strip minister first get involved though? Colonel Dobbie and colleagues had previously braved a Hyde Park pop concert one Saturday to see how it was done. His wife Flo takes up her husband's recollections of what they encountered there:

A group of gaily-dressed young Americans, hippie-style, in freaky tee-shirts, were sitting in a circle, singing ... These must be the fabulous Jesus People ... A big man in Californian gear, and wearing a string of beads around his neck, then got up and, standing in the circle, began to speak. His words were simple, arresting. 'Tune into God! Let Him turn you on! Jesus said, "I stand at the door and knock. If you will tune in, if you'll open the door, I will come in, I will abide with you." Jesus will turn you on to a trip like you have never known before.'[7]

Subsequently, the Colonel arranged a meeting to glean Arthur's advice about following up new believers after the rally. He outlined his ideas and Dobbie was spellbound; the evangelist just had to take part. Flying back to America for a TV appearance on the pre-rally Monday, Arthur returned the same day. His presence electrified Saturday's event.

From a broader angle, both rallies had a marked Jesus People feel to them.

Celia is the wife of Lyndon Bowring, the Chairman of CARE (Christian Action, Research & Education), the rebranded name of the Festival after March 1983. She was there that momentous day. Just eighteen, Celia had recently come to faith, and was with her Christian Union group. Proudly wearing the flamed Festival T-shirt, her Jesus banner was boldly held aloft. Celia paints a vivid picture: 'Every now and then someone in the crowd would cry, "Give us a J", followed by a "J", "Give us an E", and so on, until the full name of JESUS was shouted out! There was a huge range of ages, although many people of my age, late teens and early 20s. There was a sense of exuberance too. Here we were in the public square, where everybody could see us, so proud of being followers of Jesus!'[8]

John Capon notes other familiar features throughout his book, like tracts given out, 'One Way' fingers raised, and stickers plastered everywhere. One cynical *Rolling Stone* journalist, Robert Greenfield, observed orange coloured Jesus stickers pushed into the eyes of the Black Stone lions guarding Nelson's Column. Apparently, the loud 'JESUS!' shouts and impromptu singing in Trafalgar Square drowned out the reading of the Prince of Wales' telegram.

The afternoon finale in Hyde Park was particularly striking for its JPM ethos.

Country Faith opened proceedings musically at 4 p.m. Other UK Jesus People types onstage were pop star Cliff Richard, sporting his pink shirt and gold medallion, and future worship-leader Graham Kendrick. Musical troubadour Larry Norman was performing too, probably invited because of his strong allegiance to friends Malcolm and Kitty Muggeridge. Asked who his favourite singer was, Larry would often reply 'Muggeridge', simply because the journalist's prose was so lyrical. The journalist joined thousands of others in making the 'One Way' sign, causing Larry to believe he was more of a Jesus Person than a convert to Roman Catholicism.

Arthur Blessitt was given the last half-hour of the event. He spoke very powerfully on Joel 3:14: 'Multitudes, multitudes in the valley of decision! For the day of the LORD is near in the valley of decision.' Specific sins reflected the valley's spiritual emptiness, he said. Only Jesus, the real and living leader, could transport us through it. Arthur urged believers to 'go down into Soho and fill all the dirty books with Jesus tracts'.[9] Christian discipleship was based, he declared, on forgiveness, purpose, and presence. In closing, the leather-jerkin-clad evangelist gave people the opportunity to respond to Jesus. The crowd was hushed. An urgent call to Christians followed: 'Do you want to see revival in Britain? If you do, kneel as we sing, and pray.'[10] Everyone did, including the policemen. Raising their hands to heaven, Arthur poignantly led a musical version of the Lord's Prayer. Capon records that 'He had no accompaniment, his voice was not good, he seemed to have pitched it too low and the crowd responded very slowly.'[11] The volume increased, though, as the worshipping crowd gave God the kingdom, the power, and the glory.

The evangelist himself recalls an unusual report:

I heard later from those outside the compound facing the raised platform that they saw strange shafts of light fall through the darkening park so that nothing could be seen but the light playing on those thousands of upraised hands as far as the eye could see … I'm sure that angels sang with us that night and lifted their voices, too, in that great moment of praise.[12]

There was a final 'Jesus shout'. Country Faith played the closing song. Host Nigel Goodwin, pioneer of the Christian Arts Centre Group, dismissed the crowd. Litter bags were filled, making the park look neater than it had on arrival. The crowds noisily made their way home, a booking clerk at Marble Arch underground being led to Christ while dishing out tickets.

In summary, Pete Ward contends, 'The youth-orientated Jesus Movement was at the heart of the development of the festival.'[13]

Two years after the event, Anglican clergyman Geoffrey Corry reflected, 'This was a remarkable rally at which Blessitt turned around the NFOL's emphasis on moral pollution and made it into a campaign for Jesus across the nation.'[14]

Although this evangelistic emphasis was prominent in Peter Hill's original vision, the first Director of the NFOL from 1974 onwards, Raymond Johnston, subsequently steered the ship in a more socio-political direction.[15] Hill's goal, though, was to get 'people aflame for Jesus Christ',[16] both evangelistically and morally, hence a festival for Jesus called 'Land Aflame' happened the following summer; 20,000 fired-up young people were expected.

From 30 August to 3 September 1972, there was nationwide street outreach: giving out literature, performing street theatre, and playing open-air music. More centrally, in London, there were five days of teaching in the mornings, afternoon outreaches, and evenings of music and testimony. The festival leaders didn't drop the ball on ethical values either, Celia Bowring commenting, 'The momentum of Christian engagement was continuing.'[17] Believers were encouraged to engage in targeted campaigning and to influence legislation on contemporary issues.

The theme-song for the Festival, 'Light Up the Fire' by Parchment, came within a whisker of entering the Top 30,[18] with much of the airplay coming from offshore Radio Luxembourg. Old favourites Larry Norman and Country Faith played again, accompanied by future Calvary Chapel pastors Malcolm and Alwyn. The week was filmed by ABBA Productions, resulting in a fifty-minute documentary called: *Why Should the Devil Have All the Good Music?*[19]

When considering the early years of the Nationwide Festival of Light, it is worth contrasting the perspectives of two key participants.

Young Bible College student Nick Cuthbert was training at the Christian Life College in Poole, Dorset. He did a lot of the practical donkeywork in 1971. Nick also read the first of three public declarations at Trafalgar Square, in his case urging the government to recognise moral pollution was more dangerous than environmental pollution.[20] Subsequently, he and his wife Lois have been involved with various Christian ministries in Birmingham. His positive opinion is that the festival was 'a vehicle for the spirit of the Jesus Movement'.[21]

Raymond Johnston was the first full-time Director of the festival from April 1974 onwards. A year later, Peter Meadows of *Buzz* magazine interviewed him, initially suggesting the festival may have left behind 'the early image with heavy overtones of the American Jesus movement'. He then quizzed its director about whether that move was intentional or not. For Johnston, it certainly was, simply to avoid identifying with just one section of the Church's life. However, Johnston wistfully concedes, 'I do hope that we haven't lost the support of those youngsters' – their passion for Jesus, he concluded, was a real provocation to older folks.[22]

* * *

What, then, is the lasting legacy of the Nationwide Festival of Light today?

The immediate aftermath of 1971-2 left many good deposits behind, such as the platforms given to musician Larry Norman and evangelist Arthur Blessitt. Plus, other Jesus festivals were spawned in localities across the UK. However, the Festival's direction intentionally veered away from evangelism. For example, at their anniversary rally in 1976, the leaders agonised over how Britain had insufficiently returned to Christian values over the previous five years.

I think the biggest legacy today, then, is the healthy balance between social action and evangelistic outreach amongst Christians and churches, living as both salt and light in society. Sharing Jesus is undoubtedly high on the agenda today through courses such as 'Alpha' and 'Christianity Explored', plus the training and modelling of lifestyle evangelism. For instance, during the recent pandemic, many explored the gospel in our church through the 'Alpha' course on Zoom.

In parallel, CARE being moral influencers with truth and compassion is still a high priority today. Under new CEO Ross Hendry, this vital ministry continues to impact our culture for Christ. For example, the excellent Leadership Programme will equip fifteen young people for work in the public square in 2023-2024. Campaigns currently address bioethics, Artificial Intelligence, and modern-day slavery, not forgetting small boats of refugees coming across the Channel.

With my Jesus People background in mind, allow me to reflect. Persuading fellow UK citizens that God's values are positive, as enshrined in the Ten Commandments, is important. However, it seems that our temporal concerns can sometimes trump eternal considerations. For example, we may find ourselves rightfully tackling issues of hunger, but be blissfully unaware of the 'famine of hearing the words of the LORD' predicted in Amos 8:11.

Winter 1971-72

10.

Turned Onto Jesus But Turned Off the Bad Trip

In December 1971, the front cover of the charismatic magazine *Renewal* carried a prominent photo of Arthur Blessitt carrying his cross in Trafalgar Square. Its theme was 'The Jesus People and the Churches'. This issue proved a first-rate opportunity to carry an advert for 'Britain's No 1 Street Paper' in the middle pages. The name of the paper was *Vibrations*, and it boldly declared, 'We are Jesus People and we're going One Way. Join us.'[1]

A classic graphic of the 'One Way' finger points upwards, and a headshot of Jesus sits underneath it. The slightly mysterious 'Jesus People' behind this paper was a group called New Life Foundation Trust – a Christian drug rehabilitation charity.

New Life Foundation Trust was started by ordained evangelist Vic Ramsey in the winter of 1964 after he had watched too many young people going downhill fast by thrill-seeking through drugs. Two years later, his team's Sunday evening 'Late Night Special' outreaches started. They drew 'beatniks, "the drifters", students, tourists, prostitutes, alcoholics, and junkies'[2] to a basement room in Orange Street, Soho. This was right near the bright neon lights of Leicester Square in London.

In this non-churchy experiment, Jesus followers introduced themselves on the streets and invited people back to the basement. On the very first night, twenty-five young men made their way forward for counselling, nineteen of whom were pill-takers or addicts. That same year, Billy Graham was in town for his 1966 Earls Court Crusade and was encouraged by his visit to this venture. Ramsey's ministry subsequently progressed into the residential treatment of addicts, and that same year he wrote *They Call it a Fix*.[3] Six years later, Ramsey was appointed Drugs Consultant for the Munich Olympic Games.

Ramsey's ministry published a sixteen-page tabloid newspaper called *His Paper,* geared towards the Christian youth.[4] However, this was supplemented by the seeker-friendly *Vibrations,* a street paper published as a cooperative venture with the mission agency Youth With A Mission (YWAM). The *Renewal* magazine advert was packed with hip language and included two references to 'revolutionary' and 'revolution', and another that identified its target as the 'Jesus People'. It was advertised as a 'revolutionary Christian newspaper for the street scene'.[5] The first edition, priced at just 3p plus postage, apparently had to be reprinted five times.

Vibrations was also widely used by the evangelistic Jesus Liberation Front and was 'largely inspired by (with borrowings from) the American Christian magazine *Hollywood Free Paper*'.[6] It contained thrilling stories about those who had lived a drug lifestyle and were freed by Jesus.

Later, in the August 1972 edition of *Buzz* magazine, another full-page advert appeared. Its cartoon graphics were drawn by a Jesus Family artist, Steve Spicer. An evangelistic rally at Westminster Central Hall on 25th November 1972 was publicised. The advert's language was decidedly hip, claiming, 'Man, you can use it in street outreach.'[7]

Additionally, Ramsey supported the opening of a 'converted pub' called the *One Way Inn* on Earls Court Road. Led by a man called Tony Ferguson, it too was a hub for evangelistic activity and counselling young people.

While Ramsey's hands-on ministry was largely confined to the UK, it had many similarities with YWAM's ministry to people on the 'Hippy Trail', which developed their culturally appropriate Dilaram Houses in Europe and Asia.

YWAM and The Hippy Trail

In 1956, a twenty-year-old Bible College student named Loren Cunningham had a vision of young believers from all denominations being sent to the nations. He subsequently led a youth mission to Hawaii in the summer of 1960, and later that year YWAM was born. Loren married Darlene Scratch two years after. By 1966, the movement had ten full-time staff, but by the seventies, that number had increased to fifty.

Floyd and Sally McClung had been American YWAM missionaries since 1967. Their story of Dilaram Houses starts three years later, as recorded in Floyd's book, *Living on the Devil's Doorstep: From Kabul to Amsterdam.*[8]

In 1970, the McClungs encountered globe trotters on the so-called Hippy Trail in Delhi. Many young people were trekking from Europe to India, lured by the fascination of Eastern religions.

'These were the lost and lonely children of the sixties and early seventies.'[9]

After chatting with Loren Cunningham for spiritual guidance, and then getting prepared logistically, the couple drove a team overland to Kabul the following year. This was the place where all the Hippy Trail paths converged. After arriving, the city-based expatriate pastor Dr Christy Wilson persuaded them to stay on and minister to this lost generation, and medically serve their health needs. For example, drug-related abscesses needed to be drained, which Sally quickly learned to do. The team began to demonstrate Jesus' tangible care by opening a clinic and publishing *The Dysentery Daily* news sheet.

The couple subsequently adopted hippy-style clothing. For many newborn Jesus Freaks, the church was culturally too straight for hippies on the Trail. So, having previously started a 'Dilaram Tearoom', that year they began to rent the first residential 'Dilaram House'. Its name was prayerfully chosen as the Farsi translation for 'a peaceful heart'.[10] Some people simply called it 'the Jesus house'. Its twenty-three rooms were 'a home for converted hippies to grow in God … and a place for Christians to minister to them in a relaxed, easy-going atmosphere'.[11]

Soon, though, a changed government with no time for hippy dropouts meant the population in Kabul abruptly diminished. Thus, the team started to explore opening Dilaram Houses elsewhere along the Trail. A second opened in Kathmandu in Nepal. 'Similar homes', says McClung, 'were to be opened and run in London and New Delhi for several years, each seeing many travellers and dropouts come to Christ.'[12] The Dilaram House in London started under Paul and Mary Miller's leadership in London in November 1977 and ran for seven years. Their emphasis was similar, reaching young people with the travel-bug, but also focusing on those wrestling with alcohol and sexual addictions.

If we track back to Europe in 1972, we find that YWAM had undertaken their largest-ever outreach at the Munich Olympic Games. One thousand team members were joined by young people from forty other organisations. Munich was widely recognised as the European drug capital at this time, and the outreach had a definite Jesus People vibe to it. During the Games, Bob Owen recounts a typical story: a young man called Wolfgang was miraculously freed from withdrawal pains through prayer from none other than British addiction specialist Vic Ramsey. Author Bob Owen partnered with him and later commented, 'As Vic prayed, you could just feel the tension releasing within this man. You could feel all the knots in his abdomen untie … shortly afterwards, he lay down and slept like a baby.'[13]

Meanwhile, following the Munich Games, freshly converted young people were involved in establishing further Dilaram Houses. For example, JPM historian Richard Bustraan recounts: 'After the Olympics, and with the help of new JP [Jesus People] recruits, YWAM went on to establish large and enduring works among drug addicts in Denmark in 1972 and in the Netherlands in 1973.'[14]

Both Vic Ramsey's UK-based ministry, and that of YWAM's Dilaram Houses, were comfortable accommodating hippy speak and wearing hippy garb to reach those in the grip of drug abuse. However, this wasn't a view shared by everyone. There were groups on either side of the Atlantic adopting quite the opposite approach.

Teen Challenge

David Wilkerson's Teen Challenge was founded in the late fifties. At the time, he was an Assemblies of God pastor in a country church. In 1958, a high-profile murder trial of gang members prompted him to start a ministry for younger people struggling with drug abuse. A year-long residential programme began in December 1960 in a house in Brooklyn, helping youth to live disciplined drug-free lives. His story is told in his book *The Cross and the Switchblade*.[15]

Later, there were huge tensions between Wilkerson and some of the earliest JPM leaders.

On one infamous occasion, Wilkerson interviewed four leaders of the Living Room for a TV programme on Oakland's Channel Two network, later aired on 7 December 1967. His aggressive questioning probed their approach to continued drug use as new believers. Did they truly preach Christ as the Saviour from sin? To him, at best, they had a laissez-faire attitude to drugs. To be fair, some drug use was continuing through dope smoking in the Living Room and their communal house in Novato.[16] Occasionally, LSD was 'dropped' too.

Wilkerson boldly labelled them 'psychedelic ministers', whereas current scholar Andrew MacDonald notes that others defended them for not ditching their pasts instantaneously: 'While examples such as this reveal the inherent messiness of cultural adaption, many of the movement's most notable leaders emphasized grace for those struggling with the transition between the two worlds.'[17] Eventually, the residents of the Living Room did give up dropping acid, then stopped smoking pot too.

Wilkerson subsequently wrote a strong critique of hippies and Jesus People converts in his 1969 book *Purple Violet Squish*.[18] However, his attitude seemed to noticeably soften in the early seventies. In 1971, he had stopped ridiculing hippies but was cautious about unsanctified new believers who, he claimed, 'had not been to the cross'.[19] The following year, he published *The Jesus People Maturity Manual*, which implicitly accepted the JPM as a viable movement of the Holy Spirit. According to scholar David Di Sabatino, this manual 'offers the "Jesus person" his insights into several different areas, including sexuality, drugs, music, and rudimentary theology'.[20] Additionally, the church Wilkerson pastored – Melodyland Christian Centre in Anaheim – welcomed many Jesus People converts in the early seventies.[21] The pastor simply wanted to ensure they were disciples committed for the long haul.

Life for the World Trust

Frank Wilson's Life for the World Trust was a UK ministry, founded in 1967, but sharing a similar ethos to Wilkerson's work. Their rehabilitation centre was first based in north London but later moved to Gloucestershire. It claimed a sixty to seventy per cent success rate with drug users.[22] Frank wrote two books in the seventies, *Counselling the Drug Abuser* and *House of New Beginnings*.[23] In terms of sponsorship, it featured as 'This Week's Good Cause' on BBC Radio 4 in early 1974.[24]

Kenneth Leech, the contemporaneous author of *Youthquake,* had some perceptive things to say about the ministry's distinctive ethos: 'The refusal to use drug jargon about the Gospel is shared by a British evangelist, Frank Wilson … influenced a good deal by David Wilkerson.'

Leech then quotes Wilson from a 1973 newsletter:

'The last three years have been years of popularity of a certain kind of "Jesus style" Christianity. Slogans like "Turn on to Jesus" and "Stay high on love" have become familiar to thousands of Christians. The one-time "old-fashioned" evangelical has come out of his cocoon and fitted into this new "Jesus Revolution".'

Wilson proceeds to argue that drug users who become Christians completely dispense with their previous habit by embracing the age-old gospel. You don't have to shout slogans or wave banners to follow Jesus either, he contends.

The work of his team, Wilson concludes, 'has gone on quietly in the simple power of the Holy Spirit who is revealing the Christ of Scriptures to young people and satisfying them'.[25]

Wilson was distancing himself from the negative Jesus People ethos disliked by Wilkerson, in contrast to Vic Ramsey's more positive approach.

To unpack this more fully, in the late sixties Wilson met Pat Prosser, a volunteer taking collected furniture from his Baptist church in Woking to the Northwick Park rehabilitation facility. He was Wilson's eventual successor, relaunching the Trust's ministry in 1993.

Prosser makes an informed guess as to what lay behind Wilson's ministry philosophy:

'The way Frank felt about the Jesus People Movement probably felt like the way he later viewed the Jesus Army: having a view of addictions that said once you'd prayed for someone, they would instantly be OK. A contrast would be Jackie Pullinger, who would spend three days praying in tongues over someone, but the following eight years discipling them thoroughly.'

Prosser concludes by saying converted addicts 'need lots of after-care in dealing with long-term underlying issues, and in gaining a heart-knowledge of Jesus'.[26]

Regardless of differences in approach, there is no doubt that new ministries emerged, both in the USA and the UK, that recognised the gospel imperative to set captives free from drugs in Jesus' name.

* * *

So, what is the legacy of those involved in drug addiction ministries and how did they mirror certain marks of the JPM?

Jesus People didn't wait for people to come to church but were out on the streets to serve people practically, demonstrating and declaring the good news of liberation through Jesus. Perhaps a parallel in the UK today would be *Street Pastors*. This ministry was pioneered by Revd Les Isaac in Brixton, London, in 2003. Serving on the nation's streets between 10 p.m. and 4 a.m. at weekends, these sacrificial volunteers care for struggling people, including those suffering the effects of drug and/or alcohol abuse.

Communes to initially disciple people were widespread in the JPM, giving Jesus followers a family in which to mature in their newfound freedom in Christ. Likewise, a ministry in Clevedon near Bristol today, with long-term roots in Life for the World Trust, has a similar ethos. At Andrew House there is room for eleven men, who are recovering addicts, to stabilise their lives. It is the direct successor to the Caleb Project, both successively run by converted addicts Ron and Pat Norman.[27]

Finally, YWAM still runs its six-month Discipleship Training Schools (DTS) today, including in the UK. Trainees might not know about the historic roots of these Schools. One of the early YWAM leaders, serving during the Jesus People days of the seventies, was an American called Leland

Paris. In conversation, he asked a new believer he was discipling about his religious background. Perhaps surprisingly, the young man replied, 'Drugs'. Leland soon consulted his cousin Loren Cunningham and other leaders and concluded that he would launch a three-pronged training programme focusing on the Bible, character development, and mission work. It was, and is, DTS. How good that in God's kingdom, constructive Christian identity replaces the destructive allure of substance abuse.

Winter 1971-72

11.

Norman is as Happy as Larry on the Road

It was the winter of 1971. A couple were getting married three days after Christmas. The photogenic man and woman both had strikingly long blond hair. They had first met in August when Larry sang at a Jesus Festival on the beach near Los Angeles. Pamela was determined to marry him from the outset, sketching their first encounter in a cartoon with speech bubbles. Larry was intrigued by her but felt the former model and airline hostess was too vain. Over time, he softened. Mr and Mrs Norman tied the knot.

After a whirlwind honeymoon in New York City, the second 'honeymoon' was a concert tour of thirty-eight gigs over thirty-five days in the UK. Even as they stepped off the plane from Chicago O'Hare, the Normans were public property at Heathrow. The grass didn't grow under their feet though. The next stop was Lancaster University, where Larry's promoter hadn't seen such a big response for Pink Floyd or The Who.

Larry Norman was born on 8 April 1947 in Corpus Christi, Texas. Brought up in a Southern Baptist home, he put his faith in Jesus aged five and started performing his songs publicly four years later. At eighteen, he graduated from high school, dropping out of college the following year. In 1966 he joined the psychedelic rock band, People!, as their main songwriter. He quit the group in 1968, claiming tensions with bandmates about their growing allegiance to the cult-like Scientology. That same day their first album hit the record shops.

Soon afterwards, at a Friday night prayer meeting, 'Norman had a powerful spiritual encounter that threw him into a frenzy of indecision about his life [and] for the first time in his life, he had received what he understood to be the Holy Spirit.'[1] In July 1968, he moved to Los Angeles, witnessing daily on Hollywood Boulevard, and feeding and clothing new converts. Larry was also involved with the Salt Company coffeehouse outreach. According to JPM expert Larry Eskridge, 'Back in Los Angeles, Norman continued to be in major demand in the local Jesus People scene, appearing at coffeehouses and rallies and occasionally taking up the pen for a column … in the *Hollywood Free Paper.*'[2] To earn his crust he wrote two musicals satirising the counterculture.

In 1969, Larry was offered the part of hippy-tribe leader George Berger in *Hair* but turned it down because it glorified drugs and free sex. That year he first met Randy Stonehill, who months later came to faith in 'Norman's Kitchen'.[3] Larry's solo album, *Upon This Rock,* was released in December 1969, ironically selling badly. He celebrated the new decade by launching his One Way Records label.

Larry was featured in the *Son Worshippers*[4] documentary in February 1971, and was interviewed for *Time* Magazine's Jesus People issue that July, and fast became a recognisable JPM face. Unlike safe Christian lyrics, author Steve Rabey wrote, 'Norman's songs explored racism, militarism, secularism, the war in Vietnam, NASA's $25million space program, social and economic justice, free sex and sexually transmitted diseases, and the boom in Eastern, occult and New Age religions.'[5]

Meanwhile, if we jump over to the UK during the seventies, we need to fasten our seatbelts for a whistle-stop tour of 'Larry World'.

In September 1971 Larry, still single, flew over to perform for the fledgling Nationwide Festival of Light, launching what Gregory Thornbury calls 'a reverse British Invasion for Jesus'.[6]

Early the next year, accompanied by his new wife Pamela, Larry returned to a media frenzy, performing thirty-eight consecutive concerts. The Normans rented a flat in Park Lane – not the prestigious thoroughfare, but a lane in the leafy outskirts of Carshalton. *Upon This Rock* had its first UK release in 1972, and Larry struck up a friendship with Cliff

Richard when they both played the Festival for Jesus. The following year he recorded *So Long Ago The Garden* at George Martin's (The Beatles' producer) famed Air Studios. He also met prostitute Hope Valentine in Mayfair, leading her to Jesus as recounted in the song 'Come Away'.[7] Meanwhile, Stateside in 1974, Larry's marriage started to flounder, which cut his touring life short.

The second half of the decade saw Larry developing a close friendship with the comedian Dudley Moore.[8] He also gigged to raise funds for Tear Fund and the Arts Centre Group. On 15 April 1976, he and Cliff Richard did back-to-back concerts supporting Pete Townshend's charity to help addicts break free. The following year, Larry's well-publicised World Tour kicked off, with five dates in the UK. Two crises hit him in 1978: his marriage seriously unravelled (the couple divorced on 2 September 1980); while an apparent accident inside an aeroplane left him with physical injuries and partial brain damage. The following year, though, he surprised Greenbelters by rocking alongside Randy Stonehill[9] and also initiated his own Phydeaux record label in the UK. As the decade ended, Larry was living in rural Herefordshire, recording locally at the Chapel Lane Productions studio. He had come full circle and was effectively single again.

Larry Norman had a widespread impact on the UK church, but in this chapter, I aim to answer two relevant questions: What influence did Larry have on the UK and vice versa? Was Larry a Jesus Person, and to what extent did he flesh out the ten marks of the JPM? I will conclude by highlighting his legacy on this side of the Atlantic.

For the everyday Jesus follower, Larry's greatest impact was his live gigs. He would drift onstage, dressed in jeans and a leather jacket, displaying his long blond hair with an acoustic guitar slung over his shoulder. The songs he performed were overtly rock, and the lyrics poignantly earthy, for instance mentioning individuals contracting gonorrhoea on Valentine's Day whilst seeking the ultimate sexual encounter. They would often bitingly critique contemporary Western culture too. Larry's focus, though, was always on Jesus the Son of God. He advised concertgoers to look into him rather than crystal balls. Songs were punctuated with the raconteur chatting about his faith-journey. When the gig ended, Larry would invariably stick around, listening to individuals' needs and scribbling down their names and situations for prayer. He was quite offish with autograph hunters though.

Four brief cameos illustrate how the enigmatic Larry both provoked and encouraged people deeply.

Glasgow's 1,500-seater Tent Hall church regularly put on evangelistic youth events. At his 1972 gig there, Larry first removed the Bible from its lectern and then proceeded to sit on the pulpit, dangling his legs over its side. The pastor eventually demanded Larry get down, inspiring boos from the audience. He was the talk of the town. It was one thing removing the Bible from its hallowed spot, but it was blasphemy to place your bum on its sacred resting-place.

Larry filled the Royal Albert Hall six times. On Saturday 6 January 1973, he was in an abrasive mood. Performing 'Sweet Sweet Song of Salvation', Larry's fans were singing and clapping along. Twice he ordered the stunned audience to stop, exclaiming, 'So don't buy my records tonight, and don't ever come to one of my concerts again … because you're supposed to feed the poor.'[10] He was tired of performing for purportedly affluent Jesus People and fearful he would be viewed as an Elmer Gantry money-making evangelist. 'It was time for him to say goodbye to the Jesus movement and the Christian subculture.'[11]

Conversely, author Ralph Turner remembers a mid-seventies concert at the Jesus Centre in Birmingham. After the show, Larry stayed an extra hour to chat and play, and Ralph was happy to miss the last bus: 'He asked us what Birmingham was like to live in and what we wanted to do with our lives. He talked about needing to chat to people to "keep it real on the road".'[12]

Squash coach Charlie Campbell-Wynter recalls a May 1981 gig at London's Dominion Theatre. He had expected to be bored, an issue hampering him from following Jesus, but he said, 'It blew my stereotypical idea out of the water, as the way I looked or acted was not important, but my heart before God. At the end of the concert, I decided to ask Jesus into my life to forgive my sins.'[13]

In a genuinely two-way relationship, Larry himself was also impacted by his UK sojourns.

First, they gave him a fresher, more critical perspective on his own home country of America. Second, he had a bigger following in the UK, as a big fish in a small pond. Third, he described his relationship with the UK to music journalist Mike Rimmer as being 'like a romance that kept growing'.[14] Pressed further by Rimmer about being an enthusiastic Anglophile, Larry added that he was charmed by the English writers Charles Dickens and G.K. Chesterton, inspired by English culture and history, blessed by English friends like journalist Malcolm Muggeridge, but that he could live without our carbohydrate-filled shepherd's pies!

Larry ministered in the UK, and at two key junctures lived here, from 1971 until performing his last gig in Waterlooville, Hampshire on 16 July 2005. So, to what extent did he identify with – or perhaps did others identify him with – Jesus People in the UK? More widely, of course, Larry was associated with the movement's prolific 'One Way' sign,[15] and had written debatably its most popular anthem, 'I Wish We'd All Been Ready'. He was also a widely photographed Jesus Person.

Many UK commentators view him as central to the JPM: Greenbelt Festival's Martin Wroe describes Larry as 'the popular spokesman for the late 60s and 70s Jesus Movement'.[16] While Larry's friend and intended biographer Steve Turner portrayed him as a figurehead for the emerging JPM. Meanwhile, Geoff Shearn of Musical Gospel Outreach (MGO) said this after first listening to *Upon This Rock*: 'Larry set a new standard of creativity for us, and he was significant as he was one of the leaders of the Jesus Movement in California and he represented something that was radical, expressive and passionate for Jesus.'[17]

British writer and academic Rupert Loydell appears more nuanced in describing the Larry he loved as a real friend, but one who could cynically manipulate things as he wanted.

On one hand, 'he did church concerts, he did Christian tours, he played at Greenbelt, but then claimed he was doing something different, or made stuff up about "being banned for talking about Jesus at Greenbelt"'. On the other hand, 'the Jesus Movement embraced him, and he needed that embrace to sell records and have any musical presence at all'.

Loydell concludes, 'He didn't "sit comfortably" anywhere though. He was too disorganized for the secular world, who would not tolerate the way he turned up late or unprepared; and he often upset mainstream church audiences. But he fitted right in at the edge of things.'[18]

Perhaps unsurprisingly, Larry's self-perception was quite different. Interviewed by British journalist James Tweed about his JPM credentials in 2004, he claimed, 'No, I was never really a Jesus Freak. I didn't really fit the profile of the Jesus Movement followers, I'd been an active and activist believer since the 50s, so I wasn't one of the new converts with neurotic, hippie theology.'[19]

Elsewhere, Larry claims Jesus People were ninety per cent nice kids who had been saved at the ages of seventeen or eighteen, rather than ex-druggies and Hell's Angels.[20] Bizarrely, he had experienced 'conversion' from church culture to hippy culture, rather than the other way around.

How, then, does Larry's ministry square with the ten marks of the JPM?

Larry had a strong orientation towards the person of Jesus Christ. The Bible was central to his narrative, as reflected in his trilogy of albums.[21] Larry was patently a contemporary Christian music pioneer, widely regarded as the father of Jesus Rock, but not always warm towards its commercialisation. Street evangelism was in his blood from his early years under his father's influence, such that before playing the Royal Albert Hall he would anonymously walk the nearby streets, giving out fliers and sharing Jesus. Larry would say his spiritual life accelerated when he was overwhelmed with the Spirit's power at the age of twenty-one, but in terms of spiritual gifts, he interestingly denied being an 'evangelist'.

Communal living was never an issue for Larry and Pamela, who often lived 'on the road'. However, they did open their home to host a Bible study that was part of the early Vineyard Christian Fellowship history. Literature-wise, Larry's main focus was the spoken/sung word, but he readily gifted seekers with Bibles and his CD liner notes famously stirred purchasers' thinking.

Also of interest are Larry's respective viewpoints on end-times teaching and church ambivalence.

Regarding the first, there is no question Larry's eyes were fixed on what God was presently doing in Israel as it related to biblical prophecy. His anthemic 'I Wish We'd All Been Ready' fleshed this out, as did songs like his 'Six Sixty Six',[22] a track about the predicted Antichrist. However, Larry also expressed a strong dislike of what is termed 'Christian escapism' and the strategy that panics people into getting saved before Jesus' soon return.

Additionally, Larry was more than ambivalent about the Church, and often particularly evasive when interviewed on the subject. However, he openly admitted to walking out of church when he was nine after not liking the hymns and singing. Constructively speaking, 'fellowship' was simply a gritty everyday reality for Larry, which he enjoyed with family and close friends. Attending church services, rightly or wrongly, was never a priority.

* * *

In conclusion, what are the major legacies Larry Norman has left behind in his second home in the UK?

Christian musicians are sometimes portrayed as amateur, but Larry modelled professionalism in his vocation, earning praise from hard-to-please seventies' journalist Michael Jacob who described him as 'the only singer/songwriter on the Christian pop scene capable of finding success in a wider sphere'.[23] Many artists who subsequently produced 'cover' versions of his songs agreed, as did fans like U2's Bono in the new millennium.

In the UK music scene of the 2020s, Larry has proved inspirational to the award-winning Christian punk band 'peter118'. Peter Field's group are often criticised on social media by regular punk bands, but take great heart from the fact that 'Larry, from a working-class background, stood out doing Christian rock in the early seventies, going against the norm, a bit like my [Peter's] band'.[24] As highlighted elsewhere in Chapter 18, Larry also inspired a young Dave Bilbrough to break the mould of worship music in his day.

Time will tell the number of lives still being transformed by Jesus through Larry's ministry. During the 2020 UK lockdown, singer-songwriter

Paul Paulton and his wife Jeannie produced creative online videos daily, squeezing the light (he says) out of songs like 'Come Away', 'A Note From Mr God' and 'The Tune'. More recently, in Spring 2023, Paul revealed his recent writing about the biblical story of Adam in the Garden had been directly inspired by an occasion when Larry prayed privately for him in 2001.

Larry may just have parallels with Abel, in that, 'he still speaks, even though he is dead' (Hebrews 11:4).

Winter 1971-72

12.

Bow to the Monarch Who United the Kingdom

It was early 1972, and Christian 'happenings' were occurring across the UK...

A new drop-in Jesus House started above an electrical shop in historic Bath; hundreds of young Brummies squeezed in for the Saturday night 'Youthquake' in the city's cathedral; a big Jesus March was brewing in the hearts of two Glaswegian scientists; a young Irish lass 'Tekoa' was about to leave the Children of God colony in Bromley; and a newly converted four-piece Welsh rock band had a fresh name brewing.

In 1801, two parallel pieces of Act of Union legislation were passed: one in mainland Great Britain; the other in the whole of Ireland. In the south, Eire later withdrew from the union in January 1922, leaving six counties behind in the north. The United Kingdom remained intact, perhaps more accurately today, somewhat united...

At this juncture, though, King Jesus was drawing new followers together into the one body of Christ.

In this chapter, I merely want to send five postcards from different parts of the UK, their messages giving a snapshot of what it was like to be a Jesus Person in the early 1970s. Apart from briefly highlighting the individuals' present contexts, I will intrude no further.

The first postcard was date-stamped from the spa city of Bath.

Phil Proctor worked with kids who had slipped through the Social Services net. Located over an electrical shop on Lower Bristol Road, and known simply as '74', the surrounding community called it 'The Jesus House'. The name stuck. According to community member Gerard Kelly, soon the clientele changed to 'recovering addicts, Hell's Angels, fugitive criminals, and a circus-like array of musicians, storytellers, artists and bemused hangers-on'. Some were brought along by street preacher Joe O'Hara, dressed in purple with his beat-up guitar. Others had previously journeyed with, for example, the cult-like Divine Light Mission.

'There was a large front door and a bigger back door,' Gerard remembers, and that, 'many came to know Jesus and a good number stayed the course.'[1]

Cotswolds-born Eddie Tustian[2] was part of the number that remained on track with Jesus. One of thirteen siblings, he was disabled from birth. During the 1967 'Summer of Love', Eddie went to London to work as a civil servant, living a double life by getting to bed at three or four in the morning and smoking dope. He first encountered the hippy tribe in the capital. Eel Pie Island, in the middle of the Thames, was his home along with two hundred others – it was the largest commune in the UK. Jagger's Stones and The Who had previously played gigs in the island's hotel. Many communards ran around naked. Eddie considered himself a super-hippy.

He arrived in Bath on 13 December 1970, just before winter broke. Eddie had accumulated numerous gurus but was frustrated. Early the following year, he and a friend met two Jesus Freaks, who gave the pair their address. Finding nowhere to 'crash',[3] they gave up trying at 2 a.m. Arriving at Jesus House, an unwashed and wary Eddie was greeted by a resident who ushered them upstairs to be greeted by the founder. The long-haired, but washed, Phil Proctor asked them, 'Do you want a cup of tea? Food? A place to crash?' Accepting the offer, Eddie was not 'preached at', but vigorously debated with Phil over the ensuing days, many of his questions being answered. Eddie then had a climactic encounter with Jesus, sitting on the settee opposite him and speaking to him personally. The super-hippy declared, 'Previously Jesus had been my guru. He asked me if I'd give myself to him. It was like leaping on his lap and being cuddled.'

Things changed after Eddie joined the community, driving his duck-egg blue three-wheeler. The police knew his location through previous drug charges, and on one occasion, officers arrived from Swindon to a false alarm, consequently hearing Eddie enthuse about life in Jesus. He quickly grew in his foundations in Christ. However, after eleven months the community blew a fuse and shut down. This resulted in an exodus of forty new Jesus Freaks to nearby Hay Hill Baptist Church, nurtured by youth workers Paul and Jill Tatman.

Eventually, Eddie became a social worker amongst kids on the streets and in schools, dealing with issues like solvent abuse. Subsequently, he taught the Bible and its Jewish roots for Christians to students at Bath City Church and studied at nearby Trinity College, Bristol. Reflecting on hippy culture today, Eddie feels their 'love and peace' longings were genuine and it was the Holy Spirit's 'wind' engaging people who had spiritual questions. He wrote songs like 'Show Me Where the Meanings Are' to address this curiosity. As for the JPM, he thinks the revival wasn't so much outreach *to* the streets, but a variation, 'it was the street itself talking to the street'.

Let's move on to our second postcard. It was written in England's second city of Birmingham early in 1972. In late 1971, Arthur Blessitt arrived and seventy young people were saved. Plastering his Jesus stickers everywhere, the Council quaintly labelled them 'stickers of an ecclesiastical nature'.[4] Two months later, the 'Youthquake'[5] event exploded.

Revd David MacInnes had been on the city's cathedral staff for three years. Previously, in 1966, he had led boarding school student Nick Cuthbert[6] to Jesus. Cuthbert was currently in Manchester, organising a sizeable Jesus March. Anticipating a significant youth movement, the clergyman recruited him to Birmingham.

In January 1972, Saturday evening's first Youthquake was hosted in the cathedral. MacInnes felt the building 'appeared far too big for our purposes',[7] but by Easter, 800 young people were turning up. Teenagers sang together on buses and trains, and walkers plastered lampposts with red stickers en route. On arrival, people grabbed any seat they could and, after pews had filled up, came 'hassock time' – people flinging kneelers into the aisles for latecomers to sit on; the cathedral was packed to the gunnels.

The event was 'primarily for teaching young folk who are becoming Christians and yet for some reason aren't being taught about the Christian Life'.[8] Its format was simple, if not occasionally disorganised; Nick hosted the meetings and his wife, Lois, accompanied on guitar-led worship.[9] People lined up to share what God was doing in their lives. MacInnes taught basic discipleship to hungry youth from the Bible. The goal wasn't evangelistic, but 'many people came to faith, although we never asked for a show of hands or had altar calls or counted conversions'.[10]

In January 2020 Nick told me:

'I look back on it now as a golden period of revival. Generationally, we saw something of a harvest that hasn't been seen since ... We know what revival tastes like, and, in the present tense, know that this is not it. It will be obvious when the spontaneity starts again.' For him, Youthquake was not 'manufactured', despite the hard work, nor was it celebrity-orientated, but it was 'a people movement from the bottom'. It wasn't about Holy Spirit manifestations either; it was simply the tangible freedom to share Jesus and see kids converted.

Speaking of his colleague David, Nick says: 'He had been at the cathedral for about three years before this happened and things felt incredibly hard going. Afterwards, he knew the difference. There was a sense of ease, as David knew things weren't wholly due to him. Suddenly it broke out...'

Finally, Nick recalls two poignant contemporary events. The first was when Nick led a clergy meeting in nearby Lichfield in November 2019 and two vicars sat beside him. Youthquake's impact was lifelong for both men, one commenting, 'I owe my spiritual life to that period.' Recently, Nick was attending Gas Street, the church led by Tim Hughes in Birmingham; the young vicar spontaneously calling him up to share about Youthquake. Afterwards, there was utter silence in the place, Tim concluding, 'This needs to happen again!'

Nick's legacy today is coaching leaders through the Leadership Academy which he set up with friend Chris Stoddard. Meanwhile, Lois has written their life story in *Sunshine and Shadows*.[11]

This book is about the entire UK, so I have the joy of adding three other cameos from Scotland, Northern Ireland, and Wales to the collection.

The third postcard is postmarked 'Glasgow'. This was the city where two medical laboratory scientists were hatching plans for ventures like a Jesus March. What did the Jesus People scene look like there?

Andy Scarcliffe[12] became a Christian in 1966 aged fifteen but felt he was straddling both his 'sacred' Christian culture and the 'secular' youth culture. Years later, he was hitch-hiking across Europe when someone in a German youth hostel showed him the edition of *Time* Magazine of 21 June 1971. It was 'The Jesus Revolution' edition, and it blew his mind. Andy now felt able to integrate both cultures more easily. He remembers:

> I came back home and got involved in the UK Jesus Movement that was emerging. Arthur Blessitt came to Glasgow,[13] and we organised Jesus Marches, coffee bars, and outreach meetings ... Larry Norman appeared on the scene, with sophisticated songs that were more than sermons-to-music/Christian propaganda. They reflected the ups and downs of life which flew in the face of much of the triumphalist worship songs that were being sung in the new movement.

Magnus Magnusson produced a TV programme on the JPM, which featured Andy, his friend Jim Givan, and Arthur Blessitt too. Newly arrived in Glasgow, the Children of God were represented by Moses Berg's daughter and key leader 'Faith'. This radical group, though, had split the Christian community in Glasgow down the middle. Andy comments, 'They shared the flat that we were in, in the West End of Glasgow. Some thought they were brilliant, but others sensed there was something seriously wrong with them.' The following summer they were outed as a cult.

Andy worked with Jim Givan[14] at the Royal Hospital for Sick Children, meeting with nurses on Wednesday nights for Bible study. Jim recalls, 'We had seen what was happening in the States and as we prayed, we felt led to organise a Jesus March through the city of Glasgow.' The march's theme was the Glasgow City motto, 'Lord, let Glasgow flourish by the preaching of Thy Word and the praising of Thy Name'. Andy was arty and produced Jesus stickers for it. Adverts appeared in the *Glasgow Herald* but with minimal effect. Launch meetings were then held in the nearby Bible Training Institute, police permission was granted, and the March had a memorable turnout.

Meanwhile, believers would regularly meet in city cafés, discover there was a meeting on, and go along. The local Christian bookshop, Pickering and Inglis, was a great connection point for advertising speakers and concerts. Once, at an open-air rally in Loch Lomond, there were water baptisms conducted by the supportive English Methodist minister, Rae Whittle.

After nursing, Andy became a Baptist minister. Now formally 'retired', he's still communicating Jesus creatively. He reflects, 'My own perspective of the Jesus Movement was like that of the USA: most of the people involved were not from drug-addled back-grounds but were middle-class church kids who were discovering a new culturally relevant, confident expression of their faith.'[15]

The fourth postcard has a photo of the seaside village of Portballintrae, County Antrim on it. Here is the travelogue story written on it:

Hilda McVitty,[16] a young woman from County Donegal in the Republic of Ireland, was living in London in early 1972. She was imminently about to move on from her Children of God commune, but not from the group itself. Hilda had become a Christian in her mid-teens, later going to London to work for Lloyd's Bank. One Sunday in 1970, ending up at Speakers' Corner in Hyde Park, she met the Children of God. An 'all or nothing' person, they were everything she wanted. The next night she went to their Bromley colony. Chatting with members, Hilda said, 'I'd love to join you sometime.' Their response was to quote Jesus' words about putting your hand to the plough and not looking back.[17] She joined instantaneously and was quickly renamed 'Tekoa'.

Being part of the hundred-strong community for two years, life was heavily controlled; Tekoa couldn't even visit the loo without somebody outside. Early 1972 was a huge turning point. The restless Tekoa moved from Bromley to three successive locations. She was increasingly perturbed

by two current emphases: *Mo Letters*[18] being read more than the 'old hat'
Bible, and women yielding their bodies for conversion in 'flirty fishing'.

Moving to Dublin, things got worse – Tekoa felt both isolated and
troubled by doubts. Chatting to her American leaders until 4 a.m. didn't
resolve her questions; Tekoa left the house crying, guitar on her back
and slept under the stars. Someone had told her about an alternative
commune in Donegal. Eventually locating it, she gingerly knocked on
the door; Chris Orr answered.

As for this young man, his family were wealthy. At only six years old,
his father had gone off with a younger woman. Consequently, his mother
came to know Jesus. She opened their main home in Portballintrae to
people with psychological problems and a second in Donegal called 'The
Jesus Community'.

Chris had self-confessedly lived a sordid life. However, one weekend in
May 1972 he had become a believer through Albert, a visiting American
pastor. Encouraged to relate to God as his friend, he remembers, 'I …
made the decision that when everyone would leave [Portballintrae] on
Monday, that I would stay and take time to recover from the mess of a
life I had led until now. I needed a place of refuge and quiet, and to me
there was no better place than Donegal.'[19] That summer he was drug and
alcohol-free. Chris loved the unspoilt beaches and lonely walks. Due to
the political 'troubles', his mother soon joined him in Donegal.

So, Chris opened the door to Hilda that sunny morning in April 1973.
The former was reading the Sunday papers in the sunroom. Looking out
to sea, he says, 'I suddenly got this feeling that I was going to meet my
wife.'[20] A hippy girl with long auburn hair and pretty eyes walked up the
path, asking to talk to the community leader – it was 'Tekoa', now calling
herself Hilda again. Subsequently housed at the Portballintrae house, the
couple quickly fell for each other, marrying on 17 December after just
two weeks of engagement.

Parts of Donegal are quite isolated, so the newlyweds eventually
pioneered community churches across the county while nurturing
their four children. Moving to Londonderry in 1986, they were part of
Cornerstone City Church, later transferring to the city's Vineyard fellowship to support its young pastor. Chris was a TV cameraman for many

years. Hilda makes friends all over the world via Facebook. As a couple they have a big heart for refugees, serving them firstly on the Greek island of Lesbos before moving their ministry to Athens.

The final postcard is from Bangor on the north Wales coastline.

Well-known Welsh musician Arfon Wyn Humphreys[21] is usually known by his first two names. In early 1972, he was halfway through a degree course in Education at Y Coleg Normal in Bangor when his four-piece rock band was in transition...

In the late 1960s, the North Wales scene displayed strong countercultural features. May 1967 saw the release of The Beatles' epoch-making *Sergeant Pepper's Lonely Hearts Club Band* album. In Bangor, later that August, the group attended the spiritual retreat of Maharishi Mahesh Yogi, the founder of Transcendental Meditation.

'This made a keen influence on us to explore spiritual matters,' Arfon commented. By this time, he had denied his Welsh heritage and early church roots feeling that 'Welsh Chapel religion was a straitjacket to our minds and lives as we saw it'. Music, though, was a profound spiritual search for him. Arfon had loved Blind Faith's 1969 song, 'In the Presence of the Lord' but felt jealous that, unlike Eric Clapton, he had not yet found a way to live that way.

At university, Arfon was a hippy-like figure, with his long blond hair, jeans, military coat, moccasins, and a desire for communal living. He took as many drugs as possible but was spared from heroin. 'LSD had been disappointing in not revealing any true spirituality we could cling to,' says Arfon, but 'Speed (amphetamine) was another story, giving us euphoric energy to philosophise all day and night.'

Spiritually speaking, he and his musical friends 'searched in meditation, Buddhism, and other routes, but not in Christianity'. Arfon further recalled, 'We talked about all manner of beliefs and religions and were always stunned by the thought of a Creator, a Creative Being behind all the Universe.' There were, however, trendy Jesus People in Bangor at that time with their transatlantic influences. They peddled magazines and comic-style Chick tracts as part of their street witnessing.

Sometime in 1971, Arfon recounts, things changed:

After a long night taking amphetamines, we as a foursome of wild rock musicians tried to relieve our 'comedown'. We wandered aimlessly towards the peaceful Church Island on the shores of the Menai Straits. Raining heavily, mirroring our dreary inner experience, we found a church door open and ventured in for shelter. There, to our great surprise, we saw the sun shining through a stained-glass window depicting Jesus himself. Underneath were the words, 'I AM THE RESURRECTION AND THE LIFE'. Our lives would never be the same again. We never touched drugs again after that day but went out into the world celebrating the Saviour who had found us.

For this reason, the following year the band was renamed Yr Atgfodiad, or The Resurrection. They were the first to play heavy rock Christian music in the Welsh language; they performed both on television and at the National Eisteddfodau in the 1970s.

On reflection, Arfon contrasts his newfound faith with his early Chapel background, 'Jesus was a man not afraid to turn the tables on materialistic hypocrisy in the Temple. A spiritual revolutionary. Such an attractive leader: "Greater love has no one than this, that he lay down his life for his friends."' He concludes, 'Jesus was just up our street; organised religion in his name was definitely not.'

Now retired, Arfon works on music projects with young people who have learning disabilities and people struggling with dementia. He still plays with his folk-rock band, Y Moniars, and has just won a seat as a county councillor for Plaid Cymru.

* * *

Generally speaking, it's unusual to reply to postcards. If I had done so, it would probably have been taking a leaf out of the apostle Paul's book: 'You show that you are a letter from Christ … written not with ink, but with the Spirit of the living God, not on tablets of stone but on tablets of human hearts' (2 Corinthians 3:3).

Spring 1972

13.

God Doesn't Lead His Children Down Blind Alleys

It was the arrivals hall of Terminal 3 at Heathrow Airport on Monday 17 April 1972. A father and 'daughter' had submitted their American passports, navigated through customs, and were safely on British soil. They were then driven to Bromley in Kent, furtively moving into a quiet suburban bungalow. The father, ostensibly a retired businessman, was David 'Moses' Berg, leader of the dispersed Children of God. His 'daughter' was co-leader Karen Zerby, then called 'Maria' within the group. As his lover for three years, her birth certificate certainly did not include his paternity, hence the cloak and dagger secrecy.

London was becoming the headquarters of this radical community. An affluent property owner would finance their youth ministry. The following year their true colours would come out in the wash. For now, though, most UK Jesus followers welcomed them.

So, what were the historic roots of the Children of God?

David Brandt Berg was born in Oakdale, California, in 1919. The son of two evangelistic preachers, he initially failed to follow in their ministry footsteps. Berg married Jane Miller in Glendale, California, on 22 July 1944, and together they had four children: Linda, Paul, Jonathan, and Faith.[1] He was briefly a schoolteacher before becoming the PR director for the Texas-based Pentecostal TV evangelist Fred Jordan. Eventually falling out after a decade of working together, the two parted company in the mid-1960s.

In 1966, Berg and his family set up 'Teenagers for Christ', a travelling musical evangelistic team. They were youth-friendly rather than geared towards hippies, but the project didn't succeed. In December 1967, an invitation came to join his elderly mother in California; she was serving part-time at The Light Club coffeehouse in Huntington Beach. Mrs Berg died the following year, and the venture was taken on by her family and started attracting a hippier clientele. The renamed 'Teens for Christ' was birthed in July 1968, effectively headed up by Paul, Jonathan, and Faith as a revolution for Jesus, despite their innate conservative tendencies. According to visitors Kent Philpott and Dave Hoyt, they kept themselves apart from other Jesus People. Culturally, Berg led the way in adopting the hippies' native dress and endorsing their anti 'system' message. His community was opposed to the established Church and criticised what he termed the 'Divided States of America'.

In early 1969, Berg received a 'revelation' that an earthquake would sink California into the sea, understandably causing negative reactions in their neighbourhood. By the spring, the community of fifty disciples had departed. The following day, Berg began his adulterous relationship with his new twenty-three-year-old partner, Karen Zerby.[2] After a short stay in Arizona, Berg and now seventy followers made their way to Laurentides, north of Montreal in Canada. This sojourn was formative for the Children of God.

Berg now portrayed himself as a Moses-figure spending forty days on the mountain:[3] a new nation was being formed out of the ashes of the old. 'Moses' also received his fresh revelation of 'Old Church, New Church', viewing the former as a lukewarm establishment, but the latter as God's radically innovative work. His wife of twenty-five years, Jane, was now 'Eve', representing the cruelly discarded old while his new partner Karen, now 'Maria', symbolised the warmly welcomed new…

A newsman aptly called the group the 'Children of God' (COG). Berg liked it and the name stuck.

By February 1970, the community was now 200 strong and based back in Texas, leasing buildings and a ranch from Fred Jordan. The following January, the COG appeared on NBC's *First Tuesday* TV series, in an episode entitled 'The Ultimate Trip'. It positively featured a silent vigil, attracting many young hippies. However, FreeCOG was formed that summer to forcibly liberate people from the group. A second fall-out with Jordan followed later that year – the 'New Church' was evicted and on the move again. Consequently, Berg instructed his disciples to break up into missional community outposts termed 'colonies' and go elsewhere. This included the nation of Mexico, the city of Amsterdam, and the suburbs of London…

The Children of God first arrived in England in July 1971, as 'the spearhead of the Jesus Revolution'.[4] They were given a rent-free factory in Bromley for their international HQ, courtesy of property developer Kenneth Frampton. Having been inspired by a BBC Jesus People documentary earlier that year, he viewed the COG as key to reaching youth nationally.

Mr Frampton also gave the group two dormitory houses in Grove Park, and 150 members resided in nearby Bromley. A total of 3,000 had dispersed across the USA and Europe.[5] The COG produced *New Improved Truth*, an underground newspaper that included cartoons and articles which unpacked their 'New Church' ethos. In secret publications, though, 'Mo' claimed the Old Testament referred to him by name![6]

Renewal was a popular magazine at the time amongst UK charismatic Christians. The title of the December 1971/January 1972 edition was 'The Jesus People and the Churches',[7] prominently featuring the COG. Lead journalist, J. Edwin Meyer, highlighted mixed reactions to the group: some were magnetised towards a Bromley pilgrimage while others were concerned about the group's exclusiveness. Leader 'Eliaphaz'[8] counter-argued that the reason for keeping themselves apart from established churches was because of their stiff worship and lack of witness. Meyer suggested churches bridge the gulf by learning from the COG rather than trying to take them over.[9]

Editor of *Renewal*, Michael Harper, was more cautious in his concluding editorial, 'The Jesus People – a Warning'.[10] Rejoicing over the JPM's impact on both sides of the Atlantic, he nonetheless gave cautionary advice about the COG: 'When Christian movements are outside the Church, they are in great danger from pride, a sectarian spirit and theological confusion.' He concludes, 'We need to see that the Church is flexible enough to contain such dedicated people, and that they themselves will be humble enough to share their new joy with their fellow believers.'[11] Little did *Renewal* know what the following year would bring…

1972 was a crunch year. Its first half saw encouragements in mission, such as witnessing teams at both the Lincoln and Bickershaw festivals, winning 2,900 new converts and recruiting thirty-two workers. One discouragement, however, was that NBC's once positive slant on the COG was retracted on a new programme called *Chronolog* after reporter Bob Rogers received reports of immoral leadership. This was then picked up by the BBC.

In the UK, things started to go seriously pear-shaped in June. Dave Hoyt was a JPM pioneer but, frustrated organisationally, had joined forces with the efficiently run COG in May 1971.[12] However, being unsettled in Seattle meant Dave wanted healthier family surroundings and new evangelistic opportunities. Thus, the family flew into London later that year, after a flight marred by a fuelling crisis and a minor fire on the left wing.

Over the coming months in Bromley, though, Dave became increasingly rattled: absolute loyalty was verbally expressed in slogans, he was physically isolated from his family, and *Mo Letters*[13] increasingly pictured alongside Scripture. Working in the print shop, Dave saw secret *Mo Letters*, and 'reading them, David Berg introduced himself as being God's end-time prophet with special revelations'.[14]

Hoyt wrote directly to Berg to voice his concerns. Refusing to shelve them, he was then led before an eight-strong tribunal where a letter was read out accusing him of being demonised.[15] Quizzed about his need for a change of heart, Dave replied that he wouldn't put anyone above God. He was mocked, then led back to his tiny bedroom, with a guard stationed outside. At 4 a.m., the coast was clear, so Dave escaped under cover of dark. Tragically, he had to leave his family behind.

Soon afterwards, two COG members unsuccessfully tried to kidnap him in a new Christian friend's restaurant. He was quickly introduced to Kenneth Frampton, who already had serious misgivings about the group. Hearing Hoyt's story, and viewing the *Mo Letters* first-hand, the businessman eventually terminated his support. In the process, Mr Frampton published a short pamphlet, *Beware the Children of God*, accusing Berg of heresy and malpractice.

By September, though, the duo of Dave and Mr Frampton had become a trio after Dave's friend Russell Griggs joined them. He was the former leader of the Jesus People Army in Vancouver and, like Hoyt, converted to the COG before subsequently fleeing the group.

In quick succession, a Christian umbrella group, Bromley's local MP, and the sensation-hungry media were on the case. Following advice from the trio, in early September the Evangelical Alliance[16] hosted a press conference. Its two-fold aim was to warn people of the dangers of the COG and to offer help to worried parents of new members.

Politically, MP John Hunt tried to axe this unwanted American influence by getting the Home Office to deport the COG, portraying them as a confidence trick perpetrated upon unthinking and impressionable youth. The Home Office concluded that, despite an unorthodox lifestyle, 'local police have found no evidence to substantiate allegations that the organisation has been guilty of any breach of the criminal law'.[17] The matter was dropped.

Back in the world of 'breaking news', the TV and broadsheets were on full alert. America's NBC worked in partnership with the BBC[18] to host a televised press conference, airing both viewpoints, but leaving the public to decide. COG members were given ample space to set the record straight. Conversely, individuals like Frampton and Hoyt were interviewed, as were people who had lost family members. The result was screened on BBC's *Nationwide*, informing the British populace that the COG was a cult with deceptive beliefs and practices. In response, the group claimed open persecution and began shutting up shop in Bromley.

The Sunday People tabloid was hot on the heels of the COG too. Undercover reporter Trevor Aspinall's sting had planted a new young 'member' in the Bromley colony two weeks earlier. The journalist subsequently visited, posing as the lad's 'concerned father'. At the factory door, leading member Mary Lamb claimed he was nowhere to be found. Leaving, though, they saw the reporter's 'son' standing by a bus stop nearby.

'The Shocking Truth about the Children of God' was published on 24 September 1972.[19] The article quoted Kenneth Frampton as giving the group multiple properties but losing two of his four sons to the group in return. He couldn't support their leadership anymore. Aspinall outlined his three concerns: young people separated from the world 'system', brainwashing using quirky biblical interpretations in *Mo Letters*, and a nepotistic leadership structure.

The following Sunday, 1 October 1972, 'The Moment This Girl Was Lured from Her Family' was published,[20] featuring the stories of two young girls.

Eighteen-year-old Nicole Caplan, who had hastily joined COG four months earlier, was now in France helping dropouts, subsequently asking her father to sign a property over to her that he owned in Spain. Wendy Hunt lived in a large house in Grove Park, occupied mainly by COG members. In their heavy-duty thinking, her unresponsiveness to Jesus had directly 'caused' her dad to be seriously ill.

On the same theme, but far more recently in 2020, adult businesswomen Petra Velzeboer and Dawn Watson shared their experience of growing up as young girls within COG families: not only were their minds controlled, but their young bodies were abused by so-called 'uncles', causing them to seriously contemplate suicide.[21]

Meanwhile, back in the early seventies, the Christian magazine *Crusade* featured an interview between editor Colin Duriez and Berg's daughter, Faith. The latter claimed that Duriez was immature in not being revolutionary enough, that the mainstream Church was beyond the pale, and audaciously concluded, 'The true Jesus movement *is* the Children of God.'[22]

Youth-orientated *Buzz* magazine joined the fray too. Originally, despite the COG's militant tendencies and funny ideas, they had cautiously welcomed the group to these shores. In November 1973, however, they published a well-researched article, 'The Children of God: A NEW SECT IN THE MAKING'. It warned of clear parallels with the Jehovah's Witnesses, summarising that, 'according to the evidence relating to the Children of God, you are currently seeing a new sect emerging'.[23]

Leading scholar Larry Eskridge reflects that 'intensifying scrutiny of the British media and the real possibility of greater government surveillance were signals to Berg that the British Isles would not long serve as an alternative home base for the COG'.[24] They thus relocated their headquarters to France in January 1975.

It is fascinating to view the Children of God through the lens of the ten marks of the JPM. Before discovering they were a cult, all ten marks were obvious. Things that especially stood out were as follows: their memorising Scripture verses daily, close-knit community in their 'colonies', a doom-laden world 'system' being overthrown in the end-times, taking Jesus to wherever people were, and their vast amount of literature production.

However, cracks increasingly began to appear in the wall. The biblical Jesus, superior to the original Moses was surpassed by the twentieth-century 'Moses';[25] Scripture was supplanted as the final authority of faith and practice by the latest *Mo Letters*, even when they called for religious prostitution. Their communities became exclusive 'secret societies'; they were 'Church hostile' and sectarian from the outset, not merely church ambivalent; and street evangelism eventually included 'flirty fishing' – women giving sex in return for conversions. It seems their radical nature had led them down the path of dangerous extremism. Eventually, the COG was disowned, not just by more traditional churches, but by the Jesus People they had purportedly identified with.

* * *

So, what legacy did the COG leave behind for today? Inevitably, it will be a bruising one for many individuals and families who were involved. The words 'sect' and 'cult' are used about the group in this chapter. In terms of a brief definition, the roots of the COG meant they were originally a sect, having their different ideas on the fringes of Christianity, but it later became more of an isolationist cult, Berg's new exclusive revelations being followed without question. Regardless of definition, while God was powerfully at work within the wider JPM, the devil didn't stand idly by.

As much as it would be great if the Children of God hadn't caused such damage, their presence in the UK increases our awareness of cults here today. I suggest that every Christian should be more aware of the New Testament's teaching about false prophets and false teaching, to avoid their grip. One balanced book I have used, *The Marks of a Cult*,[26] highlights what warning signs to look out for in identifying such groups today, such as 'finding new secrets', being 'slaves to the structure' and viewing 'the outsider as enemy'.[27] Pastorally, though, disagreement with your fellow 'Christian' doesn't make them a cult member.

As I write, in the UK today, one Anglican and two Methodist church ministers are being investigated over safeguarding issues, the former leader's church labelled a 'cult' by some journalists. More widely, other church leaders have recently been proven to be bullies. These issues should be explored rigorously, dealt with fairly, and learnt from compassionately. They don't mean that their denominations, streams, or churches are necessarily cults though. Nonetheless, all leaders need ongoing accountability, and followers need wisdom about where they pledge their allegiance.

I would not put the non-Trinitarian Mormons or Jehovah's Witnesses on the same level as the COG. I have distant family members in America who are part of the Mormon Church, and I seek to show them friendship before any rightful debate. I am also provoked to ponder how I respond to handwritten letters we receive from a Jehovah's Witness couple living a few roads from us. Even when addressing issues of truth, 'gently instruct' is a good guideline from 2 Timothy 2:25.

Summer 1972

14.

Experience a Good Spree with Little Retail Therapy

It was a big dilemma to find a trendy name for a youth festival in the summer of 1973. Christian marketing experts offered fifty suggestions – two punchier ones being 'Bang on!' and 'Hit it!' – the notion perhaps being that believers 'bang on' about Jesus whilst 'hitting' people with a floppy black Bible! One name temporarily adopted was the enigmatic 'Outspell', but could it be confused for 'Outspill' misspelt? The agony of giving a week-long evangelism training course in London a name. Two leadership friends cooked up 'Spre-e '73' – the 'Sp' standing for spiritual and 're-e' for re-emphasis; the National Secular Society promptly altered it to Spurious Re-evangelism.[1]

When the word is looked up in the dictionary, more shockwaves hit us. Its etymology speaks of a 'lively frolic or a bout of drinking'.[2] Maybe not the best word for a festival of Jesus followers faced with the youthful temptations of booze. However, as one biblical wisecrack points out, 'How about the early Christians on the day of Pentecost? They were accused of drunkenness.'[3] The name sticks, approved by twenty-four men and just one woman, an MP's wife. 'Spre-e' it is then.

Explo '72 is the important prelude to Spre-e '73. Maurice Rowlandson participated in the first but headed up the second. Originally a surveyor, he had been involved with Billy Graham's ministry for many years, then in 1961 he was recruited to run the London office for Graham's Evangelistic

Association. Five years later, pop star Cliff Richard was one of the 40,000 people coming to faith at Earl's Court through the evangelist. Both men were heavily involved in the UK Spre-e '73 event.

The previous event was put on by Campus Crusade for Christ (CCC) in June 1972 in Dallas, Texas. Up to 100,000 young people attended daily for evangelism training and street outreach. There was fresh music and inspiring teaching from Billy Graham in the evenings. And the core idea? Attendees were to go home and invite five other people to neighbourhood events – producing a domino effect in the evangelisation of the USA by 1975, and the world by 1980. It was no surprise that some observers spoke about militancy amongst Christians.

Described as the equivalent of Woodstock with a religious twist, a God-twist, or even better, a Jesus-twist – CCC's leader Bill Bright capitalised on the highly publicised secular rock festival of August 1969.

Popular Christian rock musicians took part, including the JPM's self-deprecating solo artist Randy Matthews; he joined forces with Chuck Girard's harmonious Love Song, and the long-haired troubadour Larry Norman.

Girard recalls this as the event that put Love Song on the map, coinciding with the release of their eponymous first album. He remembers, 'We went like we usually did, no contract, no hotel arrangements, and no expense money.'[4] They played alongside Larry Norman at an outreach event on Thursday 15 June. On the following night, they performed at the Cotton Bowl before Billy Graham preached. Chuck concludes, 'I believe that night was a defining moment in Christian music and changed the mentality of the whole church at large. Suddenly, guitars, drums and all kinds of modern instruments began to be considered to be acceptable for the first time.'[5]

As for evangelist Graham, until then, many Christians had apprehensions about hippy converts but were consequently reassured by his ringing endorsement of what God was doing in their lives. If it was fine with him, it was fine for them.

For Larry Norman's biographer, Gregory Thornbury, 'In terms of pop culture, the Jesus movement had arrived.'[6] Leading JPM scholar David Di Sabatino adds, 'Explo organizers exaggerated that the crusade was the "most significant Christian event since Pentecost." Regardless of the rhetoric, Explo '72 represents the most visible event of the Jesus People Movement.[7]

Returning to Maurice Rowlandson, he was utterly blown away that week. Immediately afterwards, Rowlandson asked Graham if he could speak at the UK equivalent of Explo; Graham was interested but could only make it in 1974 or the following year. Back in London's Camden Town, a letter landed on Rowlandson's desk from the evangelist on Thursday 23 August 1972: 'I have one week free in 1973, August 27 to September 1, and I think the desperate spiritual need of Britain is against further postponement.'[8] Maurice rang the Earl's Court Arena – it was free that week, as was the iconic Wembley Stadium. Twelve days later an ad hoc committee of twenty-five was convened, meeting on 23 October. The following month, evangelical youth leaders joined a planning team. Spre-e's wheels were in motion.

It was not a problem-free journey though. Over the August Bank Holiday, the Festival of Jesus took place in London. December's *Buzz* magazine suggested the forthcoming Spre-e '73 would almost be a carbon copy of this event. Might its organisers be doing a takeover job? Joint Secretary Steve Stevens, however, countered this in print: he was enthusiastic about Spre-e '73 happening but stressed the need for Christians to be salt as well as merely light.

1973 started with a bang. On the afternoon of Saturday 27 January, Spre-e '73 was launched in London, with JPM musician Randy Stonehill performing and an Explo '72 sound strip shown. February's *Buzz* magazine asked readers to submit songs for a competition to find a theme song; Ivan Thurlow's 'Let's Join Together!' was chosen.

Over these two months, *Buzz* entered the fray again. Their January edition expressed positivity but warned that 'for those who are yet again hoping for a world-shaking panacea, they are all, we fear, in for a big disappointment'.[9] To be fair, in the February issue, space was given to a lengthy response from Maurice Rowlandson. Declaring a greater sympathy for American positivity than for British negativity, he nonetheless agreed 'that no man-made event can organise the blessing of God'. He went on to personally conclude, as on the day of Pentecost, 'I believe that God can take man-made situations and pour His blessing out upon them.'[10]

In March's issue, Pentecostal pastor and columnist Tony Stone reflected that 'in 1972, with the Jesus Revolution, and the great outreach in evangelism that many of us were swept off our feet getting stuck into … it was hard to settle into a good training programme for the new converts'.[11] After the event, his Southampton church saw a hundred people find Jesus and Spre-e provided the programme for discipling them.

However, there was more 'trouble at mill' later in the spring. Billy Graham's organisation had received lots of letters critical of Spre-e '73, so the evangelist flew across the Atlantic to allay their fears.

For the third time, in June, *Buzz* put their oar in yet again. The editor highlighted a long catalogue of weaknesses: the 'short notice' of planning, a lack of wider consultation, the wisdom of mass training, a vast financial outlay, flamboyant American publicity, and a simplistic *Four Spiritual Laws* booklet. They gave just qualified support: 'In short, not everything in the Spre-e garden is lovely but those who keep away for that reason will be cutting off their evangelical noses to spite their faces.'[12] The Spre-e team had the insight to get the Musical Gospel Outreach (MGO) leaders quickly on board, and the August edition of *Buzz* included a full-page programme timetable.[13]

On Sunday 15 July, a worldwide prayer day took place six weeks before hordes of zealous young Jesus followers descended on the capital. Put on by the Billy Graham Evangelistic Association, the main events took place daily at Earl's Court Arena from Monday 27 to Friday 31 August. About 11,600 young participants were trained and activated during the week, a long way off the target of 100,000. The training included witnessing on the streets every afternoon. Saturday's final celebration at Wembley Stadium was attended by 30,000 enthusiastic young people. Famous converts from both sides of the Atlantic were wheeled out. The rather uninspiring 'Let's Join Together!' was performed by the Swedish choir Choralerna. Graham preached against the background threat of an Armageddon-like Third World War launched by Russia on China. He concluded, 'There is a little bit of Watergate[14] in all of us … Jesus Christ is the answer, there is no other.'[15] The call to stand in commitment to Christ followed and many answered the call.

So, what was Spre-e '73 really like for the ordinary delegate?[16] Most found it fantastic. To give a mild flavour, here are some highlights:

On Monday, many sang as they travelled. One group of young Presbyterians from Coleraine, Northern Ireland, consistently did so during their arduous fourteen-hour trek. The first thing to greet them, however, were opening-night problems with the amplification.

During the next afternoon's outreach, Sharon, from Hyde in Cheshire, was chatting with a girl in a coffee bar, praying quietly as she listened. Giving her new friend a copy of John's Gospel, the girl said she wanted to accept Christ and she did so.

Wednesday saw a sixteen-year-old girl looking forward to street witnessing, but because she was ill the plan was scuppered. Her GP visited her, enquiring about the *Buzz* magazine at her bedside, and they chatted about Jesus for half an hour. The lost opportunity was snatched back.

Meanwhile, the next day, church-going nurse Paul came to faith. He later apologised to Christian friends for hypocritically deluding them that he had been a believer. That evening, three Heavenly Angels bike-riders, displaying their believing 'colours', joined in with the worship.

Finally, on Friday, after Graham had preached about the end of the world and pointed to Jesus, there was singing and dancing on the London Underground as people found their way home. Earlier in the week it had been forbidden as the platform announcements couldn't be heard for the noise.

Saturday was the final day. Christian journalist Brian Rice had previously been to a seminar on the occult. That afternoon he was confronted by a male witch, who told him that if he stepped onto the Wembley turf his coven would kill him. Brian gently led him by the hand onto the well-tended grass, continually pleading Jesus' name. The man stayed for thirty minutes, then left. Who knows what became of him.

What JPM features were in evidence at Spre-e '73?

Considering the ten Jesus People marks, the mornings were very Bible-centred, street witness occurred over two afternoons, and contemporary worship was a large component of the evenings. Regarding the latter, Peter Meadows, editor of *Buzz*, commented, 'The musical programme is merely the surfacing of a movement that has been evident in the churches for the last two years. Until now we have only seen the tip of the iceberg.

Spre-e has made it all visible.'[17] In the USA, the pinnacle of the Jesus People had been two years earlier in 1971. Both organisers and attendees were pro-church. It is questionable how overtly charismatic the event was, but it seems very little. Notably missing from the event, though, was any sizeable contingent of converted hippy-types.

In terms of other JPM influences, Spre-e '73 piggy-backed on Explo '72, again featuring Billy Graham. He continued to endorse what God was doing in his book *The Jesus Generation*, published that same year. It was both remarkably positive and constructively critical. However, Graham genuinely believed that contemporary Jesus People would help set up his final kingdom on earth.

There were a few identifiable Jesus People figures on stage, such as British musical duo Malcolm & Alwyn and solo performer Graham Kendrick, all three having a measure of Calvary Chapel connection. (The former pair are both Calvary pastors to this day.)

The Upper Norwood-based Jesus Family also attended, selling tickets for their *Lonesome Stone* rock-musical and offering *Everyman* magazines for just 10p. Meanwhile, in the Exhibition area, Sonrise Outreach sold masses of badges, stickers ('Jesus loves you') and posters ('Fight truth decay'), together with their best-selling T-shirts ('Jesus One Way'). They had grossed £1,000 by Wednesday. Their Jesus Liberation Front leader, Geoff Bone, was there too, arguing that Spre-e '73 was only scratching the surface of what God was doing nationally and it shouldn't stop there – the enthusiasm for Jesus must be taken back to local communities to see an outpouring of God's Spirit in 1974. Geoff said with hyperbole, 'There's an expectancy in God's people which will soon explode and make the Reformation look like a firecracker.'[18]

Nonetheless, from the opposing perspective, Technical Director David Payne (from MGO) was more downbeat. He reflected, 'I wouldn't make wild claims for Spre-e any more than I would for the Jesus movement generally, which has been overplayed no end. I don't doubt there is a genuine moving of the Holy Spirit among today's youth, but it's been glamourised and exaggerated out of all proportion.'[19]

Much ink was spilt in the following weeks and months about Spre-e '73. Aspects were seriously called into question, such as the £350,000 expenditure, its apparent personality cult, perceived mindlessness, and the gospel being trivialised. Individuals' lives were undoubtedly changed though; some were even baptised the very day after Spre-e had ended.

However, one final reflection is worth serious thought. Journalist Tony Jasper, himself a Christian, argued that Spre-e 'was in part shaped by, and expressed something of, the Jesus revolution which tore through parts of America during the late sixties'. Nevertheless, he proceeded to shrewdly highlight the attempt to blend old-style teaching and new-fangled music to attract the young, concluding that, 'Two different worlds met at Spre-e.'[20]

* * *

What aspects of Spre-e had a lasting impact on the UK today?

Speaking of Spre-e '73, previous youth specialist Pete Ward pointed out that, 'The Jesus Movement encouraged the tendency within evangelicalism towards festivals and large events as a means of encouraging young people in the faith', but upon further reflection, argues that it 'only served to isolate Christian young people in an increasingly distinctive and attractive sub-culture.'[21] Christians love gathering the clans, whether in football stadiums, holiday camps, agricultural showgrounds, or openly marching in the streets. In the UK, the JPM-inspired Greenbelt Festival has just reached its fiftieth anniversary, while in 2019, youth festival Soul Survivor shut up shop after twenty-six years, commemorated by a fireworks display and a massive thunderstorm.

One associated (perhaps more negative) legacy is the exacerbating of 'celebrity culture', symbolised by the high profile of Cliff Richard and Johnny Cash at Spre-e '73. Tony Jasper commented, 'Famous musical converts were to be wheeled out as if to say, "Look, they believe and you've loved their music, so don't buy their album, save your soul instead."'[22] Does the living God seriously need a leg-up from celebrities in his global rescue plan?

Evangelism training is a final positive legacy, stretching back to the apostle Paul's teaching about evangelists being given to 'prepare God's

WHEN JESUS MET HIPPIES

people for works of service' (Ephesians 4:12). One good example today is Through Faith Missions, a team led by my friend Daniel Holland, who equip UK leaders and churches to communicate Jesus naturally to lost people. In June 2023, he took a team of six to a Heavy Metal festival in Leicestershire. I wistfully wonder whether this equipping legacy is as much prioritised today as slick and 'happening' worship events might be…

Summer 1972

15.

If it is Too Hot in the Kitchen, Don't Get Out

The idea for The Kitchen emerged from a festival but, perhaps unexpectedly, not a culinary festival. It was a five-day Festival for Jesus held in central London between Wednesday 30 August and Sunday 3 September. Real food was on offer though. On the final Sunday evening, there was a four-hour worship meeting in Trafalgar Square. During the midway interval, dozens of bread loaves were informally shared out to remember Jesus, as well as free snacks for the tramps and dropouts who had gathered. Londoners were hungry…

Perhaps it was the theme song that caught the imagination of the two posh cousins and their guitar-playing American friend. It was Parchment's 'Light Up the Fire', and it almost got into Radio Luxemburg's Top 20, peaking at only number thirty-one in the official BBC charts. One of the recurring lyrics spoke about opening the door before Jesus returns. Eighteen months later, the doors of The Kitchen would swing open, offering wholesome simple meals accompanied by 'the bread of life'.

Who, though, were the three characters directly inspired by this Festival for Jesus?

The story of The Kitchen begins with two aristocratic hippy cousins living in London. The first, Mickie, was seven years older than Phil…

Michael Richard Anstruther-Gough-Calthorpe, perhaps understandably, was usually called Mickie. Born on 30 October 1943, he was the middle son born to the 2nd Baronet of Elvetham Hall in Hampshire[1] and his wife, Nancy. Historically, the family had sixteen hundred acres of land in fashionable Edgbaston, Birmingham. Indeed, the city coat of arms has a Calthorpe fur stripe[2] on it. The baronetcy, though, became extinct in 1997, the final baron having died without a male heir.

Mickie lived in South Kensington, in a mews house at 16 Petersham Place, an area surrounded by embassy buildings and close to the famed Imperial College. Vocationally, he was an artist and designer, also involved in his family's property business. Mickie came to know Jesus in 1971, probably influenced by that year's Nationwide Festival of Light.[3] After his conversion, every Monday morning for three years he met up with Gordon Scutt, Festival for Jesus organiser and family friend. They spent these times growing together as brothers in Christ. Very much a people-person, Mickie quickly displayed the ability to reach others for Jesus.

His cousin was Philip Lawson Johnston, whose mother was also an Anstruther-Gough-Calthorpe. He too was from a privileged background, born in 1950 to Lord and Lady Luke. The family firm, Bovril, had been started by his great-grandfather, and his father was an International Olympic Committee member. Phil's home was constantly filled with music and his chosen instrument was the guitar.

At the age of thirteen, Phil had been confirmed at boarding school by the Bishop of Ely. He was then educated at Eton College but inoculated against religion through the daily chapel services. In 1966, Phil accompanied his parents to hear Billy Graham preach at Wembley Stadium; he went forward during the appeal, but the effect was short-lived.

In his own words, 'I was a child of the fifties and a teenager of the sixties and so grew up in the era of The Beatles, Stones, and the "permissive" push at the boundaries of conventional behaviour.'[4] After pitiful A-level results, Phil ended up at a 'crammer school' in Brighton, intending to improve his grades. During this patch he started adopting a hippy-type lifestyle, engaging with the pot, acid, and music of the drug culture.

Afterwards, following a wild three months in Florence, Phil returned to study History of Art at the Inchbald School of Design in London for a year. Instead of an art career, though, Phil trained himself in glass engraving, his vocation to this day. In 1968, Gordon Scutt (initially a friend of his brother, Andrew) invited Phil to an outreach supper at Chelsea Town Hall. After the meal, Anglican clergyman David MacInnes spoke about Jesus being our friend.

'It was as if he was speaking to me personally in the midst of about four hundred others,'[5] Phil recalls. Praying a prayer of commitment, Phil joined a weekly Bible study for city pinstripes. Culturally, being long-haired and weed-smoking, the experience didn't last long!

Two and a half years later, he bumped into his cousin Mickie at a party in London. Swapping notes about their similar journeys, the older cousin had come to faith six months earlier than him. Phil was invited to his relative's mews home, where barrister Sandy Millar was speaking. After most people had left, Mickie sat Phil down and explained the Holy Spirit's work to him. After prayer he was instantly filled with 'a penetrating peace',[6] understood why Jesus had died for him, and crowned him Lord. He was no longer what he lyrically describes as 'a wandering vagabond',[7] but had experienced a wake-up call to the love of Christ.

The Kitchen saga continues with a couple of American musical missionaries coming to London and meeting these two cousins.

In September 1971, Chuck Butler entered Mickie's world, sleeping at his home while his band were performing for the Nationwide Festival of Light. Country Faith were back the next year, playing at the subsequent Festival for Jesus. Phil eventually met the American guitarist-vocalist for the first time that summer. The Festival made a deep impression on the two cousins; it paralleled American Jesus People festivals – good teaching, contemporary music, and a clean-up operation. 'There were rallies at Tower Hill, Hyde Park and Trafalgar Square, and a flotilla of boats motored down the River Thames draped with "Jesus is Alive Today" banners.'[8] Importantly, relatives Mickie and Phil had connected with Chuck.

During the five-day Festival for Jesus here, Chuck proposed to his girlfriend Carol over the phone; she was back in the USA. The couple married in the States in December 1972, arriving as missionaries on a six-month visa in June 1973. Where would they stay? 16 Petersham Place, of course. There wasn't much space or privacy for newlyweds, but they coped. God was at work amidst this hive of activity.

Not long after the Butlers' arrival back in the UK, gatherings for informal praise started up at Mickie's mews house. Beginning at 8 p.m., straight after their respective church services, he and six single friends[9] encountered Jesus together. Chuck ministered in music as Phil vividly remembers, 'While he led, I sat next to him, copying everything he did, and following him on the guitar.'[10] So, when role model Chuck and his wife abruptly returned to the USA in November, everyone turned to Phil as 'worship leader'.

Fellowship was not everything though; the Festival had inspired them to radically look outwards for a welcoming venue to offer food, music, friendship and Jesus. Nothing came to light.

On one occasion Carol asked, 'What about using the garage below your flat?'

Mickie's response was, 'Unfortunately, it's rented out for the next 100 years.'

Carol boldly replied, 'Well, can we pray about it?'

The trio, including Chuck, descended to the garage. An unnamed Lord X's Silver Cloud car was parked there. Mickie gave voice, 'It'll never happen. Lord X has his Rolls-Royce parked here, the contract is solid, and there's no way out.' So, they prayed…

That very night Lord X met his Maker! His chauffeur visited the next day, picked up the Rolls-Royce and severed the contract. Mickie's response was, 'What?'

Carol concludes, 'We watched the chauffeur back the car out of the garage and drive away, then picked up three brooms and swept out the garage.'[11]

Mickie proceeded to remodel the empty garage: a kitchen and eating area developed below; a suspended staging area above, decked with cushions. The colours and materials were inspired by the décor in King Solomon's temple. The Kitchen was launched in April 1974,[12] after the Butlers had left. From Monday-Thursday people would drop in for lunches and suppers, contributing what they could afford. Chatting together, people unexpectedly got Jesus on the menu, tasting his goodness for themselves. Sunday evenings were Spirit-filled worship times led by Phil, and God's cloud of glory was regularly expected.[13]

The third part of The Kitchen drama involves a party-loving colonel's daughter called Pippa Hislop and an atheistic first-year Cambridge University undergraduate called Nicky.

The pair had met in London before either were Christians. Pippa recalls being given Nicky's number when wanting to take a friend to a nightclub. He was a member, so Pippa rang him and asked if he could get them in. Nicky was having some friends round for supper and invited them too. They went along, subsequently becoming friends.

Later, a few days after her friend Nicky had come to faith, the pair met again at a house party. The overly zealous Nicky remarked, 'You look awful. You really need Jesus.'[14] Pippa thought he was mad.

That spring, Pippa was invited to The Kitchen. Working as an estate agent's secretary, she had no direction in life. She enjoyed the friendly atmosphere of The Kitchen, not leaving before being the first person to sign the guestbook. On a subsequent occasion, Pippa was chatting with Mickie when he read John 10:10 to her: 'I have come that they may have life and have it to the full.' The verse leapt off the page. Pippa returned home and committed her life to Jesus.

Pippa's 'friend', of course, was future husband Nicky Gumbel. A first-year law student at Trinity College, Cambridge, he was reading the New Testament. After attending evangelistic meetings at a 'Christ Alive' mission, Nicky came to faith on Monday 18 February 1974.[15] Months later, he was at his parents' home in London for the summer vacation, situated three hundred yards from The Kitchen. Finding his way there, he was warmly welcomed and was consequently filled with the Holy Spirit.[16]

After Nicky's graduation in 1976, he was looking for a church to settle in. No surprise that he became involved at The Kitchen, just as Pippa had previously. Sandy Millar was appointed curate at Holy Trinity Brompton (HTB) that year and gathered young people who were hungry for renewal into midweek small groups. So, the pair joined in. Reflecting on this era recently, Nicky had seen many of his immediate circle attending HTB on Brompton Road instead. It snowballed into a rapidly growing movement that ended up eclipsing The Kitchen.

Two years later, in January 1978, Nicky and Pippa were married. He then spent a decade working as a barrister but, following theological training, became the curate to vicar Sandy Millar. A succession of previous curates had run a more in-house style 'Alpha' course, but Nicky took it on in September 1990. Publicly launched three years later, the evangelistic course has now gone viral globally.

Surveying this narrative of The Kitchen, in what sense did it reflect the JPM?

Firstly, leading Jesus People were involved. For instance, the very first Calvary Chapel overseas missionaries Chuck and Carol played an integral part through their friendship with Mickie. Over six months, they taught Scripture and mentored Phil as a worship leader, the baton falling to him when they left. In the mid-1970s, the cousins flew over to California to stay with the Butlers. Visiting their church, Phil sang one of his songs. He was subsequently baptised in the Pacific Ocean by Country Faith group member and pastor Tom Stipe.

Chuck Smith also ministered on occasion. St Paul's, Onslow Square, was the church for The Kitchen crowd in the early 1970s. Sandy Millar recalls the conservative Chuck preaching there to just ten people from 1 John. Other Californians, including Smith, were invited over by Mickie to The Kitchen, consistently focusing on Jesus' second coming.

Secondly, many marks of the JPM were present in their community. There was an informal hippy-type feel to The Kitchen. Its participants were Bible-based and Spirit-welcoming, certainly focused on the Lord Jesus. Worship music on Sunday evenings was contemporary too. There were no communal houses, but a sense of relational community was never absent.

The most fascinating mark is that of church ambivalence. All team members were regular church attendees but had differing perspectives.

On one hand, in 1975, Phil and his two-year-old band, Cloud, started being committed to St Paul's, Onslow Square. When the fellowship merged with HTB the following year, they transferred over to Brompton Road wholesale, leading worship more regularly than before. Phil felt The Kitchen was not a proper church, given both its limited twenties-thirties age bracket and the fact it drew people from different denominations. HTB curate and regular speaker Sandy Millar agreed.

On the other hand, Mickie was keen on fellowship, but, as historian Andrew Atherstone says, 'Calthorpe, in particular, was wary of institutional churches.'[17] Mickie's view was that the future of the Church of England lay with Chuck Smith, this being 'all part of God's plan to have mercy on the Church one more time!'[18] His ambivalence was displayed in the fact he went Stateside to train for ministry with Calvary Chapel in the late seventies. Subsequently invited to join Chuck Smith's staff, Mickie narrowly escaped.

In essence, then, The Kitchen was more a flourishing sizeable house group than a church.

* * *

So, what was the deposit the JPM-like Kitchen left behind fifty years on?

The Kitchen was not the sole cause for the 'Alpha' course that flourished from 1993 onwards. However, Phil Lawson Johnston believes 'the fact The Kitchen's ministry was based around food led directly to the importance of the Alpha meal'.[19] Historian Andrew Atherstone goes further and claims, 'Here was the ethos of Alpha in bud – conversations about the Christian faith, with friends, around a meal, in an informal relaxed atmosphere.'[20] This tiny seed first showed signs of sprouting in the garage of a mews house at 16 Petersham Place, and its legacy is flowering internationally today.

The mould of worship was significantly broken too, cascading down from Chuck Butler to Phil Lawson Johnston through to trainee worship leaders at Worship Central in London today. Individuals' lives were transformed. A good example of this is Ed Pruen, who was preparing for ordination at King's College, London, in 1974 and was invited to The Kitchen. There the Holy Spirit's presence transformed him. Life-changing worship prompted him to help lead worship alongside Phil. He still does so today – a living example of being retired but not redundant. Everyone Ed knows from those days is currently walking with Jesus. He concludes, 'I still think of The Kitchen as the springboard into a lifetime of ministry as an Anglican priest.'[21]

Finally, what about the four key players in this story?

Phil reflects, 'I believe the Jesus Movement had a profound effect on how we did church – the joy of throwing off the shackles of only traditional worship and rather churchy ways of doing things.'[22] Chuck and Carol returned for three years in 1980, planting three new churches in the process: Calvary Christian Fellowship in Silksworth near Sunderland is still going strong today. Mickie died young in 1990, having battled with multiple sclerosis for more than a decade. His legacy is amply celebrated on his gravestone: a visual carving of the Holy Spirit as a dove with the name 'Jesus' inscribed underneath and capped by the well-known verse from Isaiah 40:31 about God renewing our strength…

Autumn 1972

16.

The Extended Family Whose Door is Always Open

It was 6.30 p.m. on Saturday 4 November 1972 and the ferry was setting sail.[1] The location was the Belgian port of Ostend, and the destination Dover, seventy miles across the English Channel. A group of thirty dishevelled hippy types had embarked on the crossing, their tickets paid for by a newly acquired friend and wealthy businessman. They were accompanied by their two trusty VW camper vans, known as Type 2 Transporters or 'Hippie vans'.

On arrival, one of the vans was discovered to have a teaspoon for an ignition key. This was quickly picked up by an attentive British Immigration official, who locked this VW up in a local detention centre. Their kind benefactor gallantly drove down from London to the rescue, vouching for them and sorting their visas. This was the fledgling Jesus Family, tired out after eight months of eventful European wanderings. And their friend, Kenneth Frampton…

The story starts more than three years earlier in San Francisco.

Jim Palosaari was a drunk bartender and actor, disillusioned after the 'Summer of Love'. Sue Cowper was studying English Literature and dabbling in anti-war protests. Meeting after a march they started living together. Both felt the city was atmospherically 'heavy', so headed north in a Dodge sleeper van.

Approaching the rural wilds of Cathcart in Washington state, they camped at a 'tent revival'[2] with free parking, greeted by the well-groomed

155

Pentecostal preacher Russell Griggs. On the fourth night of preaching one message, he was tired. Innocent observers, Jim and Sue were unconvinced. Russell then appealed for people to receive their salvation. Jim noticeably shook, grabbed Sue's hand, and the couple went forward to receive Jesus. They eventually ended up training in nearby Seattle for a year with the Jesus People Army led by Linda Meissner.

The next stop was Jim's birthplace Milwaukee, where the now-married couple started a ministry from scratch in the hip Brady Street area. Jim, Sue and five other believers comprised the residential Jesus House on Frederick Street. They reached out through a Christian coffee shop in an abandoned hardware shop and developed a rock band called The Sheep.

At one Jesus Rally, thirty were converted. Within eighteen months, there were 150 disciples now inhabiting a hospital building, spiritually grounded through a forty-week discipleship training course. One night, at a Sheep gig in Chicago, Finnish pastor Leo Muller invited them to do a fortnight of ministry in Scandinavia. The sizeable group divided four ways, the Palosaaris' thirty-strong team flying out on Wednesday 10 May 1972.

The charter flight arrived safely in Copenhagen[3] for their 'International Jesus People Music Concert' tour. After performing in Stockholm, they trekked to Finland's capital city Helsinki, which especially welcomed hippy preacher Jim because of his Finnish roots. Jesus was made known. Soon, though, the airport departure lounge loomed again.

In a forested pit-stop location on the way, Jim's arm was twisted by his wife Sue and team member Fred: it was an eleventh-hour afterthought to 'miss the plane and keep on going in Europe'.[4] Their aircraft was detained, the group reversed their vehicles and waiting sponsors had egg on their faces...

A gig at the Hahn USAF base in Germany beckoned. On arrival, they were introduced to the eccentric and alcohol-fuelled Herr Faust, residing in the nearby hamlet of Lautzenhausen. He offered the believers his ex-brothel front room for free for two months. Berlin was the next stop and its imposing wall was used as a great visual aid of sin's impact on human beings.

Their last new home after Belgium was a youth-club-cum-disco in The Hague, Holland. Everyone was demoralised, ministry opportunities had shrunk, and deep soul-searching was rife. One momentous day a young boy delivered a telegram that would change everything.

It arrived from the previously unknown Mr Frampton on 1 November 1972. Just eight simple words.

'Come to England. Post haste. Money no object.'

This caused sighs of relief and hoots of excitement. Three days later, the group boarded the *Roi Baudouin* ferry sailing from Ostend to Dover. Happily awaiting them at the Queen's Hotel in Crystal Palace, London, were deep-pile carpets, piping hot water, and a full English breakfast.

Kenneth Frampton's back story is fully told in Chapter 13. Essentially, after sponsoring the Children of God and discovering they were a cult, he severed his links with them. In the process, he met Russell Griggs,[5] previously a Children of God leader, who had subsequently exited the group in Texas. Mr Frampton asked him where he could find the genuine article rather than a counterfeit. Leading scholar Larry Eskridge recounts, 'Griggs told Frampton he knew of a "real" group of Jesus People who were within relatively close proximity of England.'[6] Somehow, his telegram reached them.

Mr Frampton provided four properties, enabling the Jesus Family to focus on outreach. The primary one was a four-storey Edwardian house at 56 Beulah Hill, Upper Norwood, where the fifteen residents were packed in like sardines. A massive gospel mural adorned the lounge wall. 'Jesus is Lord' sat above the front-door letterbox.

A Bromley house accommodated three married couples, while another couple and their children lived in Frampton's factory building. The fourth property, 41 Westow Street in Upper Norwood, became 'The Living Room': a mixture of a craft shop, an office and printing facility, a small music venue, and an open house for seekers.

The Jesus Family's heyday was between early November 1972 and late August 1974 when they left for the States. They were a missional community of the day. To give a flavour of this era, I will highlight stories about their internal community life and external missional life.

Community-wise, 'Beulah' admission was given after a fortnight's trial. The workload was divided in an ad hoc manner. Private property and personal money were voluntarily surrendered to the 'common purse'.

There was a store of used clothing and new clothing was bought as needed.

Capel House band member and resident Nick Stone reflects, 'They were into discipleship and dedication to Jesus. Here were people living it out. As individuals they were not worried about clothes, food or where they were living. This was an opportunity to minister. It was a complete lifestyle...'[7]

Another Brit, Ray Harris, joined Beulah for the outreach but amusingly recalls guys sneaking in to raid the kitchen during the night on the third day of a week's fast. More seriously, he recalls that because there were so many young Christians there, care had to be taken about welcome, especially recalling the example of an aggressive homeless man perceived to be demon-possessed.[8]

Jacky Hughes said, 'I quite liked living in the Jesus Family house for a while.'[9] She recounts sensing God telling her to marry house member Jeremy Hughes but even after being discouraged from being with him, the two would sneak off to nearby woodland to meet up. Jacky loved the evangelism though.

Leader Dave Hoyt reflects on the pros and cons of their commune living: 'The relational benefits of learning from one another, working and serving together was amazing ... On the flip side, being "I" centred and confident of "always being right" required internal adjustments and a considerable amount of self-correcting.'[10]

Margaret Stevenson,[11] from Bungay, Suffolk, was disheartened trying to follow Jesus as a teenager. Band Capel House performed at her folk club, inviting her to meet the London-based Jesus Family. That weekend she joined them for a beach baptism, prayed to be saved with team member Rich Haas, and was promptly immersed fully clothed. Margaret was different inside. For her, the discipling missional community was magnetic.

Outreach was in pole position for the community with leader Jim Palosaari viewing it more highly than church renewal. People were drawn to Jesus by various creative means, including the rock-musical *Lonesome Stone*, to which I devote Chapter 19.

The Jesus Family were also *On the Buses,*[12] using two successive repainted

London buses to attract people. One story was 'Scotland Yard busts the bus'.[13] Essentially the police stopped the colourful hippy vehicle anticipating drugs were on board. Questioning its passengers, Karin Bienge was asked how she made her money. She worked for Jesus; he met her needs. Karin proceeded to tell the policeman of Jesus healing her from morphine addiction. The police uncovered the 'stuff' alright, but it was a Gospel, plus free tickets and a poster for *Lonesome Stone*.

Everyman was the street paper used to engage people in conversation. The first edition shared their God-travels and the gospel in cartoon format; the second asked why the devil should have all the good music (advertising *Lonesome Stone*); the third raised the question, 'If God was real maybe we would…'

One day, team member Matt Spransy was witnessing in Upper Norwood using *Everyman*. Meeting a young trainee from London's Transcendental Meditation (TM) school, they shared a coffee. Matt then communicated Jesus positively rather than knocking TM. Coming back to 'Beulah', the devotee rejected his beliefs and received Jesus as Lord.

Blues-oriented country rock music was a magnet for young people, pounded out by The Sheep, who pointed non-believers to the good shepherd. They played gigs in schools and youth groups and at The Living Room. Their sole Brit was thunderous drummer Nick Malham.

In June 1971, he was unjustly detained by the police, but the charges were eventually dropped. Subsequently, he read the Bible for eight months, then turned to Eastern religions and back to drugs. A friend radiated love and peace, sharing Jesus with him. In March 1972, he received forgiveness according to the Bible's truthful promises. Nick's story travelled.

It was a typical Friday night at a pub in Upper Norwood. 'Last orders' had just been called before chucking-out time at 10 p.m. Where is good for a late-night coffee, snacks, and live music? The Living Room at 41 Westow Street, of course, is open until 1 a.m. This neutral venue on the high street enabled curious seekers to connect with accessible believers. An early version of 'An Evening with the Jesus Family' was hosted there, along with intimate gigs by The Sheep and Capel House bands. Later it hosted a Christian bookstore and sold leather and crafts. That's what we call low-key reaching out at its best.

Jesus Family members also regularly witnessed in favourite youth haunts Soho, Trafalgar Square and Piccadilly Circus.

Allan had gone into a Soho brothel pretending to be a customer!

'A young girl, a spunky firebrand, came for him and took him into her room. He sat down and quietly said, "I've come to tell you about Jesus."' The brazen but stunned girl listened to the Jesus story, quickly getting her 'mother', the madam, to hear. The latter surprisingly assured Allan: 'Oh yes, we're Christians too. My "daughter" will be retiring in a couple of months…'[14]

While the women's Christian profession displayed minimal convincing fruit, Allan's story exhibits the boldness to go anywhere with the gospel.

After twenty months of the Jesus Family's missional community life, the picture changed on 2 September 1974, when the *Lonesome Stone* squad took to the skies for a USA tour. It was a hinge moment on both sides of the Atlantic.

Stateside, the musical's sixth and final gig was in Lancaster, Pennsylvania, on 22 December 1974. The rock musical and its team had run out of steam. The team disbanded, many returning to their families. But the following year the frontier pioneers Jim and Sue Palosaari started their Highway Missionary Society[15] which pursued Acts-style community, creation care, street evangelism, and yet another band, Servant.

About eight UK team members had gone to the States: some returned home to London straight away; others received hospitality in the small town of Wales in Waukesha County, Wisconsin, before flying back the following spring.

The second half of the seventies saw huge changes back in the UK. Gerd and Karin Bienge led the little house-based church of twelve as Beulah Hill Christian Fellowship, while Gerd studied at nearby Spurgeon's College. He was supported by local adviser Phil Booth, of Radio Worldwide, especially in leading Bible studies. JPM pioneer Kent Philpott was also a strengthening figure, much later appointing elders during one visit from the USA, but some members were concerned about his choices.

Community members started doing regular jobs. The Dales Bible Week was launched in 1976, stirring the church family greatly. 56 Beulah Hill was finally demolished two years later, with a Thanksgiving Service occurring on

Saturday 17 June. Thirty strong by then, the church temporarily squashed into Gerd and Karin's flat. Later that year the little-used Thornton Heath Baptist Church was discovered locally, which had twelve members and no pastor. Merging, they renamed the combined fellowship Beulah Baptist Church. Still going strong today, as part of the Newfrontiers network of churches, they have been called Beulah Family Church since 1 July 1998.

Reflecting on the ten JPM marks, the Jesus Family were typical. They focused truthfully on the biblical Jesus, unlike presentations like *Godspell*, and they modelled communal living in both London and Manchester. Additionally, they lived a balanced charismatic lifestyle; reached out through their *Everyman* street papers, and the contemporary music and arts of *Lonesome Stone*. However, their focus was broadly on youth rather than merely hippies, and second-coming teaching was less strident than in the USA.

One interesting mark is 'church ambivalence'. The Jesus Family worked hard to integrate new believers into existing churches; but they also found themselves planting new house churches as needed.

PhD student Roger Curl noted encouragingly that, 'They criticised the early Jesus Movement because it had cut itself off from the church.'[16] Fellow Anglican clergyman, Geoffrey Corry, claimed their initial Seattle roots 'produced a moderate form of the Jesus Revolution which is interested in establishing a relationship with the churches'.[17]

Moreover, Jim viewed the Church as a prototype of God's new society. However, he did critique the existing churches for their lack of fellowship, discipling, and authority, brusquely claiming, 'The church is so organised that I believe it leads to death.'[18]

* * *

In terms of current legacy, the tangible Jesus Family has long since disappeared. However, current friendships between previous members, both in the USA and the UK, indicate a strong level of kinship that has sustained many as disciples over the decades. They are still 'family' today.

One unusual legacy, perhaps, is modelling a mission that travelled widely as it was blown along by the wind of the Holy Spirit. The Jesus Family were flexible enough to follow his leading on 'the Way', an Acts-like journey for sure.[19] This is a challenge to UK churches today, which may have an overly structured model of mission based on business. Nonetheless, the community discovered other lessons the hard way.

The flip side, then, is a warning about ensuring care for individuals, especially during revival times when God is rapidly at work. In retrospect, many recognise the serious lack of pastoral care, especially for those 'left at home', such as women (some single, many married) and children, and others who 'held the fort' at Beulah. Unceasing activity can lead to a lack of self-care and, in some cases, terrible 'burnout'. No wonder Paul urges Timothy, 'Watch your *life* and doctrine closely' (1 Timothy 4:16).

Finally, there seems to be a fresh surge of interest in intentional communities today. Although short-lived, and comprised of naturally flawed people, the communes in both south London and the Greater Manchester area seemed to disciple people well. The only other UK example is that of the Jesus Army, which finished so tragically in 2019. Positively, for instance, in our town today the local Vineyard church is currently practising community houses for young Christians in the eighteen to thirty-five age bracket.

Winter 1972-73

17.

God Has a Squad That Motors at Full Throttle

It was early 1973 in Melbourne, Australia. The temperature was mid-twenties Celsius. Many of the bulging internal walls of 265 Canterbury Road had been demolished; more extensive space was required, the place was regularly full to the brim. Hundreds of new believers gathered on Monday nights; travelling dropouts found faith and stayed overnight. The key leader was flying off to the States for six weeks. What might he discover there?

The place was named the Jesus Light and Power House, a community for the outsider and disaffected. Since December 1972, it had been open twenty-four hours a day, seven days a week. Sometimes, more than 500 people gathered, many sitting outside. Launched by John and Glena Smith, it was a missional 'church' as you may not have known it before. At its heart were God's Squad bikers; it was their official property and clubhouse, a meeting place to study Scripture, and the leather-clad guys were responsible for its safety at night. They were hardly 'easy riders' though…

John Smith[1] was an Aussie and Methodist pastor's kid, born in 1942. He came to faith as a teenager through grasping the parable of the prodigal son. In 1968, newly married to Glena, he was pastoring three churches and teaching thirty hours of English and History at school. His politics were very right-wing, but his messages became increasingly socio-political.

In 1969, John was appointed full-time evangelist with Campaigners for Christ in Melbourne. Influenced by evangelistic coffee shops like the

Drift Inn, he perceived the culture gap for new believers to be extremely wide. John explored other possibilities for evangelism, reflecting aloud, 'In doing so I found myself in the vanguard of something called the "Jesus Movement."'[2] Old-style churches had the stigma of being outdated and inward-looking, but outsiders were interested in Jesus. Links subsequently emerged with both American and Australian Jesus People.

John connected with Carl Parks of the Jesus People Army in Spokane, Washington. They published joint issues of his street-paper *Truth* for two years, adding on indigenous Australian material. Christmas 1971's edition featured a provocative image of the crucified Christ together with the headline 'Happy Birthday, Jesus'. The partnership lasted until undefined 'cultural differences'[3] caused their division in 1972. John also corresponded with Jack Sparks from the Christian World Liberation Front in Berkeley, California, inspired by his *Right On!* paper. In 1973, Sparks later spoke at Melbourne University through John's invitation.

Meanwhile, back home, John had bumped into the earliest Australian Jesus People in August 1971. The key figure, John Hirt, led his House of the New World community in Sydney. Meeting up at a large annual youth event on the Gold Coast in Queensland, Hirt was impressed by John's speaking. The original God's Squad chapter was part of his community, their name inspired by the American TV detective programme *The Mod Squad*. Led by biker Paul Eddison, they reached fellow bikers for Jesus. The following year John Smith bought his first motorbike, a Honda 500cc. Soon after that, he and six friends became the Melbourne branch of the God's Squad, taking their colours on 13 May 1972. They were full members by August, following three months' 'probation', and John was their first President.

So, 'Smithy',[4] as he was often known, was both a Jesus People pioneer and God's Squad leader in early seventies Australia. How did his vocation unfold locally?

In early 1972, the family witnessed at the 40,000-attendee Sunbury pop festival, the 'Woodstock' of Australia. It was a pivotal moment: there were hundreds of chats about Jesus, and some new converts baptised in the river, including one member of an outlaw biker group. Returning to Campaigners for Christ, John was sacked with three months' notice, 'allegedly because drugs and sex, and rock 'n' roll mark such festivals so they "are not a suitable place for a young evangelist to be"'.[5] The family were now flying solo.

Their fledgling home-based community then published the *Truth and Liberation* street paper in March 1972. Printing 10,000 copies, the $450 cost was miraculously paid for by two out-of-the-blue cheques. The family quickly outgrew their modest-sized home. Four months later, the Jesus Light and Power House (JLPH) was launched in rented Methodist premises in the North Bayswater area. Smith highlighted the fact that 'the move out of our home marked an explosion in our activities'.[6]

Biker-friend Paul Eddison captures the scene well:

The fast-growing community of Jesus People meeting at the JLPH consisted of a unique assortment of Jesus 'freaks', counterculture drop-outs, bikies, ex-druggies, students and 'straights' (those from more conservative backgrounds). By December 1972, the house was open 24 hours a day, seven days a week. God's Squad members and associates were rostered to look after the house of an evening. People would call in from all around the country. It soon became apparent that many were considering the JLPH to be their spiritual home.[7]

In late 1973, Smith flew out to the USA 'to connect with the rest of the [Jesus People] tribe'[8] in person. Berkeley, California, was home to the previous student radicalism, which had dissipated by that time. Here John met Jack Sparks, being inspired by his preaching on the steps of Sproul Plaza and his 'church' that had devolved into community houses. John went back to Australia, feeling called to teach the Bible straight-forwardly – beginning in Acts – and to focus on authentic community. The Melbourne believers thus became an alternative 'church' on Sunday mornings. Constructing their mud-brick facility, the name Truth and Liberation Concern effectively replaced Jesus Light and Power House.

After just over a decade, unnamed 'internal leadership problems raised their heads',[9] resulting in the Smiths painfully exiting the ministry in November 1982, accompanied by their biker friends; John and Glena were badly broken up. After a year's wilderness wanderings, the hundred Christians found a disused Anglican church in inner-city Melbourne and began St Martin's Community Church and the God's Squad remained a vital part of it.

However, this is a book about the Jesus People in the UK, and it is now time to speed across to the third continent of Europe.

In 1986, John made his first trip to the Greenbelt Festival in England at the time when the vicious Hurricane Charley visited our nation. He roared in to preach at the open-air communion on Sunday, pleading for Christians to tackle major social issues of the day. Being extremely gregarious, he first met Steve Spicer on this occasion, a vital prelude to the forming of the UK God's Squad nine years later.

Steve was from a Brethren church background but had a brief involvement with the Children of God before connecting with the Jesus Family, and one of its leaders Dave Hoyt. He was then part of the front-of-house team at the *Lonesome Stone* rock-musical in London. Steve subsequently became Programme and Visual Arts Manager for the Greenbelt Festival, his skills being in graphic design and multimedia. He and his wife, Ruth, live and worship in Bath these days and have three adult children.[10]

Before meeting John, Steve was a biker too, riding alongside his good friend Sean Stillman. The pair were active in grassroots mission as leaders of the Christian Motorcyclists Association (CMA). God's Squad was on the radar, but Steve was initially sceptical about both their overtly male emphasis and their attitude of 'the easiest to get on with, the hardest to get into'. Meeting John Smith altered all of that, Steve says:

I remember clearly the first time I met John Smith… It was his first visit to Greenbelt Festival … John appeared at the CMA stall we had, a press entourage following close behind him. They were looking for a big bike to have as a prop for a photo shoot. Mine was the biggest, a Guzzi California, which, with John on it and the rest of us gathered around it, was photographed, and duly appeared in the colour section of *The Daily Mail*, the UK's second biggest selling tabloid at the time. John disappeared with the press. When I rode over and met him later that day, he greeted me with, 'Keep it up!' or something similar and gave me a signed photo of himself.[11]

Meanwhile, thinking they needed to be part of a biker group with higher commitment levels, the two friends shopped around for further affiliation. Sean was keen on the God's Squad right from the start. Steve had reservations, so investigated the Californian Christian club, Soldiers for Jesus,[12] but it didn't seem a good fit. So, it was back to square one for the friends.

John Smith frequently made visits to the UK, often staying at Steve's home between speaking engagements. Their increasingly close friendship involved beer, cigars and good banter. Steve was not as overawed by John as many were. The Australian then brought other God's Squad members with him to biker shows and clubhouses, demonstrating how to relate well to other clubs.

Recalling 12 August 1995, Steve says, 'Eventually, on another visit to the UK, he turned up before a show with our patches. There was much to be excited about for the four of us! Jayne Stillman got the job of sewing the patches onto our jackets before we went off to yet another motorcycle club event.'[13] 'Patches', by the way, are the important insignia that identify the biker's club membership and territorial location. God's Squad UK had launched full throttle, aiming to minister relationally to the outlaw biker fraternity. The Squad's roots and history are succinctly described on their website: 'Since its birth, out of the counterculture Jesus Movement days of the late 60s and early 70s God's Squad has continued ... to devote its efforts among those on the fringes of society.'[14]

Bringing the story up to date, Steve eventually stepped down from the God's Squad, partly because of extreme pressure on his marriage and family life. His friend Sean is currently International President of the God's Squad today, supported by his wife Jayne, and recently published his fascinating story in the book, *God's Biker: Motorcycles and Misfits*.[15] There are currently three chapters in the UK: South, Central, and South Wales.[16]

Historically, the origins of the Australian Jesus People and the beginnings of the God's Squad are deeply intertwined, their longing being to reach people on their turf, not on the Church's turf.

In terms of JPM marks, they displayed the majority of the ten.

There are just three exceptions to the 'rule'.

First, John Smith's doctoral thesis indicates it was not primarily hippies being reached in the early Jesus People days in Australia, but rather the existing Christian youth culture that was being revitalised.[17]

Second, regarding the God's Squad particularly, outreach naturally took place more 'on the road' than in the streets. For example, on one notable occasion,[18] John and his friends motored over to a coffee bar in Gippsland to chat with people. There they encountered the Count,[19] a wild guy who rode with Satan's Cavalry. He aggressively tried to break up the party. The police – no great fans of bikers – were called. Before they arrived, three God's Squad members bundled the Count under a table and physically muzzled him. The police duly arrived, enquired about the 'trouble', and being told there was none, departed. Then, in the wee hours of the morning, the now sober Count came to know Jesus.

Third, back in the context of the UK today, the mark of 'church ambivalence' has been wonderfully countered by Sean Stillman's inspiring community in Swansea. Originally a draughtsman, Sean later became an ordained Baptist pastor. The seed thought for Zac's Place was embedded in his mind in 1996, based on the story of Zacchaeus, the friendless tax collector who encountered Jesus.[20] It was originally a community meeting above the Duke of York pub but later developed as a tribal gathering for the 'ragamuffins' of the city.

After eight years in ordained ministry, Sean had been struck by the reality that both bikers and others from fringe groups found 'church' difficult, despite being genuinely converted. He poignantly reflects, 'If you were to reverse the roles, it would be like asking your average churchgoer to step inside the local biker's clubhouse. A mixture of fear and discomfort would prevail.'[21] After moving to Swansea, Sean pledged to change things, even if it meant messier church life.

On one Tuesday night, Jenny, a forty-year-old homeless woman carrying the visible scars of drug and alcohol abuse, comes into the pub. She's in a disruptive mood today. Despite some measure of care, it's been a bad day in court, and her mobile phone has been taken from her. Things could get difficult. Suddenly, team member Glenn carries a bowl of water from the kitchen and starts washing Jenny's feet. She softly begins to sing, 'Yes, Jesus loves me…' I won't spoil the rest of the story for you.[22]

* * *

The God's Squad came directly out of the JPM, so what is its legacy today?

An important one, celebrating the group's golden jubilee year, is the book *God's Squad: The First 50 Years*, recently published in Australia in late 2022.[23]

Another legacy, though, is the modelling of appropriate ways to reach outsiders with the gospel – relevant both for countercultural hippies in their day and outlaw bikers in our own day. Unlike Peter, as an apostle to the Jews, Paul was sent to reach gentile outsiders, subsequently integrating them into the early church.[24] This poses the vital question as to which 'tribe' feels most excluded from the gospel in the UK today. Some might say men, in which case the sometimes-controversial God's Squad policy of membership still being limited to the male gender could be strategic. Another legacy, especially from Zac's Place, is to encourage the UK Church to gladly release people who are cutting-edge pioneers into their ministries, as Sean's originating church in Reading did in his early days. Sometimes we can unhelpfully put people in human boxes, hampering their Spirit-driven creativity and innovation.

The last word goes to John Smith himself.

'Smithy' died of prostate and pancreatic cancer in 2019, aged just seventy-six. In an interview with *Sight* magazine the year before, he was directly asked what his legacy would be. His poignant reply?

'My legacy will be in the lives of thousands of people who will never be the same. That's what matters to me.'[25] Numerous individuals would shout a loud 'Amen!'

Spring 1973

18.

Make Way for the Two Troubadour Worship Leaders

It was London in April 1973. One young man was about to board a flight to California, having just released his first UK album. The Tannoy system announced the flight's departure and he made his way to the gate. The West Coast beckoned, and an unknown Jesus People, too. Meanwhile, back in Romford, Essex, a young teenager was strumming a guitar in his bedroom, an instrument that had lain dormant under the stairs for years. An early-day Jesus follower, in three years' time he would be leading thousands in worship at the Royal Albert Hall.

Who are these two mystery men? The first wrote 'Shine Jesus Shine' in 1987, which became the anthem for the first March for Jesus venture which he described as 'a prayer for revival'.[1] The second composed 'All Hail the Lamb', enabling the worship of Jesus as the unique sacrifice, who is now enthroned at the Father's right hand. Both were later impacted by the Jesus People Movement, although from different stables. In case you haven't guessed, they are Graham Kendrick and Dave Bilbrough.

Graham came to faith aged five or six and a decade later was teaching himself to play guitar and compose songs. His band, Whispers of Truth, played at youth coffee bars, singing about life's emptiness but with Jesus as the answer. His brother Peter and sister Gill were part of the group, a 'psychedelic' band inspired by early Pink Floyd and The Beatles. Musically, there were some unusual chord sequences and tempo changes. Lyrically, the words were subtle, but not confrontational, drawing people into the biblical story. Whispers of Truth gigged from the mid-sixties until 1969 when Graham headed off for three years' teacher training in Avery Hill, south-east London. While there he first met the ubiquitous Clive Calver, whom he later partnered with in church-based missions. Following graduation, he took a gap year to try his hand at full-time music.

While still at college, Graham had signed as an artist to Musical Gospel Outreach, with manager David Payne running his diary. Then, in 1973, he joined Clive Calver in a new initiative, the 'In the Name of Jesus' travelling evangelistic team. Three years later, he began working with British Youth for Christ until 1979, before basing himself for four and a half years at St Michael le Belfrey church in York (an Anglican church led by David Watson). After that, he went on to serve in Roger and Faith Forster's Ichthus community in south-east London for two decades until 2004.

The popular, annual Spring Harvest Christian festival had kicked off in 1979 and Graham was chosen as the natural worship leader. Referring to this, house church sociologist Andrew Walker reflects, 'It was dominated by the worship songs of Graham Kendrick, who in my opinion had a greater influence on British Christianity than all the new church leaders put together.'[2]

The directly related *Songs of Fellowship* book of fresh praise songs was published in 1981 and Christian youth commentator Pete Ward comments on Graham's career as illustrating 'the move from work primarily aimed at young people to music which was to be used in worship with people of all ages'.[3]

In the late eighties and nineties, he pioneered what new church sociologist Andrew Walker describes as 'Graham Kendrick's imaginative processional liturgy – *Make Way*'.[4] In partnership with Roger Forster of Ichthus, Gerald Coates of Pioneer, and Lynn Green of YWAM, this became the global March for Jesus phenomenon. Graham and his team 'mobilised millions of Christians to "take the walls off the church" and bring praise, prayer and acts of goodwill and reconciliation on to the streets'.[5]

In 1987, 15,000 people marched on the streets of London, going global across 170 nations seven years later.

But, how about Graham's gap year mentioned earlier? What caused Christian music aficionado Mark Allan Powell to comment, 'In his early twenties he became a pioneer in the United Kingdom's Jesus movement and in the British version of Jesus music that accompanied the revival'?[6]

During April-May 1973, Graham, together with bass player Simon Dennis, visited California at the instigation of Musical Gospel Outreach (MGO). They were there for a short tour featuring material from his *Footsteps on the Sea* album. I interviewed them separately in 2022 to learn about their exposure to the Jesus People.[7]

On one occasion, in northern California, they were the warm-up act for the famous Larry Norman. The pair subsequently went south to spend three days in Costa Mesa, the home of Calvary Chapel's newly formed Maranatha! Music, getting a glimpse of the JPM in its heyday. They knew next to nothing about the movement, viewing themselves as 'two innocent young musicians being taken places'. Graham particularly remembers the massive tent, which replaced the outgrown 150-seater building, where larger evangelistic concerts happened. Graham was especially impressed to see that the JPM had acquired many musically artistic individuals. He remembers that 'the bands were very accomplished, and the standard was very high compared to where we'd come from'. Simon recalls being amazed by the sheer quality too, plus the constant push to talk about Jesus. He was regularly quizzed, 'Are you born again? What are you doing here? Do you expect the rapture?'[8] The pair met Love Song's Tommy Coomes, whose family hosted a beach picnic for them and put Simon up in their home. They bumped into other Calvary musicians and groups, including future music pastor Karen Lafferty, of 'Seek Ye First' fame and the fiery, uncompromising artist Keith Green.

In our interview, Graham regularly used the words 'influence' and 'catalyst' about the JPM. Overall, he argues, 'The success of the Jesus People Movement gave encouragement and a model of a cultural revolution working its way through.' Firstly, he experienced a high standard of artistic professionalism. Secondly, Graham said, 'It gave us permission, in a way, to embrace and engage with our culture, and legitimised what we were doing.' Thirdly, a template for outdoor festivals was provided, albeit a Californian one. Fourthly, having initially viewed JPM evangelism as theologically lightweight, Graham was positively startled by the massive response to appeals for salvation. Finally, big characters like Arthur Blessitt 'became part of our world' says Graham. In parallel, Simon underlines the fact that 'the JPM greatly encouraged musical creativity', subsequently describing this as 'a church renewal which has led to a new freedom of musical expression, using many different genres'.

The two men are shrewd enough, though, to critique the JPM's influence, especially the naive idea that the movement could be exported wholesale from the States to produce the same results. In Simon's own words, 'There was an undercurrent perception that the UK would turn to faith in a new way if the record charts had plenty of Christian singers. A slightly negative aspect was that if a well-known singer came to faith, they were expected to instantly become an evangelist.' Graham adds, reputedly quoting George Bernard Shaw from 1942, that Britain and America are two nations separated by a common language. The cultural differences were even deeper than people realised.

Graham also notes particular contrasts: a Californian beach culture doesn't translate well to the colder UK; also, our mood music was that of a retreating Church unskilled in handling cultural change. Kendrick's perception, too, is that UK evangelicals have a deeper theological and biblical tradition. Evangelistically, the JPM was incredibly in-your-face, unlike Graham's more oblique approach. For this reason, he felt his low-key approach never took off in the USA, at least initially.[9] His style was too English, too poetic, and too introverted! Simon concurred, adding, 'They seemed a bit overpowering for modest Englishmen like us.'

In summary, Graham's final thoughts are worth quoting in full:

'I think the Jesus People Movement was a catalyst which helped us in the UK find our own way.' He proceeds to argue that openness to history makes you realise how deep our UK Christian roots are. He poignantly concludes, 'It was really important we kept those roots, but were stimulated and challenged by an influence from a different place.' The JPM was a transatlantic catalyst, not a movement to unthinkingly import as a package deal.

Our second worship leader had much the same mentality, but a different influence. Intriguingly that influence was the Jesus rocker for whom Graham and Simon were the support act in northern California.

Dave Bilbrough was born in Hackney, London, on 1 February 1955.

A true East Ender, he eventually moved out to Romford where he was brought up. The teenager came to know Jesus aged sixteen in 1971, the zenith year of the American JPM. I interviewed Dave in late August 2020 about his influences.[10]

In terms of church involvement, new convert Dave became part of Romford Baptist Church, a fellowship heavily interested in popular culture. Its many artistic individuals were especially inspired by Francis Shaeffer's L'Abri community in Switzerland and Nigel Goodwin's Arts Centre Group, both of whom encouraged Christians to engage positively with the arts.

'There was quite an emerging group of creatives,' says Dave, and 'they hooked in quite well with some of the modern music coming out, the creative presentation of the gospel, and people dressing and doing things informally.'

Later, some members, including Dave, left the church, feeling the Holy Spirit wasn't being sufficiently honoured and experienced. They became part of the multi-congregational Romford Christian Fellowship. Its locally based leaders John Noble, Maurice Smith and Nick Butterworth were key figures in the charismatic 'house-church' movement, emphasising relational, non-religious Christianity with a strong focus on worship music. In tandem with others in the capital, these 'London brothers' initiated sizeable gatherings for charismatic fellowship and worship in the Royal Albert Hall and Westminster Central Hall.

Meanwhile, for Dave, 'Many of the hymns and songs used language and terminology I couldn't relate to. I picked up the guitar my dad had given me and began singing and writing songs in a contemporary style. The leadership in my home church encouraged me, developed me in my calling, and gave me the freedom to make mistakes.'[11] At nineteen, Dave was leading 9,000 worshippers in the Royal Albert Hall.[12] Like the early JPM's journeying minstrels, Dave began to travel too, new house churches wanting input for their worship.

So, what was the primary influence upon Dave in those early days?

'Music was the coercive factor, particularly Larry Norman.' He remembers first seeing Larry play in the crypt of St Paul's Cathedral, almost certainly for a *Songs of Praise* TV special produced by David Winter.[13] His initial impression, seeing this fellow walk on stage, with his long blond hair and guitar case in hand, was, 'Who is this guy?' Dave was blown away though: 'I connected straight away because as a youngster it aligned with my aspirations of someone who is hip, cool, and trendy. It all seemed to make sense. Not coming from a religious background in growing up, this opened up a new way to express music in a non-traditional way.'

Dave was encouraged to believe his first songs could have some validity. Larry's 1972 record, *Only Visiting This Planet*, seemed 'a cool album', that could easily be put alongside the music of his beloved James Taylor. Norman's inspiration aided him in developing his rock guitar style too, broadening his musical range. Although not the person who led him to faith, Larry was the biggest influence on Dave amongst contemporary Jesus People.

Dave was not only influenced by Norman though, but by the JPM more broadly. The bands of Maranatha! Music impacted him, especially the well-known Love Song. He also regarded solo artists Barry McGuire and Honeytree, and other bands like 2nd Chapter of Acts, as especially 'cool' – one of Dave's favourite words. Their concert tours in the UK were fuelled by Musical Gospel Outreach's Geoff Shearn, who made regular trips across the Atlantic. For Dave, 'the whole thing was aspirational and hip'.

Back in the UK, Bilbrough was explicitly touched, as many were, by our indigenous brand of JPM. In 1972, a songbook of melody lines and chords called *Songs for Jesus* was produced, featuring early artists like Parchment and Judy McKenzie, all 'in the kind of vibe of the Jesus People Movement', says Dave. Another touchpoint was the *Lonesome Stone* rock-musical, feeding off the cultural moment of *Godspell* and *Jesus Christ Superstar.* Dave also connected with the Jesus Liberation Front co-leader Geoff Bone at the local 'Woodenstocks' – a satirical spoof on Woodstock 'that had that whole Jesus People thing too,' says Dave. In addition, Arthur Blessitt's 'One Way' stickers were floating around all over the place.

These combined JPM influences had three positive impacts on the young musician: their informality was very attractive, the artists provided great role models, and there was a broad expression of musical styles. Concerning the latter, producer Les Moir speaks of Dave as 'an ambassador of diversity', musically speaking, recalling the fact that 'this was enforced further by American prophetic figure Dale Gentry, who spoke over Dave about bringing new rhythms and new sounds, as he has continued to do'.[14] On a more negative side, Dave didn't like the fear-mongering of the

Jesus People's rapture teaching, as reflected in Norman's anthemic song, 'I Wish We'd All Been Ready'. He also perceived some JPM participants to have cultic tendencies, especially the Children of God and the Jesus Army. Of course, in one sense Dave was simply a child of his cultural moment, but was, nonetheless, directly impacted in a marked way by Larry Norman's music, and somewhat less by Maranatha! Music.

* * *

As for their legacy, Graham and Dave were musical pioneers. Strongly influenced by both the American JPM and the UK charismatic movement, they became worship leaders before the term even originated. Breaking the glass ceiling of archaic music, sung worship became more contemporary. Others, like Matt Redman and Tim Hughes, followed in their wake. Indeed, today, Worship Central equips contemporary worship leaders, and the energetic Noel Robinson offers greater musical variety. The pair have also left behind a deposit of demonstrating professionalism in ministry, including 'translating' positive aspects of the American JPM to our context. Both have blessed the UK Church by reflecting the movement's distinctly non-denominational flavour, too.

That these men are serving today is another significant legacy, still displaying a heart for unchurched people: Graham was a co-founder for March for Jesus, a back-to-the-streets worship initiative that began in London in 1987. Currently, the *Where It Began* EP was Graham's recent jubilee release, which he says, 'takes him back to the days of narrative storytelling, when coffee bars and folk clubs were his venue of choice'.[15] Dave's *Troubadour Songs* album was released in 2021, and is described by him as being 'solo acoustic, raw and unashamedly unvarnished'.[16] His ongoing 'Tales of a Troubadour' presentations offer Dave's autobiographical faith journey; clearly he intends to communicate Jesus in song to an unchurched audience.[17]

In 2023, though, might a Glastonbury headliner from four years ago have taken up the baton? Rapper Stormzy has had four number-one albums, with the quietly melodic but lyrically strong 'Holy Spirit' appearing on his latest album. Despite his provocatively colourful language, the thirty-year-old is making spiritual waves in mainstream music.

Summer 1973

19.

The Rolling Stone That Gathered a Lot of Moss

It was 8 p.m. on Wednesday 11 July 1973 at the Rainbow Theatre, London's iconic rock venue. Earlier that year Eric 'Slowhand' Clapton had played and more recently Genesis had sold England by the pound. The night before, famous jazz trumpeter and bandleader Miles Davis had performed. Tonight, though, the theatre's Art Deco frontage would welcome guests to a Christian rock musical. Entitled *Lonesome Stone*, it was a cutting-edge multimedia presentation for outsiders.

Jesus was all the rage in the West End, with *Godspell* and *Jesus Christ Superstar* on offer. Here in Finsbury Park, though, tickets were much cheaper priced at 50p to £1.50. But the front four rows were cordoned off, serious flooding having made them waterlogged. Suddenly, the expectant audience saw the lights going down. War babies are born onstage, plastic bags simulating their amniotic birth sacs; military planes are seen on the screen behind. The sounds of air-raid sirens going off and bombs falling too. Welcome to *Lonesome Stone*.

While Chapter 16 highlighted the story of the Jesus Family, the group who produced *Lonesome Stone*, this chapter will focus solely on their rock musical which arrived on the back of three wider productions.

Hair broke the mould in the late sixties, charting the experience of a 'tribe' of New York hippies. Its members were pro-drugs and sex but anti-war and their parents' religion. It ran in the West End for three years from 27 September 1968. Journalist Nigel Wilson whimsically compared it to *Lonesome Stone*, saying the latter 'is a cross between *Hair* and a Billy Graham rally'.[1]

Containing purportedly Christian messages, *Godspell* and *Jesus Christ Superstar* followed, opening in London in November 1971 and August 1972 respectively. *Godspell* pictured Jesus as an outlandishly dressed street clown; *Jesus Christ Superstar* portrayed Judas as the main protagonist, misquoting the Bible too. Both omitted Jesus' physical resurrection. *Lonesome Stone* the following year was intended to set the record straight about the Jesus of the New Testament, rebutting the scripts of both writing duos, but adopting a similar style.

So, what was its run-up like between 1972-73?

The harbinger to *Lonesome Sto*ne was a more modest production, *The Story of The Jesus Revolution: How The Jesus People Came Alive*. It told the JPM story through song, testimony, and a gospel message plus an appeal from preacher Jim Palosaari.

One night, though, Jim's wife Sue felt tired of the same old thing. She recalls, 'While on stage, holding baby Jed in my arms, the Holy Spirit helped me visualise more of our team actively participating in a dramatic show.'[2] Everybody's cameo could appear in the presentation. The idea meant Sue kept her husband Jim up through the night by describing a full-blown contemporary musical, creatively telling the story of the West Coast Jesus People. They would invite the ninety-three per cent unchurched Brits to inhabit the narrative for themselves.

Sue floated the idea to Jesus Family members, and Jim spoke to financier Mr Frampton. Soon the upstairs office in Westow Street was buzzing with brainstorming sessions. Californian scenes were recalled; on Venice Beach, Mike Damrow had bumped into a drug dealer called 'Dancing Bear', and so the character 'Bear' emerged; Dave Hoyt had encountered police violence during a peaceful anti-war march, which translated into the fight scene. The concept was quickly gestating.

Five dry-runs of the revised presentation were performed between February and June 1973 to fine-tune it. The last, in Chatham, Kent, took place on Friday 8 June and Saturday 9 June. Publicity was huge, partly because the musical included a realistic but simulated orgy scene in its depiction of hippiedom. However, Jim Palosaari argued no one would find it vulgar, 'except perhaps Christians who, for the most part, live in a dream world anyway … The non-Christians will simply find good entertainment and a lot of good music.'[3] The press featured photos of the group's flower-power bus, along with cast member, Caroline Green, who was formerly the lead actress, Sheila, in the London production of *Hair*. 1,500 young people attended the show.

Following this, rehearsals began, led by young Company Stage Manager Bill Smith,[4] at the redundant Sundown Theatre in Brixton.[5] On Monday 2 July, a press reception was held at the Waldorf Hotel in London. *Lonesome Stone* was ready to be launched.

This rescue vessel was heading for seventies' searchers whose lives were marooned on the rocks of 'materialism, dead religions, sex, new gurus, astrology, and mind-expanding and bending drugs', all to bring them 'one by one to their moment of truth in finally calling out upon God, finding the true peace and love that was to be found in knowing Jesus Christ'.[6]

The setting for the musical was the Haight-Ashbury area of San Francisco in 1967. Drug user and dealer Bear gets arrested and sent to jail, where he becomes a Jesus follower. He then returns to his countercultural friends, such as Lonesome Stone and Queenie, with this good news. Ostensibly, they are looking for love, but a mere handful turn to Christ.

This story comprised a pastiche of the various life stories of every single cast member, described by *Sunday People* journalist Peter Oakes as, 'The Cast With an Amazing Past':[7] social misfits and druggies; Dave Hoyt and Fred Gartner with long jail sentences behind them; and a con-man and drug smuggler too…

Music was provided by The Sheep. It included a mixture of homegrown songs and 'covers', such as Randy Stonehill's humorous 'Vegetables' and Scott McKenzie's epoch-making 'If You're Going To San Francisco'. The electrical equipment was more sophisticated than that used by major bands of the day. Props were large-scale, including non-perishables like 2,000 party-poppers, and perishables such as bananas, cabbages, and potatoes on alternate days. Even blood capsules were bought for the fight scene. A real explosion for the senses. The cost was enormous, including ongoing advertising on sixty per cent of London buses, costing £600,000 in today's money.

It was only on that first day that the copyright was registered at the British Museum. Initial attendance figures were not good. However, after 20 July, sales were boosted when the roof fell in at the Shaftsbury Theatre, the venue for *Hair*. This exponentially added to the show's audience.[8] Many critics were harsh, but the *Sunday People's* Peter Oakes poignantly commented: 'Lonesome Stone may never break box-office records. But if it saves a few wayward kids, it could be the most successful musical of them all.'[9]

Some well-known celebrities were involved; the newly converted Caroline Green performed, and singer-songwriter Cat Stevens discreetly sat in the audience one evening. One person whose life was transformed was Chris Smith:[10] 'I was one of the proto hippies whose life was changed, and I still hug trees and follow Jesus. I spent sixteen years serving in London City Mission, and have retired in recent years, with time to think and remember those truly exciting years.'

UK citizens are sometimes accused of being too London-centric though. Conversely, *Lonesome Stone* toured the length and breadth of the country between November 1973 and August 1974. I will now highlight the show's legacy by telling individuals' stories at successive locations.

The biggest European council housing estate was Wythenshawe in Greater Manchester, a 'garden city' with some 66,000 residents.[11] From 6 November to 2 December 1973, *Lonesome Stone* played the two-year-old Forum Hall. Despite being set in the USA, the show's fight scenes, for example, resonated with young people in an openly violent culture. Happily, many tough teenagers from low-income homes started following Jesus, experiencing lifelong transformation.

Two of the ten JPM marks, 'church ambivalence' and 'communal living', were combined in practice.

The *Lonesome Stone* team, far from being church-ambivalent, scoured in vain for an appropriate fellowship for new believers. Dave Hoyt, lead actor 'Lonesome', felt moved to stay on and disciple them. Helped by two couples from the local Mighty Flyers band, three communes were launched in redundant Anglican vicarages. The first in Stockport stood amidst the rubble of a demolished neighbourhood. The local youth found its location cool and rapidly grew there as Christians.

A commune in Crumpsall soon became a house church, led by the Mighty Flyers' manager and vocalist Dave Rees and his wife Barbara. Known as the Jesus Family, then Trinity Church, its dwindling numbers meant the fellowship eventually merged with a local ecumenical project (LEP) in the mid-eighties.

Andrew 'Bamb' Rushton[12] lived there, which for him was 'a crash-course in self-knowledge: living all together in close proximity helped me to know that I had a lot of shortcomings, much to learn'. He is still a singer-songwriter today, about to retire from teaching English.

Wythenshawe highlighted a crucial reality – sometimes, the new wine of the gospel requires a wholly new wineskin,[13] despite intentions to the contrary. Pioneer missions call for people-centred flexibility and often innovative discipling communities.

The second stop was a four-day run in Horsham, Surrey.[14]

Young resident Norman Amey[15] remembers, 'In 1973 I was an average teenager. Popular music was pushing boundaries. Many of our idols were high on drink and drugs. I had become a Christian but found it difficult seeing them [contemporary idols] living contrary to my new-found values.' *Lonesome Stone* was loud, polished, and thought-provoking, comments Norman who concludes, 'I could relate to the storyline – someone a similar age to me looking for answers to the big questions of life … the good news of Jesus was for everyone.'

After playing Cheltenham, the tour headed to USAF Lakenheath in Suffolk.[16] There they met Essex-born Ant Wren.[17] From a working-class home, and a believer of sorts since eleven, he never really fitted into a middle-class church. Ant ended up living with the Jesus Family in south London, where he grew spiritually in the community. After his colourful self-described 'Skool of life' ended in June 2015, Ant's lived-in body was transported by motorbike hearse to his funeral, awaiting a resurrection body.

The next venue was the Queen's Theatre in Burslem in the Potteries.[18]

Young science teacher Max Coates,[19] teaching twenty-two miles away, was asked to host a school visit for the cast members. He reflects, 'They were more Haight Ashbury than Hazel Grove. Neither the children nor the staff had seen anything like this when a polychromatic group of exotic rock stars got off the bus.' Many then attended *Lonesome Stone*, the local inter-school group Christalis ballooned to 250 students fortnightly, and the rock musical 'raised the bar about what the Christian faith could be'.

Sixteen-year-old John Tsang[20] was an Office Studies student, invited to classmate Kim's youth group, who was given a spare concert ticket. John recalls, 'I ended up speaking to cast member Ethel Krauss, sitting cross-legged on a table in hippy costume … Instead of the requested autograph she wrote down John 3:16.' Feeling nudged the following day, but wanting to be undisturbed, John prayed a salvation-prayer in a men's toilet cubicle. Decades later, after vocational retirement, John served as a Visitor Guide at the Houses of Parliament.

After stints playing Sheffield[21] and Liverpool,[22] the next two locations were American Air Force bases in Germany.[23] Back in the UK, the following month saw *Lonesome Stone* play the 1,500-seater St George's Hall, Bradford,[24] Britain's oldest concert hall. On 2 May, I organised a promotional Sheep gig at nearby Leeds University, where I was a final-year student; I still have the original flier today.

House-church believer David Lee[25] attended in Bradford, recalling, 'It was quite a revolution for us all … What I do remember was the hall being full every night. One evening two middle-aged ladies sat in the row before us. As usual, the show started with a bang, causing both ladies to jump out of their seats simultaneously. The real blessing, though, was getting to know some of the cast.'

Meanwhile, Birmingham greeted the Jesus Family at its Old Rep Theatre.[26] Student Colin Marriott[27] had identified with hippies, thought church was for old people, and was exploring Eastern religions. He had heard about Jesus People, personally coming to faith in a nightclub aged nineteen. He reflects, '*Lonesome Stone* was brilliant and everything I wanted at that time.' For Colin, the ultimate draw was the Christian community. Later, having escaped being recruited by the Children of God, he and five friends formed a Methodist-based community in inner-city Birmingham.

Liverpool was the only city *Lonesome Stone* played in twice[28] and June 1974 was its second visit. Thirty-year-old Christine Ellerton,[29] PA to the show's benefactor Mr Frampton, was not a Christian and felt without hope in the world. Having previously seen the London show, she wanted to meet the cast first-hand. This happened when she worked alongside the advanced 'publicity team', Steve and Ruthie Shaw, in Liverpool. They were light in her darkness, giving Christine a firm but godly shove that enabled her to take the first steps to receive God's forgiveness and new life in Jesus.

Edinburgh was the penultimate location; the rock musical played nearly a month's run[30] at the Church Hill Theatre, one of the many venues used by the famous Edinburgh Festival today.

Hosts Revd David Maybury and his wife Doreen were true parents to the cast, putting them up in their church hall at St James', Leith. Their third child Ruth remembers tripping over people praying for each other all over the house and having late-night prayer meetings with hot chocolate in the lounge.

Anna MacDonough[31] was brought up in the Highlands, the daughter of an alcoholic minister. She loved psychedelic music. Leaving home for good at the age of sixteen to live in Edinburgh, Anna adopted a hippy lifestyle but hung out with coffee bar Christians too. Paying 50p to attend *Lonesome Stone*, she loved it and went back several times, but the change didn't stick. Sometime later, falling seriously ill in trendy Amsterdam, she eventually found her way to London's Jesus Family. She joined the community and found faith. Following long battles with alcoholism, Anna is now fully restored and serves as a Street Pastor in her hometown of Newmachar in Aberdeenshire.

Plymouth-born Nigel Boney[32] moved to Glasgow at the age of fifteen and feels more Scottish than English. His experience of Christian conversion was reinforced by seeing *Lonesome Stone* in Edinburgh. He reflects, 'The show proved to me that it doesn't matter what experiences you have come through, both good and bad, you have a life in front of you. God has a habit of putting you back on the runway and you just need to trust the journey.' He must know, sadly having lost his mum and brother in quick succession recently.

Lonesome Stone gave a farewell performance at the first Greenbelt Festival in late August 1974, before the American contingent flew back to the States. After nearly four months of performing there, the musical became a huge animal that breathed its last breath … The team disbanded and dispersed.

* * *

To close on a positive note, though, through *Lonesome Stone* the Jesus Family left behind in the UK a remarkable legacy of multiple new Jesus followers for life – I should know, I was one of them!

Summer 1973

20.

Jews Given Pole Position in Hearing About Jesus

A Jewish sixth-former started identifying as a Christian at the height of summer in 1973. He had grown up in Walton-on-Thames in a liberal family who celebrated annual festivals. A striking memory for him was the Passover *Seder* meal, stumbling through the Hebrew language and needing an English translation. The young man was sent to *cheder* school on Saturday mornings to learn more about Judaism. One year the lad's birthday fell on *Yom Kippur*, the Day of Atonement; he had to spend all day at the synagogue before opening his presents the following day. As an eleven-year-old, he heard news of the Six-Day War.

Entering his teens, our young man had won a 'Headmaster's nomination' to the prestigious boarding school, Winchester College, during which time he became introverted and depressed. Religion-wise, he skipped his *bar mitzvah*. Two of his classmates, Simon and Michael, called themselves Christians, and he ridiculed them. An Anglican evangelist visited the school on a mission and the gospel message got under his skin. Who was he? His name was Richard Harvey, and he would later become a missionary to his people and lead the UK branch of mission organisation Jews for Jesus.

The story begins, though, more than four decades before this game-changing event...

Martin Meyer Rosen was born in Kansas City, Missouri, on 12 April 1932, to Jewish immigrant parents from Eastern Europe. His Yiddish name 'Moishe' (Moses) meant 'drawn from the water'. He met Ceil Starr while selling house number signs door-to-door. After courting her, the pair were married when both were just eighteen. Ceil then found *Yeshua*[1] as her Messiah, casually leaving Christian pamphlets around the house. Wanting to refute her faith, Moishe studied the Scriptures and became convinced: 'It wasn't because I thought Christianity was nicer than Judaism. Nor was it because I wanted to renounce my birthright, as many have said. Basically, I accepted Jesus, because, after searching the Scriptures, I found them to be true.'[2] Moishe was adamantly told to leave his father's house.

After theological training, in 1957 Moishe was ordained as a Conservative Baptist pastor. He ministered to fellow Jews for sixteen years with the American Board of Mission to the Jews (ABMJ). All but three of these were in New York.

A late 1960s encounter at Columbia University first nudged Moishe toward his newfound ministry. Speaking about 'Hippies, Radicals, and Revolutionaries' for the Inter-Varsity group, he joked about a hippy who smelt like a cheetah. Afterwards, social worker Bob Berk asked him, 'Did you ever smell a hippy?' Moishe had never got close enough. Thoroughly rebuked, he began to engage with them in Greenwich Village, finding many had spiritual aspirations. 'Before long, Moishe's office had become a gathering place for, as he put it, "wall-to-wall" hippies.'[3]

Moishe later spoke at Golden Gate Seminary in San Francisco. Afterwards, the missions' lecturer introduced him to people reaching counter-cultural types, such as leading JPM figure Kent Philpott. Moishe also ate with Jack Sparks of the Christian World Liberation Front, who introduced him to two Messianic believers. God's work on the West Coast seemed more fruitful than that on the East Coast, but returning home to New York, 'Moishe intensified his efforts to reach the counterculture, trying as he did so to get others excited about the possibilities.'[4]

After negotiating with ABMJ leaders, in July 1970 Moishe's family relocated to San Francisco. For three years he led his ministry, Hineni Ministries,[5] under their auspices. Meanwhile, Moishe became impressed with the communication techniques of anti-Vietnam War activists. Jesus People were prolific too, up to thirty per cent of them coming from a Jewish background.[6] In June 1972 *Time* magazine's religious section published 'Jews for Jesus' – an article referring to Messianic Jews generally. During this time, Moishe preached in the Haight-Ashbury area, clearly stating that his hearers could trust Jesus without giving up their Jewish culture.

Eventually, Moishe connected with other newly converted Jews. Susan Perlman, from an orthodox background in Brooklyn, had come to faith through Larry Norman in 1971. She was on her lunch break in Manhattan and ended up meeting him on the street, going for coffee, and was saved at his gig afterwards. Susan was a Jews for Jesus co-founder. Another, Amy Raninovitz, viewed Moishe as a mould-breaker: 'This Jesus People Movement was already happening – Moishe recognised the importance of it and looked for ways to shake up Jewish missions and utilise what he knew to reach a wider audience.'[7]

The activist in Moishe was increasingly unsettled though. Feeling AMBJ was blunted through bureaucracy and facing tension with his boss, Daniel Fuchs, he knew that something fresh was brewing and this was only exacerbated by being fired. Jews for Jesus became an independent mission under his leadership in September 1973, intertwined with the Jesus People from the very start. Moishe humorously reflected, 'I am overweight, overbearing, and over forty. What am I doing leading a youth movement?'[8]

Meanwhile, across the ocean, that same summer of 1973, Richard Harvey had been converted precisely two months earlier…

Born in 1956 in Ashford, Kent, Richard was the son of German-Jewish immigrants, originally named Hirschland. His parents then became founders of a new liberal synagogue in Kingston. As an eleven-year-old Zionist, Richard made his first trip to Israel. Subsequently educated at Winchester College, Richard was a seeker and became involved in countercultural pursuits such as reading Hesse's self-discovery book *The Glass Bead Game*. He also engaged with The Beatles' psychedelic phase; was fascinated by Leary's advocating mind-bending drugs; and went through Transcendental Meditation (TM) initiation with a mantra to chant. In due course, prompted by two Christian friends, he started to think about Jesus' resurrection and felt he 'saw' the empty tomb for himself. Following this, in 1973, Richard heard Anglican minister Keith de Berry speak. Later that night, kneeling at his bedside, he found rest for the heavy-laden through Jesus.[9] He was part of a religious revival in the school, involving seventy boys in the Christian Forum. 'Around July of 1973, I started calling myself a Christian,'[10] Richard said. He was a UK Jesus Person.

The following year, a survey revealed that there were no more than a hundred Jewish believers in England at that time[11] but, while studying at Bristol University from 1975-1978, Richard encountered some of them. Anthony Bash, the Navigators' ministry leader and fellow Messianic Jew, was an encouragement to him. Some of Richard's Jewish friends became Jesus followers. David and Rosemary Harley, leaders of the Church's Ministry Among the Jewish People (CMJ) in London helped Richard grasp what it meant to remain Jewish as a new Christian. They invited him to a conference that gathered twenty young Jewish believers at London Bible College in 1976. There, he first met special guest Moishe Rosen, who exhorted participants like Richard, 'You may only be a small number here today, but God can use you to do a lot if you let Him.'[12]

A year later, Richard heard and met the band The Liberated Wailing Wall at All Souls Church at Langham Place in London. During that trip they gave a presentation at his home church where his brother Nick gave his life to Jesus, desperately wanting what these Christians had for himself.

Following his graduation, in 1979 Richard encountered a second Messianic Jewish group, Lamb, at the Greenbelt Festival. The band was driven by American, John Clark, who met Richard and later jotted down his contact details. One day, the telephone rang; John was inviting Richard to visit the States. Along with four friends, he flew out, armed with a long list of written questions. Inspired by Messianic congregations in America, the group started the fledgling London Messianic Fellowship the very next year. Richard also walked the streets of London that summer, giving out tracts on a Jews for Jesus campaign to encourage people to probe the identity of Jesus.

Throughout the 1980s, Richard was actively mentored by Moishe but never joined Jews for Jesus. Instead, he first engaged in theological training,[13] then in 1982 joined the long-standing Churches Ministry Among Jewish People (CMJ).[14] Richard served as an evangelist with them for almost ten years. One Friday night, two years after signing up, he first met Monica Shulkind; the couple fell in love and were married under the traditional *chuppah* (Jewish wedding canopy). Meanwhile, in the States of the mid-1980s, three fellow leaders were pushing a reluctant Moishe to go international. He finally relented and Richard eventually joined Jews for Jesus as its first UK leader in 1992. He found Moishe a larger-than-life figure and didn't always agree with him, but says he 'was a genius, master strategist, and rare eccentric who could bring a new perspective'.[15]

A fascinating yarn from the 1990s gives a flavour of Moishe's influence in the UK[16] ... Richard engaged with Jews weekly at Speakers' Corner in Hyde Park. He and fellow Messianic believer Mark Greene worshipped at Bushey Baptist Church, where the Liberated Wailing Wall had been invited to perform. Moishe Rosen was there too, awaiting a European board meeting of Jews for Jesus. Two young visitors with yarmulkes arrived late and unexpectedly that night; Richard recognised them as anti-missionary hecklers from Hyde Park. Moishe got Mark and colleague Susan Perlman to engage with them after the final song, hindering them from detaining people in conversation as they left. Eventually, confronted by Moishe, the pair admitted they were trying to stop people being deceived; they were told that they were not welcome and were ushered onto the pavement. Richard was told to call the police, who reassured the interlopers this exit strategy was perfectly legal. Sitting down afterwards with Greene, Moishe explained that the pair were disruptive 'wolves amongst sheep', and that even Paul had used his Roman citizenship to positive effect (Acts 22:22-29).

Meanwhile, the 1990s was billed as the 'Decade of Evangelism' by church leaders, but many argued that Jewish people did not need to be reached. They were already God's historically chosen people, so why interfere with their religion? Jews for Jesus pressed on regardless, particularly engaging in vigorous media involvement. An advert in *The Times* in 1991, written by Mark Greene, was countered by strident Jewish journalist Bernard Levin. His article, entitled 'Clodhoppers on Crusade', rudely described Jews for Jesus as 'such slop', but Greene responded graciously.[17] In March 1992, veteran TV presenter Joan Bakewell stirred the pot further, producing a *Heart of the Matter* documentary about whether anyone could be both Jewish and believe in Jesus. A further advert was placed in *The Independent* in 1994, bringing Passover greetings from Messianic believers and containing questions based on the traditional four questions about the food of the Passover *Seder*.[18] The Jewish community reacted strongly, and Bishop Richard Harries condemned the advert. He subsequently debated with Richard Harvey on Radio 4's *Sunday* programme, arguing that one cannot be both Jewish and Christian. Harvey demurred, saying he was both... Jews for Jesus had big hurdles to jump over, both outside and inside the Church.

In 1997, after leading the UK team for five years, Richard Harvey handed over the reins to Jonathan Bernd before going on to teach at All Nations Christian College until 2012. Richard then became the senior researcher for Jews for Jesus. For example, in 2019, he responded to a Church of England report entitled 'God's Unfailing Word', highlighting theological and practical issues in Christian-Jewish relations. He commended Anglicans for repenting of past antisemitism but also defended the right to evangelise Jewish people.[19] Two years ago, Harvey wrote an accessible paper giving five reasons why Christians don't engage in Jewish evangelism, beginning with, 'I don't know where to start.'[20]

Bringing things up to date, in the 2021 census, 271,327 people self-identified as Jewish with more than half of them living in London. For Jews for Jesus, some are discovering ways to be both British and Jewish in following Rabbi Yeshua ben David. The current team 'go and tell' through street outreach, but since the pandemic, they have communicated more through social media. Their podcast is intriguingly called *Keeping Jewish Weird*. They also invite fellow Jews to 'come and see' in welcoming settings, currently re-imagining a ministry space in London to connect through art shows, books, coffee, and *Shabbat* dinners.[21] Jews for Jesus 'love and serve' practically too: ministering to the elderly, giving care packages to Holocaust survivors, and relieving poverty (especially prevalent in ultra-Orthodox circles).

One narrative to demonstrate the first strategy is Leah's story.[22] She recently relocated from Israel to London to be nearer her Jewish boyfriend.

Team member Maia initially met Leah through Facebook, then they regularly walked together during 'lockdown'. First, they chatted about Leah's secular upbringing in Israel, then shared about their families and busy lives. Leah is still looking for a community of Israelis to connect with but doesn't want to do so 'religiously' through a synagogue. Having met Christian clients at work, some of whom were Messianic believers, Maia suggested to her friend, 'Might God be trying to tell you something?' At present, Leah has not yet come to faith…

Apart from its direct genesis through the JPM in 1973, Jews for Jesus displayed many of the movement's marks.

Evangelism was out there on the streets of San Francisco, later in other cities, and now as 'live chat' on the internet. Their group, The Liberated Wailing Wall, used contemporary music, described by American Christian expert Marc Allan Powell as 'some of the finest liturgical and worship music to come out of the Jesus movement'.[23] The central message was the Jewish Jesus of the entire Bible, who clearly stated 'salvation is from the Jews' (John 4:22). In a historical context deeply influenced by prophetic end-times teaching about Israel,[24] their Jewish evangelism resonated strongly. Not every Messianic believer was from countercultural hippy roots though. Neither was there evidence of disciples living in communal houses, but there was certainly an open door at the Rosens' home. Church-wise, some converted Jews joined regular Gentile churches, while others formed Messianic Fellowships[25] like the one Richard and Monica Harvey pioneered in London. Jews for Jesus were noticeably part of the JPM though, quickly widening their scope to include Gentiles after their inception.[26]

* * *

Exactly fifty years after Moishe Rosen founded Jews for Jesus, what is their golden jubilee legacy?

The next generation of Messianic believers is still reaching people in London and the UK. Nationally, they have added to the chorus of voices against antisemitism that sometimes, sadly, comes from fellow Christians. Also fighting antisemitism is Jewish personality David Baddiel, with his

Jews Don't Count book and TV programme. The Labour Party is trying to root out antisemitism, including dealing with allegedly inappropriate remarks by MP Diane Abbott in April 2023. From the reverse angle, the group has also argued against the Chief Rabbi's insistence that there is no place for Jews having Yeshua preached to them, Harvey conversely arguing that Messianic Jews are 'the missing link between the church and Israel'.[27] After all, both Jesus and Paul indicated Jewish people as the first to receive the gospel.[28]

Church-wise, Jews for Jesus have motivated believers in the UK to discover their Jewish roots in the Bible and history, especially through their 'Christ in the Passover' presentation which is offered to educate believers in Christian churches. They are keen to teach that the Church hasn't replaced God's historic people.[29] Rather, Gentile Jesus followers have been grafted into the vine of God's people, the Jews (Romans 11:17-21). Relationally, the national team has modelled how to reach Jewish individuals for Jesus, especially those who are part of the Israeli diaspora currently living in the UK.

All because of a mission-minded, Messianic Jewish couple who turned into Jesus Freaks half a century ago.

Autumn 1973

21.

The Church That Comes Together, Stays Together

It was the first day of Autumn 1973. 'The Troubles' in Northern Ireland were at their height and had spilt over into England; in mainland Birmingham, a soldier was killed while trying to defuse an IRA bomb. The following day, British and Irish politicians agreed to establish an Executive body for Northern Ireland, hoping it would foster long-term peace. That same month of September, Belfast hosted a Christian musical from America and an IRA man came to know Jesus, warmly embracing a British soldier afterwards.

Touring elsewhere in the UK, further stories emerged. Spontaneous offerings were taken up for a family whose house had recently burnt down and for someone to fly and visit a relative dying of leukaemia on the other side of the globe. A Pakistani family without a job or home was immediately taken in to live with a missionary family who had been thrown out of Uganda.

Amidst trouble and hardship, there was hope in the form of the ground-breaking musical presentation, *Come Together*.

The story begins four decades earlier, during the Great Depression with the births of a baby boy and a baby girl. Jimmy Owens entered the world in 1930 in Clarksdale, Mississippi. As an adult, he earned his living in the jazz business but was a sailor when he met his future wife Carol. Carol Webb, an only child, was born the year after Jimmy in El Reno, Oklahoma, but in 1936 the family moved to California. In her late teens, Carol trained to teach in San José, regularly visiting her cousin Corky at weekends in San Leandro. Corky took Carol to her church, called Port O'Call, where she first met Jesus and then met Jimmy. The pair fell in love and married on Valentine's Day, 1954. Jimmy's musical talents speedily re-emerged at Port O'Call: he played in the church band, then tried out conducting the choir, getting properly trained in the process. Jimmy's musical presentations packed the place out and soon he was on the church staff.

Familywise, daughter Jamie came along in 1955, followed by Buddy in 1957. Much later, in the mid-1960s, the family moved to Glendale in southern California, worshipping at the United Community Church. There they met Ralph Carmichael, widely recognised as the father of Contemporary Christian Music. The pioneer affirmed Jimmy's musical talent and helped him to arrange two albums. Soon Jimmy was leading The Jimmy Owens Singers and appearing on the TV's *World of Youth*. Carol partnered with him, their twin passions being music and young people; they released an album for youth pastors, *Turn On the World of Youth*, in 1968.

However, two issues strongly influenced the writing of *Come Together* at this juncture: their hippy neighbours and their new church.

Firstly, hippiedom came of age during the 1969 Woodstock Festival. Carol perceived that for hippies, there 'was no welcome for them, let alone rainbows, in the churches then. Too many religious folks objected to long straggly beards and hair, and filthy feet that ruined the carpets.'[1]

The Owenses' response was their first 1971 musical, *Show Me*. Carol explains, 'The point of its message is that many churches had built cultural and class walls that kept the street people out, when they should have been out on the streets inviting them in.'[2] Satirical humour poked fun at the Ladies' Missionary Society – sending people overseas, but clueless about reaching youth locally. The fictional church should apologise, saying, 'Is all you've seen just patterns. Mere routines and pious words. When what you sought was love? Forgive me, my friend.'[3] Meanwhile, a fictional church leader was pictured surveying Woodstock's clientele, pompously contending, 'I think if only they were shaved. That then perhaps they could be saved.'[4]

The initial *Show Me* performance had teenagers and street people downstairs in the thousand-seater auditorium and praying Christians upstairs. Following an evangelistic appeal, the entire ground floor gave their lives to Jesus. The evangelist had to double-check they had understood correctly.

Secondly, in 1970, the Owens family became part of the Church on the Way in Van Nuys, California, pastored by Jack Hayford. This Foursquare Church had been founded in 1926 but, when their new pastor arrived forty-three years later, had just eighteen members. At the time, the Owenses lived fourteen miles away in Glendale. Magnetised by the church, they had been travelling to Van Nuys to worship there regularly. The family swelled their growing numbers by four (with two early teens in tow). They learned so much in the following eighteen months as the church mushroomed through vibrant worship, meaningful fellowship, and relevant evangelism.

Carol subsequently recounts, 'Then came that fateful Sunday … we were having dinner at the Hayfords' when Jack casually suggested, "Why don't you write a musical about our church?"'[5] He was suggesting they share lessons from their recent discipleship journey more widely. So, *Come Together* was born in 1972, a contemporary and interactive musical on the back of *Show Me*; Jimmy and Carol began to write, produce, and then tour. It was presented at American churches and promoted on TV. The title song urged its listeners, 'Jesus people come together, let your light shine!' Mark Allan Powell comments, '*Come Together* was the Owenses' highpoint, and by the year 2002 would remain the best contemporary Christian musical of all time, the benchmark for all other contributions to what became a major genre in its own right.'[6]

So, what did a typical *Come Together* look like for the average attendee? It was front led but with room for participation too. The whole focus was on the person of Jesus, his identity, work, and soon return. The songs were intentionally congregational, but in a mainstream 'pop' vein, which Powell describes as 'regarded as somewhat "hokey" by real aficionados of rock'.[7] The middle section of five included breaking into small groups for fellowship and prayer, something rarely practised at the time. After the grand finale anticipating Jesus' return, attendees were invited to give an offering, as there was no entrance fee.

Anyway, needing a holiday after all their hard work touring, Jimmy and Carol had a fortnight away in Hawaii. On returning home, Carol's cousin Dee rang. A lady preacher called Jean Darnell was with her. Jean was soon flying back to England, where she and her husband, Elmer, had lived since 1946. She had previously seen a vision of revival flames blazing from John O'Groats to Land's End and was waiting for God to answer the 'How?' and 'When?' questions. Dee urgently wanted to introduce the Owenses to Jean. Getting together, Jean forthrightly asked Jimmy, 'So, what is God saying to you?' He replied by talking about *Come Together*. Had Jean found the answer to her questions, to stoke the flames of revival in the UK?

1972 was the year of the Evangelical Alliance's 'Power in the Land' initiative to reach every household. The charismatic movement was thriving, house churches were being pioneered, the Nationwide Festival of Light was having an ongoing impact, and the JPM was touching the UK. Jean flew back with a film of the musical. Showing it to some friends, they felt its style was too American, but Darnell was not deterred…

It was time for Jean to rally the troops. She gathered a team of three – herself, a businessman, and an Anglican vicar. Jimmy flew across the Atlantic regularly to coach musical directors in different locations. UK churches of every ilk were getting stirred up about the musical. Pat Boone, the Christian pop star who played the lead role in the States, offered to trek over to take up the part again. Michael Allison wrote to two hundred fellow MPs to endorse the musical. He also persuaded the Archbishop of Canterbury to issue a call to prayer for the nation, endorsed by no less than Queen Elizabeth herself. Things were quickly falling into place for September 1973. The Owens family flew out to London.

The planning for the whirlwind tour was undertaken rapidly. Alongside Jean Darnell were key figures and house-church pioneers Peter Lyne and Gerald Coates, together with Barney Coombs. Anglican clergyman Teddy Saunders, who had prepared some young royals for confirmation, was another. Coates himself remembers, 'The whole thing was planned and organised within three months – with no office, paid personnel or money.'[8] The ten-venue tour kicked off at the Usher Hall in Edinburgh, 'Jean knowing that if the musical could break through the reserve of the

Scottish church, it would work anywhere.'[9] The place was packed, with some attendees standing.

Meanwhile, across the water in strife-torn Belfast, Protestants and Catholics unprecedentedly came together to seek reconciliation. A priest publicly asked for forgiveness from his Protestant counterparts, who rushed to pray and repent alongside him. Carol recalls another incident where, 'Jimmy's attention was fastened on two men standing to one side, embracing and praying together: one was a radical IRA leader; the other was an English Major in full battle dress.'[10] Back at Westminster Central Hall in London, Gerald Coates burst into tears on hearing the first few bars striking up, commenting, 'I knew intuitively this was going to be a big move of God.'[11] Other cities, such as Birmingham, Liverpool and Coventry, hosted *Come Together*, with many disappointed people regularly being greeted by 'Full Up' signs.

The following year 1974, there was a second tour with more than fifty locations taking part between Easter and Whitsun. This time only home-grown talent was involved, with Brits running things using their battalions of volunteers. A particular hotspot was Birmingham, where twenty-one localised neighbourhood presentations took place. In a sizeable corporate finale, though, the open-air Bull Ring hosted 1,000 attendees; it was a good job the storm clouds blew over during the musical. Organiser Nick Cuthbert reflects on how the event was 'picking up on the same spirit of the Jesus Movement'.[12] Moving east from the Midlands to East Anglia, the very first Greenbelt Festival was taking place. Pete Ward recalled, 'The influential charismatic musical *Come Together* was performed on the Sunday with a service of "Breaking of Bread".'[13]

The August 1974 edition of *Buzz* was jammed with stories from the length and breadth of Britain:[14] a seventeen-year-old girl came to faith in Truro Cathedral, fifty others doing likewise in Rugby Town Hall; a broken ankle was miraculously healed at Bedworth Civic Hall; folks from Holy Trinity Wandsworth were inspired by the inter-generational fellowship; a welcome 'admission free' policy meant finances had to be raised, and Leeds participants gave £100 more than was needed. In Southampton, *Come Together* proved a great follow-up to prominent evangelist Don Summers' crusade there. Good news was rife.

However, it wasn't all plain sailing. In Falmouth, the venue was changed at the last minute after discovering competition from a noisy three-piece orchestra in a nearby beer garden. Wandsworth experienced their PA amplifier blowing up forty-five minutes before launching, while in Rushden, Northamptonshire, the spotlights caught fire during the event. Two hundred of Brighton's populace sadly didn't use their tickets, frustrating a thousand people on the waiting list. For the staider folks, praying in small groups was a bridge too far.

So, having had a bird's-eye-view historically, in what senses did *Come Together* connect with the JPM? Firstly, in terms of the personnel involved and secondly, in displaying many of the movement's ten marks.

Notable Jesus People personnel were involved. Singers included the Owenses' friend Barry McGuire, famed for his apocalyptic 'Eve of Destruction', and Jesus musician Randy Stonehill, duetting with the composers' daughter Jamie.[15] Meanwhile, Calvary Chapel's 'Musicianary' Karen Lafferty[16] had sung on the first recording, Jimmy auditioning her from a phone booth on the beach. Pat Boone, certainly no converted hippy, but part of Church on the Way, played the lead role. The year before he had released *Pat Boone Sings the New Songs of The Jesus People*.

Regarding JPM marks, the musical exhibited many previously high-lighted. *Come Together* was utterly Jesus-centred from start to finish. The music was softly contemporary, and some considered the record to be the first contemporary praise album. The presentation's ethos was certainly charismatic, featuring Spirit-inspired 'body life' in small groups. As for end-times teaching, the final section provoked believers to live pure lives as they anticipated the imminent second coming of Jesus the Bridegroom.

In one sense, though, the influences of *Come Together* could be termed 'second generation JPM'.[17] To explain further: the first was countercultural hippies coming to faith; the second was Christian youth being revitalised. *Come Together* was more the latter than the former, reflected in the mainstream pop genre rather than in rock and roll. Teenager Jamie Owens was a good example of the 'second generation JPM', remembered for popularising songs like 'Jesus People' and playing at primitive Jesus music festivals. Powell summarises, 'Jamie grew up surrounded by Jesus music pioneers and so became the most recognisable figure of the Jesus movement's … "second generation.".'[18]

My friend Geoff Boland hosted an early Jesus Music programme on local radio station Hope FM until quite recently. He reflects, 'Some important musicians – previously dropping acid and smoking weed – had come to faith, and thus the catalyst for *Come Together* was the Jesus Movement of the States.'[19]

* * *

Legacy-wise, music professional Les Moir quotes an unnamed *Crusade Magazine* editor saying that *Come Together* 'had done more for the spiritual life of the church than any other event in the previous fifty years'.[20]

Relationships flourished across church denominations through believers working and worshipping together. Jean Darnell saw the musical 'as a needed agent of unity throughout the church'.[21] Ironically, it also catalysed the rapid growth of new house churches, perceived by some as divisive. Gerald Coates' Pioneer Network, launched in the mid-1970s, is still here today under new leadership. His biographer, Ralph Turner, claims *Come Together* acted 'as a catalyst, as a calling card for the house church movement'.[22] In 2017, Newfrontiers founder, Terry Virgo, reflected that it modelled 'the sort of church we were wanting to build in our local congregations'.[23]

According to MGO team member Geoff Shearn, chatting with a friend in the early seventies, it was a launchpad for 'a whole new kind of worship that's emerging'.[24] Worship-leader Phil Lawson Johnston, founder of Cloud, remembers that in 1974 London, 'Many of the worship songs from *Come Together* had a great influence on us and became very much part of our repertoire.'[25] (Phil still leads worship regularly in Oxfordshire and elsewhere.) Presentations in Birmingham directly inspired musician Nigel Swinford and Christian friends to launch the classically orientated New English Orchestra in 1976, which still delights audiences today. New church leader Roger Forster even attributes the genesis of the renowned March for Jesus movement in 1987 to *Come Together!*[26]

Winter 1973-74

22.

You Can Trust Deo Gloria to Make Jesus Famous

The thrills and spills of being a successful entrepreneur. Sometimes rapid growth necessitates restructuring your business. Just ask Virgin's Richard Branson or social media wizard Steven Bartlett. This property entrepreneur, though, had more on his mind than bricks and mortar. He also ran Deo Gloria Trust, whose declared aim was the advancing and preaching of the Gospel of our Lord Jesus Christ.

By early 1974, with 10,000 people on its 'You Need Christ' mailing list, the ministry had become unwieldy. The businessman cut the big cake in two, personally leading one half called 'Contact for Christ'. This included researching UK cults, an area grounded in his painful family experience. The businessman was Kenneth Frampton, an evangelist to the core.

Prise up the 'rock' of seventies UK youth evangelism and you will find the concealed 'crab' of Mr Frampton. He happily financed bodies such as Operation Mobilisation and Christians in Sport. As for UK Jesus People expressions, he bankrolled four projects: the Children of God, the Jesus Family, Contact for Christ, and the Greenbelt Festival.

The benefactor's story begins, though, three years before World War One. Kenneth Petter Frampton was born in Bromley in 1911 to Albert and Margaret Frampton, a family with longstanding Plymouth Brethren roots. He came to personal faith in his mid-teens. His father Albert was a builder and property developer. Kenneth was an intelligent student at

215

Alleyn's School in Dulwich. However, he was dissuaded from going to Cambridge University as his father sensed the looming Great Depression[1] and encouraged his son to train for business as a chartered accountant.

World War Two generated some formative events for Kenneth. Life in Bromley's 'bomb alley' was practically challenging. At weekends, he and his friends started a soup kitchen for resting airmen and troops outside Bromley Library. Offering John's Gospels alongside refreshments, some came to Jesus. Kenneth also wrote tracts like *Out of Darkness*, highly relevant for London's night-time 'black out'. Vocationally, he was managing director of an engineering company, which had switched from making domestic products to producing aircraft parts. Meanwhile, romance blossomed with Calcutta-born Pauline Ker, ten years his younger, and the couple married in 1940.

After the war ended, Kenneth's father gifted him a lot of money, which he used to buy up bombsites in southern England. Kenneth let them increase in value for five years before making a financial killing. He used this wealth to support his evangelistic adventures.

By 1951 the couple had five sons – Charles, Clive, Christopher, Keith, and David. They were part of the stricter 'Taylorite' branch of the Exclusive Brethren. A harsh elders' decision in 1953 affected them badly. Kenneth was put out of fellowship for dissent, finding 'his new situation gave him a greater freedom and he became aware that there were many other real Christians out there who, although they worshipped differently, shared the same love for Christ and the Scriptures'.[2] Kenneth started thinking outside the box about communicating Jesus to lost people.

His independent ministry flourished. Needing a more sustainable financial footing, on 27 March 1965 the Deo Gloria Trust was launched. Its aim? 'To seek the glory of God by encouraging the furtherance and preaching of the Gospel of our Lord Jesus Christ.'[3] Receiving his share of his father's estate, Kenneth liquidated one of his companies, placing the assets in his new Trust, the rents and leases providing a sustainable income for his growing ministry.

He then employed the Trust's first paid director in 1967, 'Taking the first steps towards being less localised and becoming a more wide-ranging and co-operative part of the emerging evangelicalism of the 1960s.'[4] The following year the experimental 'You Need Christ' campaign was launched: literature like Kenneth's *Seven Reasons Why You Need Christ* was produced to stir people's thinking; 'front page corner' adverts in national papers yielded 1,400 enquiries every month; short loop projection films were developed, utilising the expertise of actor Nigel Goodwin. In partnership with the Evangelical Alliance, a pamphlet was produced, entitled *So You Want to Evangelise!*, prompting fresh missional endeavours. Kenneth's business mind was behind 'seed funding' wider ventures.

Meanwhile, across the Atlantic, Jesus People were making huge waves, reaching the English Channel as the seventies began. There would be choppy waters for the Framptons though. In 1971, the benefactor discovered the Children of God on TV, subsequently providing them with four properties, including a large factory building. Before discovering they were a cult the following summer, Kenneth and Pauline's youngest sons Keith and David[5] had joined the group. The cost of the Frampton's naive sponsorship would cause the couple deep, lifelong heartache.

After rigorous investigation, Kenneth replaced the cult with the Jesus Family, having approached them by telegram while holed up in Holland. They too were given property, two homes and a shopfront. Their *Lonesome Stone* rock musical was financed to the tune of £40,000 in London alone. Apparently, '*The Times* called Frampton "the Angel from Purley" because he was a theatrical angel putting thousands of pounds into the show and had Christian Brethren origins.'[6] The Jesus Family were supported from November 1972 until they returned to the USA in August 1974.

Meanwhile, the Greenbelt Festival started in a Suffolk field during the August Bank Holiday 1974, initially benefitting from Mr Frampton's deep pockets to the tune of £10,000. After financing the festival for its first decade, Kenneth stopped doing so, graciously giving the executive team their own head of steam.

These two communities and one festival supported by Mr Frampton are featured in full chapters elsewhere in this book.[7] Thus I will now give more space to the fourth body, his own Contact for Christ, first launched in 1976.

Work with cults had its initial conception in 1969 when You Need

Christ published two booklets critiquing Mormonism and Jehovah's Witnesses. Adverts on *The Times*' front page produced thousands of requests for copies.

Elsewhere, while God was moving powerfully through the Jesus People Movement, a dark underbelly of cults emerged in the USA. Here in the UK this also happened, with non-Christian groups hitting the streets such as Sun Myung Moon's 'Moonies',[8] the shaved-headed Hare Krishna, and the mantra-repeating Transcendental Meditation. Supposedly 'Christian' groups like the Children of God went public too.

In 1979 Contact for Christ sponsored an international conference in Belgium about cults, which was infiltrated by bogus reporters and threatened with violence. The following year's conference drew forty European Christian workers for briefing about contemporary cults. Heavy-handed 'de-programming'[9] was current then and untrue rumours circulated that notorious de-programmer Ted Patrick would attend.

Finally, in the eighties, ex-Mormon Tom Poulson came on board as Field Officer. He led the Cult Information Centre, with a threefold mandate: ongoing monitoring; advising enquirers; and supporting exiting cult members. However, there was strong push-back to cult hostility in the late eighties. London-based Professor Eileen Barker was sympathetic to the 'Moonies', feeling peoples' adverse reactions were unwarranted. In 1988, she founded INFORM[10] to highlight the positive side of these movements.

Deo Gloria Trust countered this by co-organising a 1989 conference addressed by psychologist Margaret Singer, famed for studying the tragic People's Temple mass suicide in Jonestown, Guyana. It took place in the House of Commons, and Singer contended these groups still represented a threat to society.

In this fourth venture, then, Mr Frampton sponsored countering the bad news of cults, as well as resourcing the good news of Jesus. Given the spiritual backdrop of the JPM, this was an important heritage.

So, who was the real person undergirding these four agencies financially? Here I want to give some colourful vignettes of Kenneth's generosity through first-hand recollections of those close to him in the seventies.

Mr Frampton was certainly affluent, the main trapping of his wealth being his moss green KPF1 Jensen Interceptor. Other KPF registration numbers followed suit. However, like Brighton rock, the theme of generosity is threaded throughout the entire 'stick' of Kenneth's life.

Those he employed certainly experienced his open-handed nature.

Phil South,[11] now in his mid-eighties, worked as the You Need Christ administrator from 1969-1977. He says, 'Kenneth had no desire to do the work, just to promote and finance the efforts of others working for the Kingdom.' His focus on others, though, meant he took on too much: 'Getting side-tracked by the sound of another exciting new idea or project, he moved on rapidly … [and] it was delegated to others to complete.'

Meanwhile, Christine Ellerton[12] was Mr Frampton's secretary in his property business in the early seventies. Aware of his charitable work, Christine remembers, 'As a millionaire, it wasn't unusual for him to receive visitors looking for sponsorship or financial help for their particular project.' One example was Mr Frampton's support for what he called 'his ship', the MV *Logos*,[13] whose small photo adorned a ledge in his office.

In late 1973, Peter Holmes[14] joined Deo Gloria Trust as an administrator, subsequently helping to lead the Greenbelt Festival. He often did the talking for the shy Frampton. Peter recalls, 'Kenneth was embarrassed about his generosity but happy to give to those he knew personally: "a cash cow" in a good sense. He and Mrs Frampton opened their home for garden parties too.'

Kent Philpott[15] was a pioneer American JPM leader, flying over to serve the Jesus Family on three occasions.[16] He never forgot the Framptons' hospitality after attending their church service: 'He and his wife invited us to Silver Grange, their home, for a very lavish dinner. They served alcohol, before dinner, during dinner, and after dinner. We Jesus Freaks were stunned, and a little disconcerted, but did not refuse and drank very lightly.'

Members of the Jesus Family are the second group of people he impacted.

Dave Hoyt had painfully departed from the Children of God in Bromley, later regarding the Framptons as surrogate parents. Being homeless, son Clive and his wife Gwyneth gave Dave their guest room before their first child's birth. He was regularly invited to Silver Grange at the weekends. Later, Mr Frampton helped Hoyt secure a bed and breakfast place.[17]

American guitarist and songwriter Mike Damrow[18] sometimes viewed Mr and Mrs Frampton as royalty, but was occasionally privy to their private lives:

'I met Mr Frampton at the coffee house in Upper Norwood … The toilet was clogged up, but no one could find a plunger. Witnessing our collective helplessness, Mr. Frampton said, "Step aside!" He then reached in and cleared the thing with his bare hand.'

Swede Karin Bienge,[19] converted on the Jesus Family's European travels, says: 'I remember once in the early seventies all the Jesus Family went to his house in Purley. He lived on a private road, so can you imagine the neighbours seeing fifty to sixty Jesus Freaks getting off a large red double-decker bus? We were there for tea and to use his swimming pool too, all with our clothes on!'

Another team member was Matt Spransy,[20] 'Cosmic' in the Family's rock musical: 'There was a cast party for *Lonesome Stone* on the day of the show's premiere. At the party, we Americans were trying to teach some of the Brits, who were used to playing rugby, how to play American football. As a result, I became seriously injured with a concussion. Mr Frampton insisted I live in their home for a week until I recovered completely.'

Kenneth's generous lifestyle was contagious.

Susan Wilson Carter[21] poignantly remembers: 'Mr Frampton was a gentleman. Because I had met him, my heart was more responsive to "give all", which included my life, my loves, and my savings.'

A key couple from Milwaukee days were Brian and Mary Steinke. Their pastor son Sean[22] remembers Mr Frampton first-hand: 'He loomed large in my imagination with his estate and excessive giving. Mr Frampton's example of hospitality and generosity were a grid for our approach as a couple. Jesus People needed fathers and mothers.'

Reflecting on these vignettes it is tricky assessing Mr Frampton and Deo Gloria Trust through the grid of Jesus People marks. He wasn't 'one of them', but without his generosity, they could not have served young people as they did. Culturally, he was a million miles away from countercultural hippies.

His enormous giving flowed from his clear focus on the Lord Jesus alone being glorified and from his huge passion to see the Bible's message hit the streets, as he initiated personally in Bromley during World War

Two. Pragmatically, he was happy to endorse the use of a musical style he didn't personally own. As for literature, his lifelong goal was to write, produce and distribute it for the benefit of non-believers.

Kenneth was always a church person, despite his disillusionment at one stage. As time went on, though, his views on the end times changed hugely, sharply departing from his premillennial and pro-Zionist roots in the Brethren church.[23]

However, in 1988, God welcomed Kenneth into his house forever. It was late afternoon on 7 June. He was at Heathrow Airport, handing in his ticket for a flight to Turkey, and about to fly to the Ephesus Conference Centre he was considering supporting. Instead, he dropped down dead on the spot, hearing Jesus' 'Well done'.[24] Heaven's door was opened, as his and Pauline's door had been throughout their life together.

* * *

What, then, are the key legacies of Mr Frampton today?

In first-century Philippi, the heart of affluent purple cloth dealer Lydia was opened to Jesus, her home becoming both a base for the church and a springboard for wider gospel progress.[25] Kenneth was a male equivalent of Lydia nearly two millennia later. The UK Church in the twenty-first century needs more people like them.

Deo Gloria Trust is still thriving, chaired by the youngest son David Frampton. Its resources are channelled into evangelism and literature, two JPM priorities. For example, support is given to evangelising holidaymakers on the beaches and missional publishers such as 10ofThose. Thinking about Mr Frampton, Jesus' words come to mind: 'I tell you, use your worldly wealth to gain friends for yourselves, so that when it is gone, you will be welcomed into eternal dwellings' (Luke 16:9).

However, we all know it is comparatively easy to give money without being personally inconvenienced. The Framptons were a comprehensively self-giving couple, as reflected in them opening their home regularly and giving their time gladly. It cost them dearly at points. They model a contagious all-round generosity to us today, in what Paul calls 'the privilege of sharing in this service to the saints' (2 Corinthians 8:4).

Finally, like us, Kenneth had his obvious flaws, perhaps especially his gullible naivety and relational awkwardness. However, I view him as an unsung hero, hence devoting an entire chapter to Mr Frampton. He may appear the least likely hero, a self-effacing man shunning celebrity status. Most of the Christian public knew next to nothing about him, but thirty-five years after his death can now be inspired by his generosity. Also, you don't need to be a youthful extravert for God to use you!

Spring 1974

23.

When Jesus Says GO, Get Your Skates on Quickly

It was Saturday 20 April 1974 on the north California coast and a wedding reception was in progress for Harry and Sandy. The hippy couple had previously lived together but met Jesus five months earlier when their spiritually chaotic lives changed. They had been converted at a commune run by Gospel Outreach (GO), and fellow members who were key to their conversion were present to share their joy. They scanned the room and saw new friends like Alex and Renie Elsaesser chatting on adjoining tables.

As Harry and Sandy grew in their faith and marriage, GO was busy sending teams elsewhere to plant churches and, six years later, the Elsaessers would join them in flying across the Atlantic. They planned to reach people for Christ in England's second city, Birmingham. The story had gone from a wedding reception to this marriage of a new team, partnering together to invite Brummies to follow Jesus. Together they would look forward to the ultimate wedding reception, 'the wedding supper of the Lamb'.[1]

The GO story starts with an American man born in the Roaring Twenties:

Jim Durkin served in the Navy during World War Two. Afterwards, the self-confessed atheist, who had two Christian friends, worked in a mountain camp the Forest Service ran. One weekend his boss and fellow workers left the camp in his care, trekking home to see their families. That night, lying in his bunk bed, Jim felt the tangible presence of Jesus. He admitted his many shortcomings and received instant forgiveness.

One subsequent Sunday Jim meets Dacie at church, they start courting and marry on 19 May 1948. He becomes a Pentecostal pastor, and during this patch, their children John, James and Joy are born. After thirteen years of matrimony, though, the couple are in meltdown and Jim divorces his wife. Three years later, God leads Jim to remarry Dacie, (based on Malachi 2:14, which speaks about not breaking faith with the wife of your youth). He does so, and their marriage and finances are amazingly restored.

Jim re-starts his ministry in various churches in Eureka, northern California, supporting his family by working in real estate. One day a bunch of hippies breeze into his Sequoia Realty office, looking for property to open a Christian coffeehouse. Jim initially sends them away. After a change of heart, he gives them a rent-free property. They soon become worshippers at his church. Another similar group arrived, then living communally in an old Coast Guard lighthouse on Table Bluff called the 'Lighthouse Ranch'. In the spring of 1971, Jim buys this ranch and Gospel Outreach is born.

These young people are willing to change and have nothing else to do but grow as Jesus followers. Later that year, the Durkin family, plus thirty others, move across to the commune 'lock, stock and barrel'. Within months it 'had grown to more than 100 members and had set up businesses ranging from an advertising newspaper to a doughnut shop to support itself'.[2] The community then grew to 200 by late 1971 and reached 300 the following year.

Despite Durkin's clear Pentecostal background, 'he negotiated with the counterculture converts to forge a hybrid Pentecostalism'.[3] On Wednesday evenings, for example, there was no rowdiness, but only a silent waiting on God while praying or reading Scripture. As for the Bible, Jim's catchphrase was 'Practice the Word': hear it, confess it, do it. His prophetic messages were sometimes doom-laden about economic collapse and global war, but Jim taught positive responsibilities of money management, food storage and fellowship with other Christians. Above all, GO was deeply committed to Jesus' Great Commission[4] and being a radical sending community. Two couples ended up in the UK, the Elsaessers and the Hewats.

Alex Elsaesser graduated from college in 1968 and was faced with being drafted to Vietnam. Finding no alternative, he and his girlfriend

Renie chose marriage and the newlyweds ended up with the Peace Corps in Libya teaching English. Sadly, Renie was heading for a breakdown, so was medically evacuated to the USA. Their marriage was unravelling too. When Alex returned after completing the year, the couple went their separate ways. Heading for San Francisco, Alex was disillusioned by the drugs and violence and relocated to the beautiful Sierra Nevada mountains to work in a gold mine. To his surprise, Renie travelled 3,000 miles to join him. Newly reconciled, the couple enjoyed a fantastic life as caretakers of a 2,000-acre ranch. One day, though, their bubble burst: they were 'busted' for possessing marijuana and LSD and spent the weekend in jail awaiting trial.

In July 1972, Renie was in Cleveland, Ohio, visiting her Christian missionary sister. While there, she quietly gave her life to Jesus at a Billy Graham crusade. Sadly, Alex tried to drag her back into their previous lifestyle. Renie prayed for him, then a converted hippy witnessed to him, both occurrences combined being gamechangers. The couple ended up at The Lord's Land commune[5] in Mendocino. One morning, Alex was walking alone in the redwood forest, frustrated that all his previous paths had been dead ends. Feeling guilty for sin, he asked Jesus to make himself real and forgive him, but nothing seemed to happen. Later, he found himself at a small Pentecostal chapel in the little town of Casper, where Jesus People from the commune belonged. Worship leader Hermann led the corny song 'Smile Awhile', encouraging people to lift their hands as suggested in the lyrics. Alex thought they were crazy, but says, 'I raised my hands and that was it. My "Road to Damascus" experience. It was April Fool's Day 1973, and I became a fool for Christ.'[6]

Meanwhile, as recounted earlier, Harry and Sandy Hewat came to know Jesus late that year, marrying in the spring of 1974.

Allow Harry to relate their story:

My wife and I both came from non-Christian backgrounds – my family is irreligious, and Sandy's family is Jewish. We met at university, fell in love, and started living together. We were products of the youth culture in America during the sixties – dabbling in drugs, alternative lifestyles and various spiritualities. Through experimentation with hallucinogenic drugs, I knew the spiritual realm was very real. We did Transcendental Meditation, a Hindu practice, and various other practices. We were pseudo-hippies with a hunger to know and experience God. While Sandy was at university her older sister died of cancer at the age of twenty-three. That turned her world upside down and increased her hunger and search for God.

Meanwhile, unbeknown to them, Sandy's other sister had become a Christian at The Lord's Land commune. Harry and Sandy hitch-hiked up the coast from southern California to visit her. Harry continues:

> We ended up at the commune where she lived, and God moved powerfully in our hearts convincing us of the reality of Jesus. We saw love in action, heard the gospel for the first time and were persuaded. On 23 December 1973, we both humbled ourselves to God and surrendered our lives to Jesus – to love and follow him all our days. We separated for a time to focus on our relationships with God before marrying on 20 April 1974.[7]

Both couples would get caught up together in reaching Brummies for Christ six years later. But to tell their story is to first recount the tale of GO branching out to Germany.

In December 1974, GO sent an advance team to Germany to 'spy out the land', concluding Munich was a better base than Berlin. In November 1975, a team of seventeen gathered in Eureka, preparing to join them. The Munich church would be a launch pad for church planting, not an end in itself. Team members subsequently got to know Brian and Christine Martin, an English couple working in Munich. He was a virologist working for the Max Planck Institute. She was having a tricky first pregnancy, confined to bed for her final months. The couple were well cared for by the GO believers and their son was safely delivered. A friendship began, including with Jim and Dacie Durkin when they visited Munich. When Brian's work was completed in 1977, the family moved home to Birmingham.

That same year, GO elder Peter DePalmo had returned to northern California from Europe and was showing slides and reporting back on his continental travels. Alex Elsaesser was present and describes the impact: 'When a picture of the London City Mission appeared on the screen, the Holy Spirit came on me, and I began to shake.'[8] He concluded he and Renie were called to the UK. However, the previous German team had been sizeable and sent within months. How could they build their team?

Meanwhile, in the late seventies, Jim Durkin was on a trip home to the USA from Germany but had experienced a mix-up with his ticket. He consequently decided to fly via London, momentarily dropping into Birmingham to see the Martins en route. Together they discussed the possibility of starting a church in Birmingham. Brian and Christine eventually decided the idea was from God. However, to quote Brian, 'We started meeting in our home, at first consisting of my wife and one-year-old son, and I preached to the chairs! One or two neighbours endured this for a while but didn't stay.'[9] Eventually, the American cavalry would arrive to fortify these Birmingham groundtroops.

Back in the States, Harry and Sandy Hewat had finally caught Alex and Renie Elsaesser's vision for the UK. Both couples spent the following three years saving from their businesses to finance the move. On 11 March 1980, Alex and Harry finally arrived in Birmingham. Three weeks later their families joined them. Quickly, they connected with the Martins and their partially birthed house-church.

Early on, the Americans wrestled with the legalities of working to sustain their mission. As informed by their solicitor, 'They couldn't start a business, they couldn't have a wage-earning job, and they couldn't stay in England. The government told them to leave.'[10] Three weeks before being deported, Alex grasped, 'There were things I did not realize back in the States were real crutches for me, until they were taken away … like the freedom to make money, to provide for my family in a physical way.'[11] God then used Revd Brash Bonsall, Principal of Birmingham Bible Institute (BBI), to help them out considerably. The Elsaessers were given a rent-free flat at 5 Pakenham Road, and both Alex and Sandy started studying for the Cambridge Diploma in Religious Studies. Alex does hint their course was not exactly a faith builder. However, when the pair graduated, they gained credibility with local pastors through being BBI graduates. Meanwhile, God met Alex and Renie's material needs amazingly, including bags of food being dropped off on their doorstep.

The house-church in Selly Oak then began to grow, especially after the team started regularly leafletting the neighbourhood. A small community hall was rented but, says Brian, 'Outreach seemed difficult, and not very fruitful for some years.'[12] He thus felt nudged to pray for an annual doubling of numbers, and it happened…

Two further halls were rented, but numbers plateaued when the doubling prayers ceased. Part of this group, including Alex and some new Christians, planted a second church on the Hawkesley estate in Kings Norton. Both fellowships were involved in Billy Graham's 'Mission England' in June 1984, hiring a double-decker bus to take friends to hear about Jesus at the Villa Park stadium.

Like earlier JPM ministries, the previous lifestyles of new believers flagged up the need for holistic 24/7 discipleship. Alex reflects, 'We needed a place like the Lighthouse Ranch or some communal or cooperative house where we can really help these people get established in the Lord. Two meetings a week just does not do it.'[13] Three Christian project managers were recruited to help find a location. After one aborted attempt, the Bournville Village Trust offered them Windmill House, originally a Cadbury's summer house. Previously used by the Birmingham Association of Youth Clubs, it was a seventy-bed conference centre, on a ten-year lease for £500 per year plus VAT. Even the Trust manager said they must have 'friends in high places'. A condition was that somebody had to live on the property, so the following day Alex and their three sons moved straight in. The year was 1990, and Alex led the centre while Harry pastored the 120-strong church.

Looking through the lens of the ten JPM marks, Gospel Outreach was a good example of a northern Californian community transferred into the UK. Their Bible-centredness focused on tangibly 'doing the Word' in everyday life, not merely thinking it through. Also, communal living was utterly central on both sides of the Atlantic. Evangelism was not easy-going, though, at least not until the doubling prayers kicked in. They were undoubtedly a charismatic group, open to the Holy Spirit's gifts. The one exception was church ambivalence. Like most UK Jesus People, GO planted two fellowships that happily partnered with other local churches, also participating in Billy Graham's inter-church mission.

All three couples are now officially 'retired', but still pursuing Jesus' Great Commission vision. Alex and Renie moved to Wales in 1996, welcoming people from all over the world to their popular Airbnb. The Hewats were eventually pastors at Riverside Church locally, then cared for YWAM missionaries from Uganda, but currently support a church plant in Bournville. Brian and Christine have been asked to help a local Anglican church in their discipling and church-planting, a plan temporarily scuppered by the pandemic of March 2020.

Alex summarises the impact of the JPM: 'We were fortunate to experience an outpouring of God … an awakening among young people that would change the church forever, with contemporary worship, casual dress, and a new hunger for the Holy Spirit.'[14]

* * *

So, what was the legacy of Gospel Outreach in the UK?

One legacy, in the late seventies, was 'almost' a second GO ministry in Liverpool. Brit John Ruffle had been saved at the California Lighthouse Ranch in July 1972, later returning to The Beatles' home city in 1978. At weekends the media-savvy creative visited the Birmingham team, considering partnering them to reach Scousers. In retrospect, he views not following through as a lost opportunity. However, John is still using his skills today to touch people's lives for Christ through social media, despite health challenges.

Meanwhile, in 1996 a ministry for recovering heroin addicts took over Windmill House, with a year's hand-over period alongside Alex. 'This Betel recovery model harmonises church-planting, residential living and charitable businesses to help desperate people heal and rebuild their lives based on Christian values and a strong work ethic.'[15] Lives are still being changed by JPM-like values. Three years later the Elsaessers, then living in Wales, welcomed American GO friends Dick and Gladys Funnell to their area to pioneer the 'Wales Awakening' ministry. They continually intercede for revival legacies, both from 1904-1905 and the more recent JPM.

Finally, contemporary lessons are learned through mistakes and successes. Regarding the former, the team mentioned that young GO leaders were heavy-handed through inexperience, including failing to release women in ministry; an over-achieving lifestyle that cancels out God's restful grace; disciples not always handling the transition to 'normal life' well; and some marriages sadly failing to last. Concerning successes, they highlight the great biblical teaching they received. Strong examples of this are teachings about vital relational unity with other Christians as brothers and sisters and living a simple lifestyle without an undue focus on possessions. Such teaching has had a long shelf-life in their lives and those they once discipled.

Summer 1974

24.

The Tragedy of Calvary That Launches a Happy Chapel

It was a blistering hot summer, so much so that some people used newspapers to shield their heads from the sun. Had you done so on 3 June 1974 in Bradford, you would have missed some breaking news. The *Telegraph & Argus* published an article about an innovative venture, headlined, 'Packing them in with the Sound of the Gospel – as well as Pinball'.[1] The location was the Hole in the Wall coffee bar in Piece Hall Yard.

The four friends running the show named themselves 'Gospel Vision' and included a certain Jim King. Being extremely popular, it gathered hundreds of teenagers from as far away as Manchester. Christian films were shown every week, such as the renowned movie *The Cross and the Switchblade*. Live bands played on Saturday evenings, neither pushing religion nor church but rather focusing on a relationship with God. Four years down the line, it wasn't just coffee brewing in Jim and wife Sue's front lounge, but a fledgling Church on the Way.

Across the Atlantic, picture a thirty-eight-year-old Pentecostal pastor, bereft of hair, and disillusioned with Church bureaucracy. Since Bible College graduation in 1948, he has experienced 'seventeen years of drought',[2] but then receives a prophecy that he would become 'the shepherd over many flocks'.[3] In December 1965, he took on a struggling church in Costa Mesa, California, which grew from twenty-five to two hundred members in three years. Meet Chuck and Kay Smith.

Throughout the summer of 1967, the couple would drive to Huntington Beach, California, gawping from a safe distance at those they viewed as parasitical hippies. For Chuck, they needed both a haircut and a job, but Kay's heart began to melt. She wanted to know why they inhabited the streets, dressed differently, rejected material things, and got 'high'. Daughter Janette recalls, 'She was praying for them and hoping to find a way to understand them and reach out to them.'[4]

The Smiths began to pray about meeting a hippy first-hand. One day in January 1968,[5] Janette's boyfriend John Nicholson, a newly converted hippy, picked up hitchhiker Lonnie Frisbee and then brought him to the Smiths' door. You can find out more about him in Chapter 7. Contrary to the portrayal in the 2023 *Jesus Revolution*[6] film, it was John (not Janette) who first introduced the Jesus lookalike to Chuck and Kay – in an abrupt induction to cross-cultural mission.

Lonnie and his new wife, Connie, then lived temporarily with the Smiths. These informal missionaries saw thirty-five young people coming to know Jesus over the following fortnight. New converts needed 24/7 discipleship, so on 17 May 1968, the 'House of Miracles' was launched as the Frisbees partnered with leaders John and Jackie Higgins. New believer Cherise, a runaway from home, brought fifty-seven folks in her wake within three weeks. Members of the darkly named Diablos motorbike gang were saved. A retired judge offered the rundown Blue Top Motel, minus electricity, to house the growing community. Church-wise, space was running out too. School grounds, bought in May 1968, hosted a new 330-seater church facility, which opened thirteen months later.

1970 was a year of profound growth. Three services were drawing 1,500 people, including overflow, new staff were hired, new music groups like Love Song played, and new believers were baptised monthly at Pirate's Cove. On 17 April 1971, four leaders took two-and-a-half hours to baptise 1,000 people.[7] Baptism photos went viral, featuring in *Time* and *Newsweek*. Chuck Smith estimated, 'During the past two years more than twenty thousand accepted Christ and over eight thousand were baptised at Corona del Mar.'[8] The drought had ended.

The year 1971 was the JPM's zenith. Calvary Chapel was pushed for space, buying a ten-acre plot on which to erect a massive green circus tent. In June, the first Maranatha! Music album, the *Everlastin' Living Music Concert*, was released. 'Papa Chuck' continued teaching the Bible conversationally verse-by-verse. In October, though, Lonnie and Connie Frisbee left the staff and headed for Florida.

In 1973, a 2,300-seater brick-built facility opened, constructed by church members and converted hippies grafting together. Then came a legendary hinge moment, as Chuck recounts:

> Those who had been inwardly protesting the hippies finally found a target to vent their discontent upon. Dirty feet soil carpets, and those carpets cost a lot of money. Besides, who wants to see dirt marks on a brand-new carpet? They took it upon themselves, early one Sunday morning, to hang up a sign reading, *No bare feet allowed.*[9]

Chuck promptly tore it down, convened his board, and broke the mentality. The existing church members were on trial before the Jesus Freaks, not vice-versa! British church leader Pete Greig reflects, 'It was a defining moment ... a prophetic act of missional hospitality that would position Calvary Chapel as an epicentre for the movement about to shake America.'[10]

A greater number of predicted 'flocks' would soon emerge elsewhere in the world, including in the UK during the 1970s, 1980s, 1990s, and the new millennium.

Two British leaders were greatly impacted in the early 1970s...

Dr Martyn Lloyd-Jones, pastor of London's Westminster Chapel and student of revival,[11] was intrigued by JPM reports from California. He sent associate Richard Bennett over, saying, 'I want you to find this man Chuck Smith. I hear there is something akin to revival happening.'[12] Richard duly flew over to gather the facts. Later, 'the Doctor' and Chuck met together in London, and mutually inspired one another; Calvary pastors were soon urged to read Lloyd-Jones' biblical expositions.

Meanwhile, in 1973, Bradford-based evangelist Jim King was in the USA training at Arthur Blessitt's 'Street University'. Fellow student Irene

Feher insisted he meet Pastor Chuck, but he had already done so the week before at a 5.45 a.m. men's prayer breakfast. Later, Jim floated his vision for Bradford to Chuck, being encouraged to evangelise the city. His 'Gospel Vision' team were already doing some things, but everything accelerated in December 1978 when a home Bible study of six people was launched. The following year, friend Richard Cimino flew over to support the embryonic church, accompanied by Malcolm Wild (one-half of the previous British folk duo Malcolm and Alwyn).

So, how did Calvary Chapel touch the north of England in the 1980s?

By mid-1980, the Kings' home-based group saw fifty people perched everywhere as 'Church on the Way' was birthed. Jim's motivation was, 'I could see kids coming off the streets needed a service that was suited to their age, in music, worship and teaching. Free expression of worship.'[13] These 'kids' included Hell's Angels' bikers, punks, and prostitutes! After having rented a Baptist church, a 110-seater auditorium and Sunday School room were built. In March 1982, Richard Cimino, then a high school pastor in Costa Mesa, had brought another team over. They were given six shovels to dig out foundations, and 'returned to California physical wrecks with blistered, bleeding hands which made their guitars redundant for weeks'.[14]

The 1980s saw a succession of Californian teams hit the runway on three-week mission trips; thirty- or forty-strong, they rotated around multiple schools at once. Malcolm Wild brought fellow Calvary Chapel musicians with him. Recognising the UK's post-Christian context, the Ciminos wanted to educate secondary school students about Jesus. Firstly, by leading the morning assembly and sharing stories between songs. Secondly, they went into History, Science, Maths and R.E. lessons. Thirdly, they performed a concert at lunchtime. Every day, pupils were invited to an off-campus concert in a rented venue or church building, and 'the vast majority of those who showed up professed faith in Jesus'.[15] The church was running out of space, largely through conversions, so a larger building was erected on the same plot, and Chuck Smith dedicated it on 25 June 1989.

In the 1990s, the focus shifted from the north's trio of new churches – in Bradford, nearby Otley, and Scotland's Motherwell – to the south. In

1992, Californian defence contractor Ron Matsen brought his family to the naval city of Portsmouth for work. A gifted teacher, he began a modest home Bible study. The group grew, soon meeting in a local school with encouragement from local ministers. Resembling Bradford, the pattern was mission first, church second. Having ministered for nineteen years, in October 2011 Ron tersely emailed his fellow leaders with the subject line, 'Leaving the UK.' He did so and pastor Barry took up the reins.

Meanwhile, in leafy Buckinghamshire, the small Chalfont St Giles Christian Fellowship was thirty-strong in 1993 but needed a new pastor. Enter Assemblies of God couple, John and Julie Vickery, then in Doncaster. John had been deeply influenced by Chuck Smith's ministry while on a Californian preaching trip twelve years before. Taking the small church on, John affiliated it with Calvary Chapel three years later. In 2001, like runners from a strawberry plant, John trailed out a Calvary-related fellowship in Cardiff, his son Phil doing likewise in Oxford.

1996 saw a church started by Chuck Smith's son-in-law, Brian Broderson, in central London. Eleven years earlier, while visiting Speakers' Corner in Hyde Park, his wife Cheryl had a vision of Brian preaching in London. This impression resurfaced once more in 1993. Thus, her husband wrote to all five UK Calvary pastors, but with zero response. Eventually, John Vickery did call him. With his encouragement, Brian spied out the land in May 1995, catching the vision for himself. Early the following year, a fortnight's outreach took place, which involved Chuck Smith, musicians Malcolm and Alwyn, and a sizeable American team. Literally at the eleventh-hour, God provided Westminster City School to host Sunday services at £300 per month. The church kicked off in February 1996; the Brodersons returned to lead it in September after tying up loose ends in California. Brian was the Bible teacher, and Alwyn Wall was the worship leader.

When the clock struck midnight on Sunday 31 December 1999, a raft of new church plants and a music festival in the south-west loomed on the horizon.

In the new millennium, Brian Broderson said, 'Because we had done so much church-planting, it just became a natural overflow of what was happening.'[16] Probably half the fifty new fellowships launched were directly sent out from Westminster or through church connections there. The majority began in 2001, using young American men as missionary pastors, partly or wholly supported by the enormous Costa Mesa congregation, 'a giant monster with unlimited resources'.[17] This may explain the fact that only twenty-five per cent of UK Calvary Chapel churches today are led by indigenous pastors.

One fellowship launched in the West Country had far wider implications:

Arizona-born, Phil Pechonis had come to faith at twenty-four years old. He and his wife, Megan, worshipped at Calvary Chapel in Fort Lauderdale, Florida. Whilst there, he had two near-death experiences – almost drowning in a surfing accident and being involved in a car crash. God had grabbed his attention big time. In 1994, the couple moved to Moscow to church plant there, returning to Florida the following year to run a surf superstore and surfboard company.

In 2000, the Pechonis family was attending a pastors' conference in Merritt Island. While there, Brian Broderson challenged Phil to church-plant in the surfer-friendly Woolacombe, an area reputed to be gospel-re-sistant. The Devonshire town had an uncanny resemblance to sunny, surfing Costa Mesa on the Pacific coast. In Phil's words, 'We rented a skate park on Tuesday night and gradually began to impact the lives of skaters and surfers in the area.'[18] A viable congregation of Jesus followers soon gathered from these outwardly focused foundations.

This tiny seed quickly sprouted a festival called Creation Fest, an idea which came to Phil and three praying friends in 2001 and was later confirmed by offers of well-known musicians to perform. Launched in the summer of 2002, it was initially billed as a one-day event but then extended to three. At its heart was bold evangelism. For example, in its third year, thirty per cent of attendees were not yet Jesus followers. Phil underlined this, saying, 'The original vision is really evangelism … stirring up the pot, trying to wake up apathy in the land.'[19] Its three-fold priorities for believers were: Bible teaching, contemporary music, and inter-church unity. Creation Fest is a real gift to the Church here in the UK, in terms of modelling volunteer serving and generous financing. In recent years 'Mission Lead' Sarah Yardley, an American permanently living in Cornwall, has worked very hard to ensure fuller UK representation.

If you had attended Creation Fest in 2023, for example, you would have been bowled over by the variety of all-age activities on offer: skateboarding, working out and dancing, the arts, music and film-watching, seminars led by Brits Pete Greig on the Bible and David Bennett on gender issues, and a message entitled 'Living in the Beautiful Wild' by Sarah Yardley. All of this is accompanied by an Alpha course for seeking holidaymakers, in the beautiful setting of Wadebridge near the surfer's paradise of Newquay...

Leading music writer Tony Cummings enthused in the early days, 'We love the vibe – which, I'm told by those who remember, resembles the Jesus music events of the early 70s.'[20]

So, what kind of DNA did Calvary Chapel display historically?

They are quintessential Jesus People: hippies were reached, perhaps especially in Lonnie's day. Jesus Christ was consistently the focus, dependably preached from the Bible verse-by-verse. Contemporary music was hugely important, Maranatha! Music being launched in December 1971. Communes were vital, John Higgins eventually pioneered some 178 Shiloh Houses. End-times teaching was key, particularly elicited by Chuck's musings on Israel's Six-Day War in June 1967. Street evangelism was a feature, but hippies were also led to Jesus through music concerts and services. Church-wise, Calvary Chapel ultimately became a 'new paradigm church',[21] breaking the mould of more established churches. As for literature, new Christian Greg Laurie produced his eight-page *Living Water* cartoon tract, and 300,000 copies were distributed.

Charismatic experience is interesting though. Originally a Pentecostal, Pastor Chuck overtly gave honour to the Holy Spirit in his ministry but distanced himself from extremism, as highlighted in his 1983 book, *Charisma v Charismania.*[22] He also found Lonnie Frisbee, and later John Wimber, tricky to work with in that regard; today he might be termed a 'cautious charismatic'.

* * *

So, what are the lasting legacies of Calvary Chapel in the UK today?

One, of course, is the Creation Fest festival. My Welsh friend Jim Hillier, a pastor in Cornwall and ministry team leader at the festival, cites four positive influences he has observed: Americans humbly serving Brits; tangibly expressing church unity; facilitating spiritual turning-points for individuals, and redeeming dark features of rural West Country spirituality.[23]

I would again add to this list the sheer generosity of sacrificial giving and cheerful volunteering.

More broadly, the Calvary Chapel approach to church planting puts the proverbial horse before the cart. For example, for Jim and Sue King, telling people about Jesus was the primary issue, planting a church being a secondary 'accidental' afterthought. By contrast, in the UK today we often introvertedly place the cart before the horse; church internals trump mission externals. Further, we can positively thank Calvary Chapel, amongst others, for breaking the mould musically, both in evangelism and worship.

One challenging legacy, though, concerns leadership succession. Many UK churches today are handing the reins on to next-generation leaders. Three years after Chuck Smith died in 2013, the Calvary movement split in two. More established leaders stayed in their Calvary Chapel Association while other more progressive leaders, under Brian Broderson, launched the fresh Calvary Global Network. Succession is complex, but the presenting areas of disagreement are methodological and threefold: teaching style,[24] alcohol consumption, and women leading and preaching. The ramifications have stretched the loyalties of UK-based Calvary pastors today. I suggest two remedies: think through issues of succession biblically, wisely and practically, and perhaps bring both sides around the table to speak the truth in love.

Summer 1974

25.

Not Built on a Brown-field Site But on Greenbelt

The first Greenbelt Festival was held in the summer of 1974 on a Suffolk pig farm. Two friends constructed the site, one of them both a builder and theologian. Some helpers were likeable ex-addicts, more interested in reading their Bibles than digging post holes. Charsfield villagers were apprehensive about the impact on their properties and eagle-eyed for troublemakers. Some festivalgoers were reputedly prone to eating cats...

Nonetheless, *The Sun* broadsheet billed it 'The Nice People's Pop Festival'.[1]

An upbeat poster announced, 'Four fantastic days of sun (?), camping, and top Christian artistes in the land.' A day-ticket would cost £1.50, but it was a fiver for the entire Bank Holiday weekend. Punters were encouraged to carry a Bible in one hand and a newspaper in the other. The toilets were extraordinarily basic, but the showers were solar-heated. There was a strong police presence, however, the crowd of 2,000 were easy to handle.

Greenbelt came on the back of UK festivals like the 1958 Beaulieu Jazz Festival. Later, the 1970 Isle of Wight Festival, featuring Jimi Hendrix's historic appearance, was inspirational for one Greenbelt founder. Two years later, he and two fellow countercultural Jesus People were about to bump into each other.

Enter Steve Shaw. Before coming to know Jesus, Steve had started the band Capel House, based in Capel St Mary, seven miles from Ipswich. The three male members rented a house, paying the bills by cleaning windows and driving vans. It soon became a dope-smoking commune.

One night in 1972, Steve describes hitch-hiking home: 'A car stopped for me. The driver was a rather camp Samuel Pepys type figure: long hair permed into ringlets, droopy moustache, gold chain hanging around his neck, fur jacket three sizes too small, blue satin trousers tucked into high knee boots. As we drove along, he explained he was a Baptist minister's son and Theology graduate.'[2]

Steve and his friends were all theologically naive and had become believers after some weird LSD trips. The literate 'Pepys', whose real name was James Holloway, soon put them right.

In the late sixties, James had visited Francis Schaeffer's Swiss retreat centre L'Abri, which envisioned Christians to think intelligently and artistically. Following Bible college training, he was reading Philosophy at Essex University. James was part of the All Things New band and was on his way to a Colchester gig when he met Steve.

James had been blown away by the 1970 Isle of Wight Festival and was encouraged that festivals like this were great social levellers. The Nationwide Festival of Light the following year involved lighting beacons nationally to symbolise its moral campaign; one was held in Framlingham near the Holloway residence. Reflecting on both festivals afterwards, James 'prophesied' to his farming brother-in-law Richard Gibbons ('Gibbo'), 'You've got a field, it would be good to have a festival here.'

After their unlikely encounter, Steve and James' friendship gathered pace. James and 'Gibbo' went to Capel House to eat with the hippy gang. On arrival, Steve exclaimed to his band housemates, 'Get to my room with your Bibles; there's a bloke here who knows the truth.' James was grilled for two hours. Spiritually, the community had 'come home'.

Meanwhile, Capel House, now an acoustic band and playing songs for Jesus, was touring in a van. Playing for Geoff Bone's Jesus Liberation Front in Hemel Hempstead, they stayed on awhile afterwards, meeting Susan Carter, Public Relations person for Larry Norman's *One Way Records*. She recalls, 'I met Steve Shaw at Geoff Bone's home, told him what the Jesus Family was doing, and introduced him to Jim Palosaari.'[3]

Consequently, Capel House played the Jesus Family's modest-sized 'Living Room' venue in Upper Norwood. Steve remembers how 'Jim descended on us…' and the American quickly recruited the band to join The Sheep on a tour of Finland. After this, Capel House stayed put as part of the Jesus Family. But Steve hadn't forgotten his friend James. A reunion was in order.

It was late 1973 and Steve invited James to meet the larger-than-life Jim in London. The wheels were about to be set in motion for the first Greenbelt Festival.

On arrival, James was astonished at the spartan living environment, but soon floated his creative vision for an arts and music festival to Steve. His simple response was, 'You'd better see Jim'. The 'godfather' of the Jesus Family was in his upstairs inner sanctum and was available. James and Jim hit it off instantly, talking about groups they mutually recommended to perform. Then, hearing that James' brother Peter managed Prospect Farm in Charsfield, Suffolk, Jim famously declared, 'Heh, you got yourself a field; you got yourself a festival.'[4]

So, the festival idea was conceived. Pouring over an Ordnance Survey map of the farm sometime later, the planning group noted the area was shown as Greenbelt with Mr Frampton's secretary Caryl Brown-Constable commenting, 'If it's going to be in the country, why not call it *Greenbelt*?'[5] The name stuck.

So, what was the run-up like to that first Festival in 1974?

A team came together early that year. Jonathan Cooke, manager of All Things New, was the natural choice for festival coordinator. He had an adventurous life, 'running his own car sale business in Norwich, and at night, when not rattling around with his band, arranged concerts and discos all over Eastern England'.[6] Ticket sales were handled from a telephone kiosk by an attractive nurse from Ipswich called Linda Farrow, later Cooke.

'Gibbo', who alongside being a farmer was also the bass player for All Things New, led the site management alongside James Holloway, who was both an intellectual and a 'City and Guilds' builder and brick-layer. His brother Peter Holloway, manager of Prospect Farm, served too. Coordination-wise, Jim Palosaari was the vital link between this local team and the financier, Kenneth Frampton.

In the early summer, the Jesus Family group arrived to start rehearsals at Earl Soham Baptist Church. James especially warmed to The Sheep vocalist Rich Haas. They wandered around the village together admiring the quaint, historic buildings. Then the police turned up, identifying hip-looking Haas as an opportunist burglar. James explained he was nothing of the sort. He also enjoyed the company of The Sheep's drummer, Nick 'Machine Gun' Malham. Later, James and his band joined the Jesus Family on the streets of Ipswich before their two groups played a joint gig, the last before Greenbelt was launched. Christians were bussed in from a wide catchment area, the sizeable crowd equalling that of a previous Led Zeppelin concert at the same venue.

As for the villagers, an expected 10,000 people descending on their rural environment was worrying. Mercifully, a fifth of that number turned up, and the county's Environmental Health Officer reassured residents the organisers were fully complying with government regulations. Ironically, 'The turned around inhabitants of Charsfield made noises about looking forward to Greenbelt coming back next year ... but plans were being nurtured regarding a new Festival site.'[7] Prospect Farm was inaccessible, and the more central Odell Castle beckoned.

So, what was it like to be a festivalgoer at ground level, and how were the festival's underlying values displayed? Greenbelt 1974 gave every appearance of being like an American Jesus Festival with its JPM roots very apparent.

There were films to watch, music to enjoy, and seminars to process.

Lonesome Stone's colourful double-decker bus had a screen on its side to project late-night movies. One, for example, was *The Son Worshippers*, a homemade documentary featuring a 15,000 Jesus People march in Sacramento in February 1971.

Musically, two Jesus Family bands performed: the country rock Mighty Flyers, having just released their first album *Low Flying Angel*; and The Sheep's farewell performance, headlining on Monday night before flying back to the States. Meanwhile, the *Come Together* musical presentation was part of Sunday morning's communion service, 'probably one of the key things that followed the Jesus Movement'.[8]

Thought-provoking seminars were led by early JPM pioneer Kent

Philpott,[9] the tongue-in-cheek Jim Palosaari and the inspirational Jesus Liberation Front co-founder Geoff Bone.[10] Rock music journalist and poet Steve Turner rattled some cages with his critique of so-called 'Christian music', reflecting on an earlier article he had written, *New Mindless Christianity*,[11] which provocatively encouraged a deeper and more thoughtful artistic expression.

In terms of implicit festival values, two locomotives were running on parallel rails. In fact, according to coordinator Jonathan Cooke, 'There were ambiguities from the word go, for there had never been a clear definition of the nature of Greenbelt and its specific objectives.'[12]

On one track was Jim Palosaari and the festival's generous backer Kenneth Frampton; on the other was co-founder James Holloway and his theological mentor from BTI days in Glasgow, John Peck. Greenbelt is a fascinating window into how underlying theology affects life above ground.

Essentially, the first pair emphasised God as Redeemer while the second duo focused on God as Creator. The festival can be pictured as Charles Blondin walking the tightrope over Niagara Falls.[13] Durham's Professor of Practical Theology, Pete Ward, highlights its balancing-act: 'There were those who saw Christian music as primarily a tool for evangelism, and others who were more concerned to see Christians expressing themselves on a variety of topics through their artistic activities.'[14]

Jim was the former. Reflecting in 1982,[15] he felt there was a good balance of evangelism and the arts, pictured biblically as planting and watering (1 Corinthians 3:6), and being light and salt in society (Matthew 5:13-16). While he affirmed Greenbelt's real-world creational emphasis, Jim still stressed and maintained his historic roots in a commitment to bold 'Are you saved?' evangelism, but without the 'preachiness'. And, similarly to American 'Jesus Festivals', Mr Frampton expected a mainstage altar-call on Saturday evenings.

James, however, was more concerned with Christian expression than evangelism. John Peck's teaching was formative, with its emerging vision of Christianity, the arts and social justice. As James famously said, 'The trouble with Christianity is that it isn't *worldly* enough.'[16] Art professor Hans Rookmaker had precisely the same vision in his one-liner, 'Art needs no justification'.[17] As for music, it should not be valued for what it 'produces' evangelistically. Musical expert Les Moir comments: 'Always tinged with a challenge for musicians to get out of the Christian ghetto, the festival has played a key role in breaking down the wall between the sacred and the secular.'[18]

This tension became concrete at precisely 3.45 p.m. on Sunday 25 August 1974. James, with his non-platform-preaching convictions, encountered renowned evangelist Eric Delve boldly ascending the stage to preach Jesus (Eric usually included a salvation appeal). The former blocked the latter's path, gently but physically. Might this have been a tiny defining moment for Greenbelt?

Trawling through the following decade, how were JPM marks reflected in the festival's ethos and programmes?

Regarding hippy background, all three founders were countercultural types, Shaw perhaps the more authentic hippy. Overall, though, Greenbelt drew existing believers from their stuffy churches into a fresh Christian youth culture.

From the outset, it was certainly a Jesus-centred festival. However, encouraging attendees to respond to Jesus was discouraged, to the frustration of some.

Regular morning Bible teaching occurred. For example, in 1978 John Gladwin taught about God as Creator and Redeemer, while Richard Bewes expounded Revelation. Increasingly, the Bible was used to address societal issues with John Stott commending 1983 festivalgoers for grappling with contemporary issues such as homosexuality, war and peace, and feminism.

Contemporary rock music did feature highly, but the programmes reveal multiple genres: classical, Gaelic, folk, New Wave, rap, jazz funk, black gospel, and a male voice choir. This eclectic music was accompanied by creative poetry, drama, mime, and dance.

Communal living was a particular focus in 1982. American groups, Servant and Resurrection Band performed, both with first-hand experience to share. Servant's manager Jim Palosaari explored commune-based discipleship, while Glen and Wendy Kaiser unpacked intentional community in downtown Chicago.

An end-times focus was occasional, but not prominent. One film shown was the 1972 *A Thief in the Night*, urging a response to Jesus before time runs out. Conversely, Greenbelt's increasing preoccupation was discipleship in God's kingdom now. The 1978 gathering was termed 'the angry festival', evidenced by 'righteous indignation at the spiritual, moral and physical state of our world – and the complacent inability of Christians to do anything about it'.[19]

In terms of street evangelism, not much happens in Suffolk fields! However, Arthur Blessitt did motivate people in his 1980 seminar 'Evangelism – A Personal View'. It wasn't a core theme though.

Regarding church ambivalence, Greenbelt appeared remarkably church-affirming, although it later drew more festivalgoers from the 'progressive Christianity'[20] camp. Two key players shared their perspectives though. Executive team member Peter Holmes claimed Greenbelt 1974 'was the beginnings of a young people's church'.[21] Meanwhile, Pete Ward later argued that, for church youth group attendees, 'a visit to Greenbelt was a baptism into a new and dynamic Christian subculture'.[22]

As for charismatic experience and literature production, the former was not central in this broad-based festival, but plenty of literature was produced, including *Strait* magazine.

Overall, Greenbelt started life with definite JPM roots but seemed to evolve in a more holistic direction, having displaying socio-political leanings and broader inclusiveness about its speakers.

* * *

What is Greenbelt's legacy?

In short, the festival has just chalked up its fiftieth anniversary. However, it has long since departed from its historic JPM roots, amply demonstrated in 2023. In contrast to the Jesus People's exclusive truth claims about Christ, Beloved Sara Zaltash presented a syncretistic divine inclusivity that embraces all. The provocative band Oh My God! It's The Church promoted a sexy Jesus in a church for the naughty; they're a band that parodies Jesus People end-times teaching in their self-confessedly salacious song 'Kiss My ApocaLips'.

This huge liberal shift had been flagged up as early as 1986 by previous Greenbelt speaker and author Os Guinness: 'What we are seeing more and more at Greenbelt is a religious reflection of political ideology. We are becoming secularised without realising it … we are collapsing the faith.'[23]

Speaking of the LGBITQA+ issue, Stewart Henderson reflects in August 2023 that, 'Greenbelt has excelled in foreseeing cultural shifts; although it didn't feel like it at the time, because of the flak we attracted from sections of the evangelical wing.'[24]

The greatest positive legacy, though, is the late John Peck's theology that demolished the spilt between 'sacred' and 'secular'. In the Creator's world, Christians should grasp a Bible in one hand and a newspaper in the other. The implications for viewing music, for example, are enormous: 'Christian music' is a mythical notion; Christians pursuing their God-given musical vocations are not. No less a person than Cliff Richard argued persuasively that believing musicians don't have to consistently sing about Jesus, merely be a Jesus Person while they are performing.

A tension can be seen today in the UK in balancing artistic expression with theological orthodoxy. Greenbelt Festival tilts towards the first in a decidedly liberal fashion while Big Church Festival probably leans towards the second with a more evangelical stance. Therefore, an underlying legacy question to ponder may be: How can we hold together the twin truths of God as Creator and Sustainer of the universe and everyone in it, but also the gracious Saviour of those who place their confidence in Jesus and live under his Lordship? Answers on a (very large) postcard, please…

Autumn 1974

26.

A New Wineskin is Crafted in the Vineyard

In rural California, the autumn is the best time to visit a vineyard, especially around October. The weather is in the upper seventies, the grapes are at their peak, and the harvest occuring is being frantically picked. It is 'all system's go'. There was another bumper harvest in urban Los Angeles throughout the autumn of 1974, but a spiritual one: thirteen evangelistic Bible study groups launched between that summer and early 1975.

It had begun on LA's west side in July 1974. A leadership couple moved home to share Jesus, propelled from Calvary Chapel in Costa Mesa. They had a gut-feeling this fellowship would be different. The first location was the home of Love Song's Chuck Girard and his wife Karen, drawing musicians and actors. After simple worship and study, people were invited to pray to receive Jesus. They did so by the shedload. Trainee actor Pamela Norman then offered the flat she and musician husband Larry shared. The crop was ripe for autumn harvesting. Vineyard was emerging, not as John Wimber's 'baby' – but birthed by Kenn and Joanie Gulliksen.

Three turning points feature in what became the Vineyard movement. These involve the Gulliksens, then John and Carol Wimber, and finally both couples joining together in ministry.

Kenn and Joanie's Bible studies had exploded by early 1975. Where could the thirteen groups meet corporately? Initially, they spent Sunday mornings at the Beverley Hills Women's Club. Subsequently, a year was spent at Lifeguard Station Fifteen on the beach at Santa Monica. Chuck Girard couldn't always hear the sermon because of crashing waves, but added, 'The worship was great, with sun and surf as the backdrop.'[1] Names like 'Holy Ghost Fellowship' were suggested for the church, but Isaiah 27:3 popped out for Kenn: 'Sing about a fruitful vineyard: I, the LORD, watch over it; I water it continually.' From March 1975, the groups were branded as Vineyard Christian Fellowship…

Subsequently, seven related fellowships were planted 'accidentally', said Kenn, describing them as 'very similar to Calvary Chapel at this point, except that there was more emphasis on intimacy in worship, the gifts of the Spirit and relationships'[2] – a harbinger of things to come. Meanwhile, Bob Dylan was saved in 1978, after a six-hour conversation spanning Genesis to Revelation, before being daily discipled with others in a room above an estate agent's office.

Enter John and Carol Wimber, who married in 1955 as non-believers. John was a professional keyboardist with the Righteous Brothers until 1963, the year both came to faith and became 'fools for Jesus'. Spirit-filled in 1964, they saw hundreds converted in their Quaker church in Yorba Linda. Six years later John was on staff and studying theology. However, John and Carol had spiritual meltdowns in 1974 and 1976 respectively, yearning for greater spiritual reality and church renewal.

October 1976 saw thirsty leaders meeting in a home to experience God in worship, led by sole guitar-player Carl Tuttle. They largely used simple Calvary Chapel choruses. One night, 'while Carl Tuttle led on guitar the singing of the chorus "Praise You, Father", the worshippers were overwhelmed by a sense of God's presence filling the room. This was a turning point for the worship of the group …. Praising God led to a sense of experiencing God's presence.'[3] Praying for one another, they experienced speaking in tongues and saw demons cast out. Their Quaker overseers requested they leave the church; in doing so, they would offer their blessings to the group as they exited. Thus, on 8 May 1977, a new Calvary Chapel of 150 people was launched. The Wimbers loved Calvary pastors' gatherings: 'Hearing their stories was like listening to the book of Acts. These ex-hippies were all between ten and fifteen years younger than we were and what a difference to what we had been used to.'[4]

The Holy Spirit's power fell on Mother's Day 1980, as recounted more fully in Chapter 7. Lonnie Frisbee was worshipping in the Wimbers' church and had been asked to speak there. He did so powerfully, then led in prayer-ministry, and the place exploded. Suffice it to say, the evening was crucial in terms of power ministry.

Under the Calvary Chapel umbrella were the Gulliksens' scattered little Vineyard fellowships from 1974 onwards, and the Wimbers' charismatic Yorba Linda church pioneered three years later. However, in April 1982, underlying tensions came to a head at a pastors' retreat in Lake Arrowhead, California. Carol Wimber recalls three concerns about the two fellowships from Chuck Smith's angle: their end-times teachings weren't clear enough, there were occurrences of excessive physical shaking, and demons were being cast out regardless of whether people were believers or not.[5] Smith's fellow-pastors expressed further angst about Wimber's 'church growth' principles[6] being taught at the expense of God's sovereignty.

The parting of the ways had come: Chuck and his pastors on the continuing Calvary side, John and Kenn on the re-branded Vineyard side. Kenn was the more relational evangelist, but John was the more strategic leader. Thus, the reins of Kenn's existing Vineyard were humbly handed over to John in May 1982. The name was retained and a further six churches quickly joined them. Precisely a year later, 'Vineyard Ministries International' was birthed, and John and Carol's church moved to Anaheim.

Soon the world was the Vineyard's oyster, particularly in the UK. Two observers here spotted their JPM ancestry.

For historian Stephen Hunt, 'By reputation, much of the Vineyard's image is largely associated with the counter-culture. Indeed, it has some roots, albeit indirect, in the Californian Jesus people of the 1970s ... identified by an abundance of Christian rock music, spontaneity in worship, and casual dress.'[7]

Speaking of Wimber, Anglican clergyman Graham Cray claimed that 'his involvement with Chuck Smith's Calvary Chapel showed him an example of a form of church for the children of the counter culture (the 'Jesus People') ... Calvary Chapel saw large numbers of these young people come to faith in Christ.'[8]

Wimber's ministry had a two-fold impact in the UK, through popular conferences and radical church-planting.

As a recent Bible college graduate, I joined 2,749 others in attending 'Third Wave'[9] in Westminster Central Hall in October 1984. It was served by 200 Americans, and I remember seeing an eighteen-year-old Californian girl animatedly chewing gum while casting demons out of someone. It was mind-blowing.

The UK organisers, led by Baptist pastor Douglas McBain, anticipated a resultant army of evangelists and London-wide revival that would penetrate the four constituent nations. Only time would tell. Subsequent conferences featured topics like healing, prayer, evangelism, spiritual warfare, and worship.

It was not just England that was touched. In July 1986, eight months after the signing of the Anglo-Irish Agreement, two successive 'Healing in the Church' conferences were hosted on both sides of the border. They aimed to further heal the rift between north and south by involving unionist Protestants and republican Catholics. The following summer's conference was difficult, though, given little endorsement from church leaders and five local murders occurring soon after they arrived, such that Wimber 'despaired of helping the church'.[10]

Scotland's capital city Edinburgh hosted the 'Power Evangelism' conference in September 1987, followed by seven satellite conferences across the nation. They filled the 2,500-capacity Usher Hall, but unsuccessfully tried to be denominationally inclusive. Intriguingly, sixty per cent of attendees had hopped across the border from England.

This raft of conferences, all soaked in a worshipful atmosphere, demonstrated Wimber's ability to get under the skin of Brits.

How about planting fresh churches in the UK? In 1981, the year before the Gulliksen-Wimber 'merger', a team visited Chorleywood and York.

Before their trip, team members prayed together in Bob and Penny[11] Fulton's home, and 'Bob had a dream about ministering in the streets in England and saw a whole series of churches popping up.'[12] On arrival, this second aspect of the dream was received negatively by leading Anglican vicar David Watson in York. He envisaged Wimber's team equipping indigenous churches in power ministry. The episode resulted in an agreed embargo on UK church-planting for six years. How was it subsequently broken?

The story goes back to 1982, with John and Ellie Mumford entering the frame. That spring John was given a fortnight's study-break from Anglican church leadership in central London, trekking to California to imbibe the Vineyard. Meeting John Wimber for lunch, he was impressed by the church's Holy Spirit theology and practice, especially the elongated worship and participatory prayer-ministry. Later that summer, Ellie received impromptu hands-on mentoring from Wimber himself at Holy Trinity Brompton in London. She reflects: 'Up till that point it had never occurred to us that this was something teachable and transferable.'[13] Little surprise, then, that the Mumfords moved to Anaheim Vineyard for an eighteen-month internship from November 1985 onwards to learn more. God, they said, then spoke to them thirty-three times about returning to plant a UK Vineyard church. After many personal hindrances, the Mumfords finally flew home with two sons in tow during the summer of 1987 and started from scratch in Putney, south-west London. Giving up a steady income, settled housing, and ministerial status, they began to invite lost people into their living room. Within six months fifty people had gathered, many quickly finding Jesus. Similarly, three other clergy couples soon kickstarted new fellowships in Feltham, Middlesex, historic St Albans,[14] and urban Manchester.

Reflecting on the ten marks of the JPM, Vineyard has something of a hybrid quality.

The movement is renowned for emphasising charismatic experience, the core issue that led to the parting of the ways with Calvary Chapel. They also focus on the person of the Lord Jesus and the centrality of the Bible, which Wimber taught in his laid-back style, often from the four Gospels. End-times teaching is an interesting mark, as Vineyard had a strong eschatology, but one that emphasised the 'kingdom now' more than the anticipated 'kingdom not yet'.[15] This was yet another bone of contention with Calvary Chapel. Nonetheless, these are strong JPM resonances.

There seemed to be little emphasis on producing literature specifically for non-Christians, balanced by much for existing believers such as Wimber's books and the widely read *Equipping the Saints* magazine. As for the hippy background, some of the early Gulliksen era converts were hippies, but the Vineyard movement proper started long after the counterculture's demise. There is no substantial evidence of living in communes, but there was a vital emphasis on 'community' itself in their Kinship Groups.

I have left three other marks until now to concentrate on them as very significant areas in which the JPM-inspired Vineyard made an impact in the UK. They relate to the three 'directions' of the Church: upwards to God in worship; inwards to itself in unity; and outwards to lost people in mission.

Contemporary music 'Vineyard-style' emerged more in the worship sphere than the evangelistic realm. Its initial roots were in the informal group started in 1976 – consequently, the worship was intimate, singing *to* God not merely *about* God. As a seven-year-old, worship-leader Matt Redman had just lost his dad when first encountering this style of worship and found it life-giving and healing. Clergyman, Sandy Millar recalls taking twenty-six people to Anaheim in the autumn of 1982, noting 'the unconscious activity of the Holy Spirit during the worship times, with songs addressed to God, such as: "Lord, we love you". It was very different from the songs we had then.'[16] As for house-church pioneer Terry Virgo, he recalls Wimber singing with tears rolling down his face when they once shared a speaking platform. Other UK leaders, though, highlighted two weaknesses: namely, the subjective songs were intellectually weak and often seemed individualistic.

When it comes to church ambivalence, John Wimber was a million miles away. Warmly embracing the entire UK Church, he fleshed out inter-denominational partnership on a macro level while also encouraging all believers to 'get to play' on a micro level.

Historically, divisions were rife; protestants separated from Roman Catholics at the Reformation and house churches threatened the historic denominations' hegemony. Rightly or wrongly, Wimber treated them as one body. Charismatic church historian Nigel Scotland comments: 'Somehow John Wimber with his love for all the churches was able at this critical point to bring an irenical spirit to bear on the situation.'[17] This resulted in conference steering groups which included representatives from every church background where possible. For individual disciples, Scotland defines John's 'doing the stuff' motto for every believer as 'his encouragement to Christians to change from being spectators to being participators'[18] – being an army rather than an audience. Some UK leaders, though, feared two dangers: first, the church compromising doctrinally for ecumenical reasons; second, inexperienced people ministering to others inappropriately.

The Vineyard's *Power Evangelism*[19] was not limited to reaching people on the streets but aimed to break the church's mentality to stay hidden within its four walls. Stimulated by believers from the developing world and fellow American missiologists, particularly the Gospel record, Vineyard embraced a supernaturalist worldview. Signs and wonders accompanied the early church's preaching (Mark 16:17,20), so why not today? We sometimes keep spiritual gifts in-house today, but how about exercising them 'out there'? In this regard, Anglican church leader Graham Cray felt that John thought deeply, both theologically and sociologically. Not only that, but he also 'had the great gift of taking the truths of the academy and putting them actively in the service of Christ in the local church'.[20]

This approach is still reflected today. For example, in the 'Healing On The Streets' model pioneered by the Coastline Vineyard church in Coleraine, Northern Ireland. Previously, though, theologian J. I. Packer had cautioned Wimber against receiving 'words of knowledge' for healing as he believed this could push the Spirit's ministry beyond the written Word.[21]

* * *

The JPM-rooted Vineyard profoundly touched these three arenas of UK church life. What other positive deposits did John Wimber leave behind?

Quoting an article from January 1998,[22] two UK church leaders not prone to hyperbole reflect on Wimber's legacy.

Anglican clergyman Sandy Millar travelled back to the eighteenth century, contending that: 'In times to come it will become increasingly obvious that the church in Britain owes more to him [John Wimber] than any other single man since John Wesley.' Ground-breaking new church leader, Terry Virgo believes his influence was massive, contending that 'only Billy Graham has had more impact in England as an American preacher'. His impact is still felt in contemporary UK churches, for instance in the prominence of prayer times at the end of services.

Adding to those legacies already mentioned might be Wimber's laid-back and unforced style, his Word and Spirit balance, and his refreshing honesty. Many leaders refer to him as a hearty friend – a simple but powerful legacy.

Having pastored since March 1985, I felt mentored by John Wimber without knowing him personally and I wept openly in church after his death on 17 November 1997.

Finally, I stretch right back to Gulliksen's early Vineyard in the immediate aftermath of the JPM. Their goal was to expose non-believers to the Bible in an informal setting. In the church today, there is evidence of a somewhat parallel resurgence through the 'Discovery Bible Studies'. Usually involving the three strands of everyday fellowship, biblical story and personal application, they are currently promoted in the UK by the Bible Society and Novo UK[23] amongst others.

Winter 1974-75

27.

These Amplifiers Buzz with the Rhythms of the Cross

'Preaching while the beer spills!' screams the December 1974 headline. The location is HMS *Ganges*, a training ship for sailors. Usually, bands playing there get tanked up before going onstage. The six Suffolk hairies of All Things New pray instead. A bloke on the door says the service personnel have had a pay rise, so are quite wasted. At 9.15 p.m. the band launch their set. The dance floor is empty. It's not easy being a Jesus rock band but a Christian magazine still covers their gig.

Seven years on, a high-living young man is residing in Anderlecht, Belgium. A fan of Bob Dylan, he is stirred by the artist's new 1979 album, released after his conversion to Christ. The Holy Spirit speaks to him through the lyrics 'Gotta Serve Somebody'. On 6 December he meets Jesus. Soon afterwards, God tells him he will use media to reach hordes of people. Chris Cole starts small with local radio in Plymouth.

These are Musical Gospel Outreach with their much-loved *Buzz* magazine, and *Cross Rhythms*, a Christian radio station and now web-based ministry. The music from the Jesus People Movement played a big part in both these stories.

The apocryphal story sometimes told is that Christians adopted Contemporary Christian Music (CCM) as a direct result of the American JPM. However, it was alive and kicking in the UK before the movement emerged in 1967. Here's its story which comes in three phases…

In the first phase, the early 1960s, the historical mould of a musical hymn-sandwich was broken: the rock opera, *A Man Dies*, reaching out to Bristol teenagers in 1960. That same year Spurgeon's College ministerial student, Bryan Gilbert, launched his 'Vernon Skiffle Group' in London. One year on, Peter Honour started working full-time with Youth For Christ. Having been inspired by attending their staff conference in the USA, he promoted rallies using a new musical style.

Meanwhile, bands quickly adopted the 'beat music' of groups like The Beatles and The Animals. Their goal was to evangelise unchurched youth. Lyrically, they sometimes sang their personal stories but were often confrontational in style. Support came from local churches and leaders, while bands sometimes faced flak for 'playing the devil's music'. When opposed, they performed in Christian coffee bars like Manchester's 'Catacombs', and in clubs, prisons, colleges and the open-air. On a shoestring budget, they sold their records to mere hundreds rather than thousands.

Eventually, other genres came to the forefront: R&B band The Envoys was formed in 1963 by Geoff Shearn, later co-founder of Musical Gospel Outreach, alongside evangelist friend David Winter. Pop music was represented by the Salvation Army's group The Joystrings, who had a major television profile from 1963-69. By the mid-1960s, Greenbelt founder James Holloway, with his Baptist friends in Suffolk, started the blues band All Things New. Claiming to be the first Christian rock band, Derrick Phillips' group The Pilgrims overtly shared Jesus in 'secular' venues from 1965 onwards.[1]

The second phase kicked off with a chance encounter at a workplace in December 1964. Geoff Shearn worked in an insurance company in London. Fellow Christian, Pete Meadows, part of The Unfettered with friend David Payne, was employed by an advertising agency in the same building. One day, Geoff and Pete bumped into each other in the lift, one spotting a Scripture Union pin badge on the other's lapel. Before entering the new year, they had organised a get-together of twenty bands at an Anglican mission hall in West Ealing, simply to swap notes. Musical Gospel Outreach (MGO) was born!

The three friends produced a regular newsletter, *Buzz* – its name inspired by the sound of the band's amplifiers. The magazine first came off the press in October 1965 as two folded sheets of foolscap paper. Two years later, they hosted their first Sound Vision event at Westminster Central Hall to showcase emerging Christian musical talent. Given it was FA Cup Final day, it was encouraging that they gathered a sell-out crowd of 2,200. (Incidentally, Liverpool beat Leeds United 2-1.)

Later, in January 1968, MGO sponsored a tour of the Campus Crusade for Christ band, The Forerunners. This quickly resulted in the launch of Key Records. Rapid growth meant Peter and David had to go full-time, their office being a disused British Legion hall in Vauxhall. The friends then began to hear rumours of early Jesus People via the international media. In the late sixties, Geoff Shearn raised the funds and flew out to the USA to check it out. He was sceptical about American hippies becoming Christians but fascinated by their music. He discovered what he now describes as a 'genuine spontaneous revival'.[2]

During the third phase of the early-mid-seventies, MGO individuals flew back and forth across the Atlantic, networking with Christian musical people and arranging tours back in the UK. The latter involved Larry Norman who played here for the first time. He had been introduced to David Payne by American record company executive Bob McKenzie, who regularly jetted to London to organise string sections for recordings. Meanwhile, in the spring of 1972, MGO arranged for Larry to meet the tastemaker DJ John Peel during his newsworthy thirty-eight-venue tour.

A *Buzz* article of May 1972 featured the cross-carrying evangelist Arthur Blessitt, but the following month's magazine was wholly devoted to the JPM. An elongated colour edition was produced in time for the first Festival of Jesus that coming August and was entitled 'A Special Investigation: THE TRUTH ABOUT THE JESUS PEOPLE'. One article, 'The Start of a New Revolution', pitted male voice choirs and organ recitals against the contemporary music revolution. *Buzz*'s editor wryly concluded that 'the term "Jesus Revolution" seems to be applied to anything and everything to do with Jesus just at the moment, but if it fits one aspect of the scene more than any other, it's the music field. Jesus Music … has certainly provided a revolution – but only because the singers themselves have been revolutionised.'[3]

Throughout this third phase, MGO continued their Sound Vision events, using artists like Judy McKenzie, who poignantly sang of the empty promises of hippiedom. Meanwhile, the amusingly named 'Operation Fred' encouraged Christians to build intentional friendships with non-Christians, consequently bringing them to autumn evangelistic concerts.

God had used risk-taking musicians in the sixties, and the revolution in musical style had finally made its mark on the UK by the seventies. It was further propelled by innovative Jesus People music from across the pond. Amnesia later crept in though.

A 2019 article by Derek Walker entitled 'The Rise and Fall of Christian Music',[4] argued that Larry Norman's 1969 album *Upon This Rock* marked the beginnings of CCM (Contemporary Christian Music) in the UK. Walker's piece featured 1970s homegrown artists but sadly omitted earlier bands.

At this point, two feisty sixties pioneers entered the fray.[5] Firstly, Derrick Phillips, formerly of The Pilgrims, described Walker's piece as 'a revisionist story from America', countering it by arguing, 'This is Britain and people need to know that it happened here first.' The Christian rock scene was established long before Larry Norman arrived. Besides, two positives from the 1960s were: the bands were amateur, so weren't wrongly motivated by money-making, and they used their music as a tool for evangelism. Secondly, Peter Honour, from the early Youth for Christ days, concurred: 'Rock groups were already being used extensively in outreach, evangelism and even in big concerts before Norman.' He went on to highlight three striking examples of memorable sixties groups: The Pilgrims with Derrick Phillips; The Envoys led by Geoff Shearn; and The Unfettered pioneered by Peter Meadows.

So, 1960s Christian music in the UK was ground-breaking, the soil considerably tilled by the MGO team. Into this fertile ground popped other seeds from the States (and elsewhere). Ultimately, both were musical partners for the harvest.

Fast-forward to our second story in 1981, when something was brewing in the heart of the twenty-nine-year-old Chris Cole. A hedonistic, successful businessman, he was living in Anderlecht, Belgium. Chris also occasionally worked as a radio station DJ. Members of the local FGBFI (Full Gospel Businessmen's Fellowship International) chapter dropped by one day. Would Chris play their Christian material? He wasn't interested but placatingly agreed to attend one of their meetings; the men began to pray for him.

Chris, though, was an avid Bob Dylan fan. After the artist's conversion, Dylan had released the 1979 *Slow Train Coming* album. It was the first of his three overtly Christian-themed LPs.[6] Chris was audibly arrested while mulling over the lyrics of 'Gotta Serve Somebody' – there was a stark choice between good or evil, God or the devil. In Chris' words, this song 'was not only used by the Holy Spirit in bringing me to faith but would be pivotal in me understanding how God was using contemporary Christian music and art to lead people to him.'[7] He came to faith on Sunday 6 December 1981. Chris soon returned home to Plymouth to tell his mother, to whom he had recently been reconciled.

In December 1981, Chris received a clear prophetic message from his friend and journalist, Dr Fred Ladenius:

'Chris, the Lord says He is going to use you to reach thousands … no millions for Christ through broadcast media.'[8]

Firstly, in 1983, Chris birthed radio programme *The Solid Rock of Jesus* on Plymouth Sound FM – an hour-long programme which aired on Sunday evenings. Secondly, four years later, he became involved with the Umberleigh Rock Gospel Festival in north Devon, a festival of music and the arts, accompanied by guest speakers; he soon became Stage Manager. However, finances were so tight in 1989 that the following year's festival was cancelled. Enter Chris with a rescue-package for the event.

Then, as the 1990s kicked off, there was a third development – *Cross Rhythms*. Here comes the best authority on UK Christian music – namely, Tony Cummings. Spiritually, Tony had been a latecomer to the party, saved by Jesus in 1980, six years after the terminus of the JPM. Two years after his conversion, though, he had been appointed assistant editor of *Buzz*. Developing an encyclopaedic understanding of Christian music, Tony reviewed its albums regularly, but edited his last issue of the magazine in November 1986. After three years freelance writing and radio work,

Cummings heard of a printer called Mark Golding who wanted to start a Christian magazine, launching it with him as publisher and editor. *Cross Rhythms* had a similar ethos to *Buzz* magazine but was geared towards a more recent generation, however there was remarkably strong inspiration from, and resonance with, the earlier JPM. Nonetheless, struggling to keep financially afloat, Tony sold the new magazine to Cornerstone Vision the following year. It was bought for the princely sum of £1 from the company owned and run by Christian entrepreneur Chris Cole. However, Cummings did continue as its music editor and main journalist until he retired in 2021.

Cole now had a radio show, a rock festival, and a music magazine in his portfolio, all under the single banner of Cornerstone Vision. The first venture lasted until its closing down in 1996, later becoming a community radio station in Stoke-on-Trent from 2002 onwards. The second motored on until 2003, but then relaunched as Arrow Festival under the leadership of Church Army evangelist Captain Steve Martin. The third is *Cross Rhythms*, still existing today online with many articles featuring Tony Cummings' enormous knowledge of contemporary Christian music.

The prophecy given to Chris Cole was beginning to come home to roost. So, what was the inspiration behind his lifelong calling from God, apart from the earlier prophecy? In simple terms, peering backwards, it was the JPM.

Despite his early battles to have Christian music played on the airwaves, his wife Kerry comments, 'Chris would come to realise that what he was involved with in terms of Christian music was part of a revival in the Western world that started in the late 60s.'[9] JPM inspiration lived in converted musicians who used their familiar style but amended their lyrics to carry the gospel forward. Chris' heart was to give exposure to indigenous UK music but also to distribute American music more widely. He was especially stirred by making friends with Glen and Wendy Kaiser of the Rez Band while they were in the UK. He subsequently visited Chicago to meet their longstanding Christian community, Jesus People USA (JPUSA). For Chris, this caring spiritual community 'was the heart of the Jesus People Movement, outworking this genuine revival – the cultural core of the music working with the practical application of the gospel in serving the broken and the lost'.[10]

Speaking further of Chris' ministry, wife Kerry reflects:

> All that was developing had its genesis in the great spiritual revival of the Jesus People Movement. As it swept the world during the 60s and 70s, much was now settling and maturing. At the heart of what had been planted was the anticipation of a coming harvest. The merging of the components Chris had been given, was to become a contemporary vehicle on which to carry the good news of Jesus Christ.[11]

A harvest of revival proportions was expected.

Meanwhile, Australian friend and mentor Tony Fitzgerald worked on festivals with Chris for years. Much earlier, he had been a Jesus People pioneer in the early days in Melbourne. Reflecting on parallels in the two men's lives, Tony says, 'Chris' life had been turned around by the outpouring of God that became known as the Jesus People Movement,'[12] despite, like Tony Cummings, being another latecomer to the party.

* * *

What legacies have these two JPM-inspired ministries left behind in the UK today?

Half a century after the JPM disappeared from public view, both ministries have modelled the transition from the printed page to web-based communication. *Christianity* magazine is the long-term heir apparent to *Buzz*, and very much operates on the internet today, including publishing on-the-day news articles. *Cross Rhythms* closed their hard-copy magazine down with its eighty-fifth issue in 2005, also in favour of the web. Both still seek to be user-friendly to unchurched people today.

Jesus People had their festivals and today's legacies are still apparent. Spring Harvest, first pioneered by MGO and British Youth for Christ, is in its forty-fifth year and still going strong, while the Greenbelt Festival just celebrated its fiftieth jubilee year. Both are continuing this joyful emphasis on Christians utilising their God-given creativity in the arts and music. This celebratory aspect certainly has a place in a culture where watching the news is often a depressing experience.

Finally, the heartbeat of both ministries was to bring people to Jesus, hence the Outreach in the MGO's name and their tongue-in-cheek Operation Fred. It also fits in with Chris Cole's prophetic word about reaching millions for Christ, and his subsequent involvement in GOD TV.[13] Unfortunately, this evangelistic legacy is not especially evident in the musical realm today. However, there do appear to be fresh expectations, on both sides of the Atlantic, about another major work of the gospel touching the lost in our generation.

PART 3

The Jesus People Predictions

28.

Inhabiting the Big Story of God's Lasting Friendship

I begin my final section of this book, The Jesus People Predictions, in an unexpected way. Rather than discussing future predictions first, I want to talk about a present invitation. It is God's invitation to friendship, which is at the heart of becoming a Jesus Person, that is if you're not one already…

In John 15:13-15, Jesus defines friendship brilliantly: to be a real friend you will give of yourself; it will cost you. Trust means taking your friends' advice seriously; what they say matters. Friends share their deepest thoughts and don't hold onto secrets.

These insights are gleaned from Jesus' moving farewell to his closest twelve disciples: very soon they will miss his company. The cross beckons for him…

And not long after, his departure from planet earth.

Speaking of John's Gospel, it's important to recognise that this is no ordinary relationship. It is having God, the eternal Son, become your friend. He's not our equal. Neither is he a softy. But he *is* friendly…

What does this mean? Simply put, he behaves in a kind, non-hostile way towards his followers.

In this chapter, I highlight how friendship is one thread in the big story of the Bible. From Genesis right through to Revelation. This isn't merely a history lesson. It is a story for you and me to inhabit. One to dwell in for time and eternity.

*

God the Maker is friendly.[1] He always has been. Although one God, he is never lonely. He is a community of three persons. Father, Son, and Holy Spirit. A friendship triangle if you like. But it's not an exclusive one – he is open to adding more friends.

Human beings for starters. We have lots in common:

We mirror his image: 'So God created mankind in his own image, in the image of God he created them; male and female he created them' (Genesis 1:27).

We care for his world: 'The LORD God took the man and put him in the Garden of Eden to work it and take care of it' (Genesis 2:15).

Our lives exhibit a sense of God-given dignity and purpose in life, so we can lift our heads high.

However, he is not an egotist, as if his vanity pushes us to reflect him. Nor is he merely our employer, creating driven gardeners. The idea is to be friends together in this journey of life:

'Then the man and his wife heard the sound of the LORD God as he was walking in the cool of the day…' (Genesis 3:8). One of the best things I enjoy doing with my wife Rosie is circular walks in the Dorset countryside. Sometimes we talk; other times we don't, but we just enjoy each other's company.

God is no 'inadequate', needily craving our friendship, but he does actively want it.

Tragically, the first human beings broke the friendship. Sin is erasing him from the picture. He responded by judging them:

'So the LORD God banished him from the Garden of Eden to work the ground from which he had been taken', then afterwards, 'he drove the man out' (Genesis 3:23-24). The 'tree of life', giving human beings ongoing existence, had a 'No Entry' sign banning access to it (v.24).

We sense that distance from God. It pains him too. Alienation is for real. How can we be friends again?

The friendly God promises a way to mend this fractured relation-ship. The unfriendly serpent (the devil) had marred it for us. And we human beings had broken loose from God (or so we thought). No one could fix it but the Maker. It's mended through Jesus, the offspring of a woman. And he suffers in the process too. Listen to God's words to the serpent:

'And I will put enmity between you and the woman [Mary], and between your offspring and hers [Jesus]; he will crush your head, and you will strike his heel' (Genesis 3:15).

The first declaration of good news: Paradise has been lost. Paradise will be regained.

There is God-given hope for us flawed people, even after being shut out from his life.

This severed friendship produces all sorts of unfriendly behaviour, as described across several chapters in Genesis: callous murder, foolish drunkenness, and holding ourselves and other gods above God (Genesis 4-11). We may not be murderous drunks, but how about putting other things or people in place of our Maker? Is there a way home? Can friendship be rebuilt? It certainly can. Hold on, though, it may take a while...

It comes through three successive friends of God.

Abraham is perhaps an unlikely friend, given his upbringing in moon worship; he applauded God's creation, not the Maker himself. However, God draws him out of this lifestyle into a close friendship, subsequently recalled by calling Abraham his '*friend*' three times.[2]

God calls him to journey with him. His gracious purpose is to start by blessing him. Then, the fledgling nation of Israel. And finally, every ethnic group on the planet:

'I will make you into a great nation and I will bless you. I will make your name great, and you will be a blessing ... all peoples on earth will be blessed through you' (Genesis 12:2-3). According to Paul in the New Testament, this whole plan unfolds through Abraham's 'seed', who is Jesus Christ (Galatians 3:16).

Friendship is sometimes a rocky road though. This was no exception. Abraham's extended family grew into a huge nation, one tyrannised by Egypt for 400 years. The friendly God gave them an exit plan through Moses. He is God's second major friend in the story. Having given his people ten vital life-instructions, he had regular one-to-ones with the Almighty inside a tent:

'The LORD would speak to Moses face to face, as a man speaks with his *friend*' (Exodus 33:11).

God used his first friend Abraham to promise a bright new future; and his second friend Moses to rescue Israel and teach them how to live.

But Israel didn't play the game. They presumed on God's friendliness: he had chosen them, so they thought, 'Anything goes!', or does it?

Jeremiah the prophet gives voice to their presumptuous attitude: 'My Father, my *friend* from my youth, will you always be angry?' (Jeremiah 3:4-5). He *is* angry though. Their words are empty; they do all the evil they can manage. Hence God consistently sends prophets to call his people back into loyal friendship. His people often feign deafness though. Later, the same prophet predicts a new covenant of friendship from the inside-out (Jeremiah 31:31-34): 'they will all know me, from the least of them to the greatest' (v.34).

A third and ultimate friend is on the way. Jesus is part of the divine triangle of friendship. There are hints about him in the Old Testament. For example, King David forecasts Jesus' betrayal, putting these plaintive words in his mouth, 'Even my close *friend*, whom I trusted, he who shared my bread, has lifted up his heel against me' (Psalm 41:9). Three of the four Gospel writers identify this as the friendship-breaking Judas.[3] But we are racing ahead too quickly…

Before Jesus arrives, a further close '*friend*' (John 3:29) paves the way for him, namely John the Baptist, like a best man promoting the bridegroom.

At long last, the friendly God arrives in the person of his Son Jesus: the Maker with a birth certificate, the Creator with human skin.

He is a '*friend*' to people in life, in death, and forever.

After thirty years waiting in the wings, he bursts onto centre stage. If there's a party to attend, Jesus will be there. He does make some unlikely friends though. The religion-police soon criticise him for being 'a *friend* of tax collectors and "sinners"' (Matthew 11:19; Luke 7:34). Why doesn't he mingle with those who have got it morally sorted with God? Instead, he hangs out with promiscuous, drug-taking, rebellious, drop-out hippies – in twentieth-century terms anyway…

There is hope for sinful people like me and you!

During his three-year earthly ministry, it is clear Jesus' mission is to form friendships. Once, four mates carried a stretcher-bound paralytic to Jesus, lowering him down into the crowds from a hole dug in a flat roof. They expect healing. Jesus' first words are: '*Friend,* your sins are forgiven' (Luke 5:20). Jesus initiates friendship, not the sick guy. Unless sin is faced, it will never happen. God's forgiveness is boldly declared, and the divine-human friendship is mended.

His death, too, is about rebuilding friendship, as Jesus said prior to being crucified:

'Greater love has no one than this, that he lay down his life for his *friends*' (John 15:13).

Very soon, Jesus will voluntarily give up his life, paying the just price for our sins and restoring us to God's friendship. As Peter, one of his closest circle of disciples, put it, 'For Christ died for sins once for all, the righteous for the unrighteous, to bring you to God' (1 Peter 3:18). Paul, who first met Jesus after his resurrection, adds that, 'when we were God's enemies, we were reconciled to him through the death of his Son...' (Romans 5:10). It's a final Goodbye to alienation, and a start-up Hello to friendship.

On the third day, Jesus was raised to life again. Afterwards, seven of his twelve bereaved disciples are together. Peter has returned to his previous occupation of fishing, the others tagging along. Zero fish are caught. Jesus stands on the shore, but at first, they don't recognise him. His initial address is poignantly worded: '*Friends,* haven't you any fish?' (John 21:5). Jesus gives them a fishing lesson, there's a supernatural haul, and Peter grasps he is the risen Lord. The seven relearn the secret of taking their coach's friendly advice.

A friend for life, a friend in death, a friend without end...

It is fascinating, though, that not everyone warms to Jesus' offer of friendship. Matthew hints at this in two succeeding parables, ironically referring to individuals who don't respond well to his grace as '*Friend*' (Matthew 20:13 and 22:12). He can offer the hand of friendship, but they must take it. Similarly, at the time of his arrest, Jesus is approached by the betrayer Judas Iscariot with a culturally normal Jewish kiss. He responds, '*Friend,* do what you came for' (Matthew 26:50). Judas' warmth is sheer play-acting. Authentic friendships are a two-way street.

Although never overtly called a friend, the Holy Spirit is 'one called alongside to help' in the original Greek language. He is 'another Counsellor' (John 14:16); exactly like Jesus, so just as friendly as Jesus is. His help is seen in enabling us to grasp and respond to the Good News of Jesus. When we do that, our lifelong goal is to 'keep in step with the Spirit' (Galatians 5:25). Don't forget, earlier in Genesis, we saw the friendly God walking with people.

Jesus lived, died, rose again, and gave us his Spirit. He calls us his friends...

Then the Church was born. Did it start life as a religious structure or a socially minded NGO? The straight answer is found in the apostles' letters, just before the climactic book of Revelation.

How are Jesus' followers addressed? You've guessed it, as *'friends'*; to be precise, twenty times out of twenty-three, *'dear friends'*.

Friendship with God the Father, Son and Holy Spirit is like a waterfall: its water cascades down vertically, then spills out horizontally. Church life is ultimately friendship-based. We reflect God in how we relate together. Jesus prayed to the Father for his followers that, 'the love you have for me may be in them and that I myself may be in them' (John 17:26).

You don't have to go it alone as a Jesus Person.

James' letter has some fascinating thoughts about how divine friendship works. His case study is Abraham who 'was called God's *friend*' (James 2:23). Why his friend? First, he had been declared righteous before God (called 'justification') through trusting his promises. Second, Abraham's faith was proved genuine through concrete actions, ones that reflect his newfound friend's character. Later, James contrasts this with the fact that *'friendship* with the world is hatred towards God' (James 4:4). The 'world' here refers to society's ungodly viewpoints. Friends have shared values and guard them in their community. To quote Jesus again: 'You are my *friends* if you do what I command' (John 15:14).

Lastly, the word 'friend' is not explicitly found in the last book of the Bible, Revelation. But the reality certainly is...

The apostle John wrote both his Gospel and the book of Revelation. In the former, he recorded Jesus' promise to his twelve friends:

'In my Father's house are many rooms; if it were not so I would have told you. I am going there to prepare a place for you. And if I go and prepare a place for you, I will come back and take you to be with me that you also may be where I am' (John 14:2-3).

In short, Jesus couldn't bear the thought of heaven without us his friends there.

In Revelation, we come to the climax of the Bible's storyline. Our sinful independent streak has shut us out from God-given life, pictured by 'the tree of life' (Genesis 3:24). Now, John says that God's grace means: 'Blessed are those who wash their robes, that they may have the right to the tree of life' (Revelation 22:14). Their robes are pristinely clean through Jesus' shed blood…

The book closes, then, by rising to the pinnacle of Jesus' soon-return, a common Jesus People theme. This is followed by a warm invitation:

'The Spirit and the bride [church] say "Come!" And let the one who hears [you and me] say "Come!" Let the one who is thirsty come; and let the one who wishes, take the free gift of the water of life' (Revelation 22:17).

God is the friendly God, from Genesis to Revelation. You and I are invited to inhabit his story for ourselves. Becoming a Jesus Person is more than praying a prayer. But it may just start there…

Why not pray something along these lines to God?

'Father, thank you for making me. I am sorry for breaking our friendship. This is my genuine turnaround. Jesus, thank you for dying for me. I ask for your forgiveness. Jesus, thank you for rising again to make me right with the Father. Please grant me that status as a gift. Holy Spirit, thank you for working in my life. I would love you to fill me to overflowing now. Help me to follow Jesus, and gladly obey him, all the days of my life. Amen.'

To cap it all, find a minister, church leader or Christian friend who can help you grow as a new Jesus Person. Explore being baptised to openly mark your newfound friendship. Enjoy celebrating your friend Jesus' death, by taking communion until he comes back.

'The grace of the Lord Jesus be with God's people. Amen' (Revelation 22:21).

29.

Your Older Men and Women Will Dream Revival Dreams

In these last three chapters, I want to address the important question of whether we can expect another Jesus People Movement today and, more broadly, consider Christian expectations for a new revival. For Jesus People leaders still alive today, how confident are they about a further revival and how might their perspectives differ from those of younger leaders? What could a fresh revival look like anyway?

The JPM has prompted revival expectations in the contemporary Church. As 'revival' is the most common word in everyday speech, I will use it consistently in these chapters, even though people rarely define it carefully. As a brief refresher, I defined 'revival' in my first chapter as 'an awe-inspiring work of God within a large group of people where he restores godly faith to believers and births saving faith in Jesus in the hearts of those who don't yet believe. From there, the Holy Spirit usually impacts their local communities and wider societies.'

The idea of 'another Jesus People Movement' begs the question, simply because there is no hippy culture today – the counterculture pretty much faded away in the mid-1970s. Whatever God does today will not be a nostalgic re-run of a previous revival. In that sense, maybe he says: 'Forget the former things; do not dwell on the past. See, I am doing a new thing' (Isaiah 43:18-19).

It may be surprising to see that I devote this chapter and the next to the

USA, before returning to the UK in the final chapter. The reason for this is quite logical: most people in the UK know little or nothing about the original Jesus People, so need to hear the story for the first time – hence this book. For this reason alone, almost all the voices expecting another JPM today are from across the Atlantic Ocean.

I am not assuming all my readers are firmly convinced revivalists. Some, with good reason, could be wholly against revival as it is popularly termed; others might have important reservations, questions, or even suspicions. This is compounded by the fact that definitions of 'revival' are notoriously elastic: ask ten people and you will get eleven opinions! Maybe we can unite around the reality of seeing Jesus' Great Commission of Matthew 28:18-20 fulfilled in our day?

My clear aim is to encourage fellow Christians, regardless of age, to yearn for the God and Father of the Lord Jesus Christ to pour out his Spirit afresh today – renewing existing believers and generating new believers. As partners together, we can then grow into lifelong discipleship, in what *The Message* author Eugene H. Peterson beautifully called, *A Long Obedience in the Same Direction.*[1]

Revival history teaches that not all awakenings are 'charismatic' in the modern sense of the word; for example, they are not necessarily prophesied about beforehand and don't always display typical charismatic manifestations. Those involved would not necessarily identify with the modern-day charismatic movement either. This is far from downgrading the crucial importance of the person and work of the Holy Spirit in our discussion.

In my final chapter, I conclude by attempting to highlight lasting biblical principles about God's work, without getting unduly bogged down in one cultural or historical expression such as the JPM. Retro may be all the rage today, but I am expecting fresh outpourings of the Holy Spirit before the Bridegroom comes to claim his bride. There is a wedding feast ahead, and some invitations to get out.

I deliberately feature original participants in this chapter, followed by next-generation leaders in the following chapter. I believe it is helpful to hear the mature perspectives of yesterday's seasoned campaigners but also to listen to the voices of today's young gun revivalists. The former have not run out of steam, many getting their stories into print while there is still time. How about experiencing a greater synergy between the older and the younger in an inter-generational Church?

What, then, of us old-stagers who came to faith in the Lord Jesus in the late sixties and early seventies? Some of us are of pensionable age (if we had pensions), and many are authentic 'grey hairs' (if we have hair). Given the timeframe, others have already finished their earthly race and have gone to be with Christ, 'better by far' according to Paul.[2]

Those who are alive and kicking today have varied perspectives about the possibility of another JPM occurring in this generation. In the first category are three leaders on the more charismatic end of the spectrum, viewed by some as being contemporary prophets.

Seventy-one-year-old James Goll is a prophetic voice who heads up God Encounter Ministries. Whilst at Central Missouri State University in the Midwest of the 1970s, he was part of a Jesus House ministry on campus, lead vocalist with the band Light of the Day, and a promoter of new musical artists. These days he is not entirely uncritical of the JPM: for example, saying that Jesus People lacked training for real life in the family and work spheres and that their fatherless generation lacked the explicit message of God being a Father to his children. In the October 2017 edition of *Charisma* magazine, however, James boldly claimed: 'It's time for a New Jesus People Movement to Emerge.'[3] He argues that we are in perilous times globally but also in a season in which God is accelerating his purposes, so we need to act in faith and not fear. More recently, in his twenty prophetic pointers for 2020, Goll asserted, 'We will see the beginning of the Third Great Awakening,'[4] referring to a new worldwide youth awakening that isn't confined merely to the USA.

John the Baptist type intercessor Lou Engle is another such voice. He, too, found Christ during the JPM days – in 1975 sensing the call of God to be an instrument of revival. Lou eventually initiated 'The Call' gathering at the turn of the millennium, aiming to turn the USA back to God through prayer, fasting, repentance and worship – all in the spirit of Joel 2.

A dream before the initial Washington DC gathering on 2 September

2000 prompted Engle to subsequently claim that if 'The Call' was a genuine John the Baptist type of movement, then a coming Jesus movement would certainly follow. 'The Call' was succeeded by 'The Send' in February 2019. Lou explains this change of tack as receiving an evangelistic burden that mirrors the heart of Jesus the Evangelist. It will bring in another JPM-like harvest across the USA, one that touches the nations. For Engle, this entails Billy Graham's mantle falling on a new generation of evangelists – streets and stadiums being filled with new songs of God's salvation.

A third prominent leader fully affirms the expectation of a second JPM. Steve Backlund is part of the senior leadership team at the influential, yet somewhat controversial, Bethel Church in Redding, California. He and his wife Wendy lead Igniting Hope Ministries, famed for its practice of laughing uproariously at the devil's lies. In the mid-seventies, nineteen-year-old Steve attended college near Eureka, California, and was dating Wendy. He was regularly witnessed to by hip Christians, especially while hitch-hiking. Locally, Gospel Outreach's Lighthouse Ranch impacted his journey to faith too. One night in 1975, Steve and Wendy attended an Erick Nelson concert,[5] fully committing their lives to Jesus. In my correspondence with Steve in December 2019, he stated that he expects another Jesus People Movement to happen.[6]

My view is certainly that revival should be perceived globally, recognising there are people movements occurring today in unpublicised contexts like Iran, which currently has a million Jesus followers.[7] Whether revival will be limited to youth specifically is highly debatable, as who knows what God might do amongst senior citizens these days? As for large-scale stadium events, maybe God will save people through authentic personal relationships in a coming revival. It may, of course, be both.

Despite the enthusiasm of these leaders above, there are more nuanced voices from three other leaders with very similar roots.

Chuck Girard, founder of Love Song, is now eighty years old. In his 2020 autobiography *Rock & Roll Preacher: From Doo-wop to Jesus Rock,* he devotes an entire chapter to the JPM.[8] There, Girard addresses the question of a similar revival occurring again with some shrewd answers. He affirms that he's praying for another mass revival and that Jesus is consistently on the move. Nonetheless, he reminds his readers of Dylan's poignant lyric about the times being a-changin'. Girard shares his insight, 'I feel it is improbable that there will be a new Jesus Movement replicating what we saw in the '70s … Any new move will likely pour out of a new wineskin that will speak to the current generation in their language, and meet their unique needs, just as ours did.' Culturally speaking, he claims this will involve a lot more one-to-one personal connection with people: 'We all must do our parts in our own sphere of relationships and influence, and the reception is likely to be cooler today.' The musician concludes, though, 'I believe in revival, and I pray that people will seek to know God.'[9]

Another longstanding charismatic pastor I interviewed asked to remain anonymous. Commenting about prophetic movements he has previously engaged with, he says, 'I find they are always foretelling revival and breakthrough. This foretelling is what they – or we – all long for. They prophesy out of their own desires and want to encourage the Church.' He further noted a lack of historical evidence for revivals being preceded by specific prophecies. This well-regarded leader favours a broader view of revival, involving a far more global perspective and emphasising holistic discipleship rather than numbers. He concluded by denying that he is unduly downbeat in his reflections, but candidly saying, 'As far as us being on the verge of revival, I really don't see it.'[10] Meanwhile, he continues to pray for the awakening he thinks we so badly need…

Finally, from a post-Covid pandemic perspective comes Wayne Drain, from Russellville, Arkansas. When newly married to June, the couple led the Fellowship of Christians,[11] birthed in the early JPM days following a localised outpouring of the Spirit at Arkansas Tech University. The sole reason for them leading this community was that they alone had a house to meet in. Wayne has longstanding connections with UK 'new church' leaders since first visiting Romford-based John and Christine Noble and friends in 1979. A musician and prophetic figure, Drain travels widely.

In his blog of 14 November 2022, he provocatively asked, 'Can a New Jesus Movement Rise from a Pandemic?'[12] A few years ago, Drain felt God speak to him about a second Jesus Movement, subsequently praying it over and talking with friends to test the message. He was cautious about people thinking that he might be having a nostalgia attack. He then sensed God speak to him again, saying, 'This movement will be different from, yet the same as, the first. It will be different from the first Jesus movement in that it will be a multi-generational rather than primarily a youth movement.' It would also be global, Drain contends, not merely confined to the USA. However, 'It must be like the first movement in that the focus remains squarely on Jesus, not personalities, not buildings, not events – just Jesus.' Drain believes the pandemic has been a God-given accelerant for transformational changes in wider society, such as people protesting for racial justice. 'Why should transformation not happen through the Church?' he asks. In that sense, a new JPM can indeed rise.

I would certainly agree with the emphases above on the importance of holistic discipleship rather than counting heads and on the vital nature of rejecting celebrity culture to make Jesus uniquely famous. Such a revival would create robust, lifelong worshippers who self-effacingly transform the world.

A third group of seasoned leaders appear more mainstream evangelical than overtly charismatic in their inclinations. As stated earlier, though, revival is not limited to believers of any particular theological stable – whether pro-charismatic, non-charismatic or anti-charismatic.

Long-time Baptist pastor Kent Philpott was a young USA Air Force veteran studying for Southern Baptist ministry at a seminary in San Francisco during the 1967 'Summer of Love'. Kent began to evangelise hippies in Haight-Ashbury, alongside Hare Krishna devotee turned Jesus follower, Dave Hoyt.[13] The pair went on to pioneer a string of communal houses such as Zion House. The eighty-one-year-old still pastors the modest-sized Miller Avenue Baptist Church in Mill Valley today. Kent has done much reflection about the powerful revival that seemed to die out so quickly. He has also moved to a more overtly Reformed theology – viewing true revival as God-sent, not humanly engineered – and appears more reticent about charismatic manifestations these days. Nonetheless, Kent highlights the JPM as possibly 'The Fourth Awakening in America?'[14] After focusing on the marks of true revivals from three historic leaders, including the theologically astute Jonathan Edwards, Kent concludes,

'Despite the aberrations, the JPM yet stands as a true awakening ... Yes, I would love to see this once more in my lifetime.'[15]

Before the JPM, Kent says, 'America was living in ordinary times, but soon the times were a-changin' – Vietnam was hotting up, the "beat generation" was in full sway, hippies had taken over Haight-Ashbury. LSD and pot were everywhere, Hindu and Buddhist sects were springing up, and *The Satanic Bible* had just been published.' He continues, 'I say all this since it makes sense that the wind of the Holy Spirit would descend upon us at that point. In some four to five years the power of God was to be seen. Thousands, at minimum, were swept into the Kingdom of God.'

However, the revival seemed to be dissipating by 1972, he claims, and was probably over by 1975. Returning to my present-day question, Kent responds, 'Conditions have worsened for sure, and we certainly do need a fresh wind of the Holy Spirit. But I cannot easily say, "Yes, we are on the brink", as many in the New Apostolic Reformation like Bethel Church do. I wish that we were, and we pray for it without ceasing.'[16]

Greg Laurie is in the conservative evangelical stable these days. Senior Pastor of Harvest Christian Fellowship and evangelist to many thousands, he hopes for a similar movement today, as argued in his book, *Jesus Revolution: How God Transformed an Unlikely Generation and How He Can Do It Again Today.*[17] Laurie came to faith during the JPM in March 1970. He heard Lonnie Frisbee speak at a lunchtime Bible study at a school in Newport Beach and was faced with the crucified/resurrected Son of God. Students were then challenged to be for or against this Jesus. Greg openly chose the former, finding 'a weight had been lifted'.[18] He later became part of Chuck Smith's pastoral team in Costa Mesa. Before Chuck died in 2013, Laurie asked his mentor if he thought another JPM would occur; Chuck replied, 'I don't know. Back in the 60s, people were desperate ... So I guess the question for today is, "Are we desperate enough?"'[19]

Looking back, Laurie honours his spiritual father Lonnie but also appears hesitant about Frisbee's 'signs and wonders' legacy. However, he does believe the JPM was the most recent American awakening and longs for another in his lifetime. Such an awakening would first entail 'God coming down' and then seeing love and joy flood the Christian community, as well as 'unbelievers drawn to the community of faith and converted'.[20] Recently, Laurie happily baptised a seventeen-year-old new believer called Steven. Laurie's co-author, Eileen Vaughn, reflects that 'maybe God will bring revival for a new generation. And maybe, just maybe, he'll [Greg] get to see another Jesus Revolution before he dies.'[21]

On 12 September 2022, seventy-year-old Greg preached on Revelation 3:7-13 at his *Harvest at Home* online service, a message entitled, 'It's Time for Another Jesus People Revolution'. He began by saying America is unravelling before our eyes for rejecting God and his Word. The closest parallel is the late sixties and early seventies, with similar problems today like drugs. Social media currently pours more fuel on the fire. We can't start a revival, but we can ask the Lord to do it again. Instead of pointing the finger at Hollywood or Washington, God's finger points at his house, the Church, first.

Laurie closes his message by noting the JPM's threefold relevance today: firstly, the Holy Spirit was at work then, and wants to fill people now; secondly, signs of Jesus' return are obvious, calling believers to change their lifestyles; thirdly, God has given us an 'open door' (v.8) today – just as he previously did for Chuck Smith – which Laurie and his friends walked through. Before the monetary offering, Laurie concluded that his generation had established the present ministry for about fifty years … It's a relay race, he said, and the baton is being passed on to the next runners.

More recently, Laurie preached to 230,000 people at his summer 2023 Harvest Crusade. Out of those who came to faith in Jesus, some 4,500 were baptised at the historic Pirate's Cove on Saturday 8 July. This is the very place where he and his wife Cathe had been baptised almost half a century before. Laurie describes it as the largest baptism in American history, one of biblical proportions.

These three groups are all participants from the original JPM, still serving God today. The more charismatically inclined feel confident that we're on the cusp of a similar revival, half a century on. There are more tempered voices, however, many with important questions about a similar revival happening.

Using Laurie's sermon image, though, who are the spiritual relay runners grasping the baton today? They are both the physical and spiritual offspring of our generation.

30.

Your Younger Men and Women Will See Revival Visions

In the previous chapter, we heard from 'old hands' involved in the JPM half a century ago who believe a similar revival might occur today. How about the expectations of 'young guns' who weren't even born then? What have they been shooting for these past six years?

In 2018 Alan and Kathryn Scott moved from the Vineyard church in Coleraine, Northern Ireland, to pastor the Anaheim church John and Carol Wimber first started. Now called The Dwelling, the fellowship controversially and abruptly left the Vineyard movement in March 2022. That summer Alan Scott preached a series on revivals called 'Everything Rises', based on the picture of the 'river flowing from the Temple' in Ezekiel 47:1-12. His Biblical passage on 31 July was the parable of the weeds and was used to illustrate the JPM.[1]

According to Scott, this revival involved three million people becoming Christians, all a result of 'the Church leaving the building' – ironically, after trying to get them back in again throughout the previous fifty years! His declared sermon purpose was both to remember and expect a revival. In conclusion, Scott stated: 'I'm not praying for another Jesus People Movement – that was for that generation; this is for this generation. God doesn't do what he did in the past.' Nonetheless, Scott still has an explicit expectation of revival in our day, but not of the same-old variety.

Fast forward a year, and a youth event called The Send took place for the first time in Orlando, Florida, for more than ten hours on Saturday 23 February 2019. It was initiated by Lou Engle, partnering with Youth With A Mission (YWAM) and Christ for all Nations. Two men collaborating with him in this venture were younger radicals, Todd White of Lifestyle Christianity and Michael Koulianos of Jesus Image. A joint interview of White and Koulianos featuring The Send, was headlined the 'Jesus Movement of this generation'.[2]

Todd White is an ex-drug addict and avowed atheist who came to know Jesus in 2005. He claims 60,000 Christians meeting together at The Send is 'God waking up a sleeping giant'. For him, we believers should recognise that Jesus constantly goes with us, regardless of our location. Todd contends people don't need to become evangelists, but merely live as Christians. When he started training high school pupils in 2007, hardly anyone wanted to sign up for the practical outreach component. Now Todd's ministry is equipping thousands on the streets of American cities through his two-day Power + Love event. Revival expectations are high.

Unlike White, Michael Koulianos was brought up in a Christian home, in Orlando, Florida. He gave his heart to Jesus and was simultaneously overwhelmed by God's power, aged just twelve. He describes The Send as 'ultimately a war on inaction … an ascending movement from the presence [of God] to the world, unto the glory of Jesus'. Asked about another great awakening occurring he responds, 'I feel like the Lord is birthing this Jesus movement and a Jesus people on and off the platform, in their homes. It is what he burns for.' For Michael, revival is not about believers making a big public name for themselves, but simply about fleshing out a 24:7 lifestyle for Jesus. Might this aspect be neglected while praying for revival to somehow 'come down'?

I agree with not expecting a repeat performance of the JPM, historically rooted as it was in the late sixties' counterculture. Maybe God will do something creatively fresh today? It is also good to hear ordinary believers are being trained in everyday witness for Jesus, particularly when celebrity culture has infected the church in our media-obsessed age. Even the New Testament church faced the issue of 'celebrity' with believers in Corinth viewing Paul and Apollos as competing 'influencers' in their eyes.[3]

Meanwhile, in the following year of 2020, Sean Feucht ran for Congress.

This passionate, but controversial, upfront leader and Republican was born in 1983 to medical missionary parents. In his adult years, he graduated from Oral Roberts University, where he had founded the prayer/worship movement Burn 24-7. In 2016 he, his wife and family, moved to Redding, California. Sean was a volunteer worship leader before launching his album *Wild* on the Bethel Music label in 2018. Two years later, Feucht came a distant third in the open primary for the California 3rd Congressional District. In May of that year, he launched Hold The Line, encouraging young believers to be right-wing political activists.

Amidst the pandemic, as an anti-vaxxer and defender of freedom to worship, Feucht kicked off Let Us Worship at the Golden Gate Bridge in San Francisco in July 2020. A second event in San Diego drew 5,000 people, Feucht audaciously and publicly declaring a new Jesus movement. He expanded this conviction by speaking about his calling to focus on cities experiencing turmoil and brokenness, containing inhabitants who want to experience God for themselves. Some observers felt he was deliberately fashioning himself as heading up a new Jesus Movement, especially when he subsequently started touring the country widely. Undoubtedly, Feucht positions himself as surfing on JPM waves.

Parker and Jessi Green are initiators of what they term 'Saturate' evangelistic events. One was held recently at Huntington Beach (the place where Chuck and Kay Smith first observed 'alien' hippies). Feucht participated for a day, telling Parker afterwards that it reminded him of the JPM era, even though he wasn't actually there…

The similarities were eerie, he contended, in that hippies were getting saved amidst racial and social strife. A movement was birthed in California that swept across the USA, widely covered by the press of the day. Symbolically, Feucht led worship that night on a 1963 Gibson acoustic guitar originally used in the JPM. He certainly perceives the Church to be in a parallel season, returning to a preaching of the gospel in a gritty, raw manner. Besides, because of Covid, Christians can't be cossetted inside their churches anyway.

Feucht was recently gifted an original *Life* magazine dated 30 June 1972. It was handed to him by his Bethel Church hero, pastor Bill Johnson. The front cover was entitled 'The Great Jesus Rally in Dallas' and this issue declared a Jesus People Movement over America. This added fuel to the fire of Feucht expecting a similar revival to occur again in the USA today.

The evangelist also has friendship links with those from the original Jesus People days, notably Republican politician turned media show host Mike Huckabee. He had attended the original Explo '72 event that fed off JPM momentum, especially appreciating its contemporary music and the preaching of Billy Graham. Huckabee describes the event as a crossroads for him, guiding his life in a different direction.

More recently, Feucht's Covid-protest concerts feature in his bizarrely titled *Superspreader* movie.[4] Meanwhile, Let Us Worship is currently about to 'go large', having already touched 150 cities. Feucht believes that the movement that started with a few courageous people will burn like wildfire across his native USA, so he and his team are now heading for all fifty State Capitals in 2023-2024. The JPM taught him to dream bigger.

Feucht is extremely media-savvy and seems to court controversy but has a deep heart for Jesus. Nonetheless, his widespread claims do pose the question of him 'getting on the bandwagon' in a JPM re-run. His ministry could appear to parallel a film franchise, trying for box-office success the second time around. For me, he also highlights the divisive nature of politics for American evangelicals today; indeed, he seems to be vigorously stoking this fire. Is the gospel not able to unite Jesus followers of both Republican red and Democrat blue today?

In December 2021, Nik Walker began to reflect on the historic fiftieth anniversary of the Jesus Movement. He is an early-twenties evangelist and author based in West Virginia, already making quite a name for himself. His key question was whether the crisis-strewn American Church is prepared for the revival many are praying for. Unsure, Nik highlights vital biblical principles that seem to be absent including real home-based discipleship; an intercession/prayer movement; and an urgency about people being lost.

Looking back over history, Walker is honest about the fact that no move of God is free from imperfections, and he doesn't omit the JPM. There are strategies to learn from that era and there was lasting fruit in changed lives too. But for him, unlike famous novels, there will be no sequel. What we can learn from, though, are the foundational biblical principles that emerged from the JPM. Walker is still faith-filled about a coming awakening of epic proportions. However, it will not look or sound the same as it did back in 1971.

I would agree with Walker. In terms of the way revival looks, from a UK angle, I would suggest we receive greater stimulus from the fast-growing black majority churches, perhaps accompanied by the sound of world music too, rather than just a niche genre like rock and roll.

Meanwhile, it is Wednesday 6 April 2022. Jennifer Miskov is visiting the historic 'well of revival' at Pirates' Cove, the Jesus People baptism site. She is a revival historian and author,[5] founder of Destiny House Publishing, and a teacher on awakenings at Bethel Church. Jen recounts a momentous chance encounter that day while looking for a secluded place with God before launching her next online School of Revival. On arrival, though, the cove was self-evidently a movie set, located where Chuck Smith and Lonnie Frisbee had previously baptised hordes of young people. Jen investigated further. When the crew broke for lunch, she bumped into Jon Erwin, the director and writer of Greg Laurie's *Jesus Revolution*[6] film. She was quickly introduced to Laurie as well. Giving both men a copy of her book, Erwin noticed their film's name *Jesus Revolution* in its sub-title. He invited Jen back as an extra the next day. There she saw the baptism scenes recreated. During filming, Jen could feel God's presence on the set. She reflects that the film's timing is prophetic for a day when 'cancel culture' is so prevalent. Jen was grateful Frisbee's legacy was celebrated too. Reflecting on a significant day caused this younger revivalist to believe God may be stirring up a new JPM in our day. What he had done once he could do a second time. Maybe it has begun already, Jen surmised, if only we had the eyes to see it…

There are many and varied expectations of revival, especially amongst charismatic Jesus followers and leaders, yet in early 2023 the Christian world woke up to reports of revival occurring in a historic Methodist university in America.

On 8 February, what some call 'Gen Z's first revival'[7] broke out amongst students at Asbury University in Wilmore, Kentucky. After a regular Wednesday chapel service, a few students stayed on to pray and worship. Others began to join them in what became a largely unplanned 24/7 movement of praying, confessing sin, reading Scripture, and sung worship. After four days the services went viral on TikTok, with the hashtag #asburyrevival being viewed more than 100 million times. Was it perhaps the first social media revival? Whether or not it was, the little town of 6,000 was quickly overwhelmed with unprecedented visitors.

A missionary from Nashville, Jessika Tate, arrived on the third day. Her initial experience was muted. However, UK journalist Tim Wyatt recounts, 'After a late-night session with only a few hundred others, the following day she entered the sanctuary and was overcome with tears. "I just go: 'Oh my goodness, he's here' and I started weeping. The presence of God was just so thick."'[8]

A visiting pastor from Arkansas discovered the outpouring was not hair-raisingly crazy, but viewed it as 'more silent, it was more sombre, with outbreaks of glorious praise, all spontaneous and student-led'.[9]

What is more remarkable is that something similar had happened previously in Asbury, right in the thick of the JPM in 1970. On 3 February, the Dean, Custer B. Reynolds, asked students to give testimonies rather than hearing him preach as planned. They did so, resulting in a long line waiting to speak. A spirit of revival came upon the congregation, typified by immense joy. Classes were cancelled for an entire week before recommencing. This outbreak resulted in 2,000 witness teams being sent out from Asbury University to churches and campuses nationally.

Meanwhile, fast-forwarding to 2023, UK-born Gerard Kelly reflects on his recent visit to Asbury. This long-term leader came to know Jesus in Bath in 1973. He sees parallels between his experience then and Asbury now. Visiting the university while the outpouring was in full swing, he comments, 'I sensed an unconditional invitation to encounter the person and presence of Jesus, sensitive to the hunger of a generation.' For Kelly, its fragrance was the same as the JPM. He concludes, 'If it is a sign of something new – the first puddle of a coming rain – then we have good reason to rejoice. Will this generation have its own Jesus revolution? I pray they will, and I for one will cheer them on.'[10]

As for Asbury University, the students were sent back to their classes sixteen days later, on 24 February, but with fresh fire in their bones.

*

These past six years have seen widespread expectations from younger leaders of further revival movements like the Jesus People. However, somewhat ironically, permit me to give the last word to two seasoned JPM campaigners: the first a musician/author in his mid-seventies, the second an evangelist in his early eighties…

John Fischer 'was in at the very birth of contemporary Christian music and the Jesus movement that preceded it'.[11] In a recent Facebook post entitled 'The Last Jesus Movement'[12] John writes:

> Contrary to popular opinion, and even what I've written in the past, I am happy to report that the Jesus Movement was never over. Yes, the Jesus Movement as a historical event among the youth culture in the 1970s that was replaced by the Christian subculture in the 1980s, is over. But Jesus moving, changing people's lives, and asking us to follow Him, is still going strong, and those who are following Him are still, dare we say, Jesus Freaks…

Over-65s and Gen Z'ers should therefore gather around the same flame he concludes, because 'The Jesus Movement is alive and well! The Jesus Movement never died. Jesus is still moving.'

Cross-carrying evangelist Arthur Blessitt concurs. As an original participant he is quite sceptical of voices today that were not actually part of the late sixties' scene. For him, the Jesus Movement first began with the angel Gabriel announcing to a soon-to-conceive Mary, 'You are to give him the name Jesus … the holy one to be born will be called the Son of God' (Luke 1:31,35). The movement continued for two millennia until the American JPM emerged four years before the media eventually took notice in 1971. From Blessitt's angle, it concretely began when he and his team engaged 15,000 hippies in Griffin Park, Los Angeles, during the 1967 'Summer of Love'. Arthur believes he has been a non-stop part of the JPM to the present day. Whilst broadly supportive of what God seems to be doing right now, Blessitt thinks another movement is superfluous as he never left the original one! Whatever the case, his heart is still to encourage people to start 'a new Jesus Movement' in their local areas.

Arthur, now aged eighty-three, is still in good heart today. If he happens to bump into younger people claiming a new JPM, he will likely greet them briefly, move on to share Jesus with somebody else, and then encourage them to do likewise. Given Arthur's poor health and its impact on his walking and travelling, such encounters are unlikely to happen like they did for him in the UK during the seventies.

So, how about revival occurring in the four nations of England, Wales, Scotland, and Northern Ireland again today?

31.

The Holy Spirit Poured Out on Everyone in the Last Days

There was a God-sent revival in the USA from the late 1960s onwards – it was called the Jesus People Movement. Like many genuine revivals, it had a limited shelf-life before a 'new normal' returned. It certainly had a big knock-on effect in the UK but in the form of scattered 'pockets' of revival rather than a full-blown one. It did mark, though, a distinct sea-change in the progress of the gospel here.

So, can we legitimately expect another homegrown revival in our day, and, regardless of geography, how do we handle revival expectations today?

Before trying to answer these two questions, it's good to remind ourselves that we UK Jesus followers are no strangers to historic revivals, stretching back to the mid-nineteenth century.

In 1859 there was a powerful move of God in County Antrim, Northern Ireland, known as the 'Ulster Revival' which largely involved Presbyterians. 100,000 people became Jesus followers. It kicked off with four stirred-up young men in Autumn 1857: new converts James McQuilkin and friends met to pray at the old schoolhouse in Kells, near Ballymena, on Friday evenings. They would bring peat for the fire to keep themselves warm. On New Year's Day 1858, the first conversion of an attendee occurred, with subsequent conversions happening every single week. One example of its wider social implications was in October 1859 when a Belfast whiskey distillery, producing a million gallons annually, was put up for auction.

It was surplus to requirements. Leading revival historian J. Edwin Orr suggests this awakening 'made a greater impact spiritually upon Ireland than anything reported since the days of Saint Patrick'.[1]

The Welsh Revival broke out between 1904 and 1905 under the leadership of Evan Roberts (1878-1951), a twenty-six-year-old former miner and trainee minister. It lasted less than a year, but between 100,000 to 250,000 people were converted. Once, when Roberts was preaching, an infamous sceptic demanded access to question him – but the man's request was frustratingly ignored. Striding towards the pulpit to do so, he was abruptly overpowered by the Holy Spirit and would have collapsed on the stairs unless held up by congregation members. He proceeded to publicly cry out for mercy. The people yelled, 'He has been saved! He has been saved!'[2] Meanwhile, the revival also changed the mining industry: beforehand, pit-pony owners had given instructions by swearing at their charges; afterwards, the ponies couldn't grasp their masters' unfamiliar, cleaned-up language. Revival news snowballed, gathering momentum across Scotland and England with some claiming a million Brits were converted. Missionaries also shipped the news abroad, impacting the emerging American Pentecostal movement across the Atlantic.

In England, there was a 'forgotten revival'[3] that began in Lowestoft in 1921, eventually spreading across East Anglia. London-based Baptist minister Revd Douglas Brown enjoyed some powerful encounters with God before arriving for meetings in Lowestoft on 7 March. Christians had been praying for revival across the denominations. Brown then preached 1,700 times in eighteen months, on 370 occasions between March and June alone.[4] On his first night, ministering at London Road Baptist Church, seventy young people passed from spiritual death to life. A packed converts' gathering in mid-April drew a congregation of whom three-quarters were young people; whole families were converted too. Later, during the autumn herring season, Scottish barrel maker Jack Troup arrived in nearby Great Yarmouth to work in the fish-curing yards. Through his open-air marketplace preaching, fishermen from north-east Scotland were converted, subsequently carrying gospel nets home on their boats alongside their fishing nets.

From 1949-1953, revival broke out on the island of Lewis in northern

Scotland. God's chosen instrument was Revd Duncan Campbell (1898-1972), but many Hebridean believers had been praying beforehand. At one prayer meeting, nothing seemed to be happening. A young man stood up, fed up with waiting. He read out Psalm 24:3: 'Who may ascend the hill of the LORD? Who may stand in his holy place?'. He felt prayer was sheer humbug if we are not right with God. When he started to intercede, a power was let loose in the barn that 'shook the parish from centre to circumference'.[5] Campbell subsequently reflected, 'Revival is a going of God among his people, and an awareness of God laying hold of a community', resulting in a deep conviction of sin and unusual physical manifestations.[6] In 2019, R. T. Kendall was invited to the 70th anniversary of the Lewis Revival. He highlighted eight key factors, the first being people saved, the last being 'No sleep!'[7]

The common denominator in these revivals in all four corners of the UK was the kind of prayer that stands in the gap between God and people. He delights to respond when we display our dependence on him.

Since my birth year of 1953, there have been no notable revivals in the UK; some people, though, feel we are 'ripe' for another revival today.

John Groves is a key leader in the Newfrontiers group of churches. In 2017 he shared with praying fellow leaders the parallels between their contemporary world and the 1970s, 'a time of exceptional movement of the Holy Spirit' in the early charismatic movement. The revival insights he suggested may apply to us in a post-Covid context too.

Firstly, John highlighted the upheavals of 2017, its election displaying many fault lines in society, such as Remain versus Brexit. He went on to chart three terrorist atrocities, the Grenfell Tower fire, and other uncertainties, causing a time of 'fear, instability, confusion and shaking'. Secondly, he outlined parallels with the 1970s: 'A decade of uncertainty, change and turmoil: the Middle East crisis, terrorism prominent, oil prices quadrupling, inflation hitting the roof at 15-20 per cent. There was social turmoil, strikes, power cuts, the three-day-week, and big pay rises but huge inflation.' We might, John suggested, expect a similar scenario in the next five to ten years. Thirdly, he sensed God reminding him of his powerful move in the 1970s. John was baptised in the Holy Spirit in 1971; he came out of a more traditional church into the new 'house church' movement, one that believed in restoring Church life to a first-century Acts of the Apostles model.

'There was a lot of turmoil and pain but ultimately it was good and of God', he claims before concluding that 'the church that emerged was very different'. Finally, John surmised, 'Are we going to see a period when God will move in his church – from Restoration to Revival? We will emerge in ten years a very different church from now.'[8]

Societal upheavals, then, are no hindrance to God being powerfully at work. Indeed, sometimes they are a prelude to heaven-sent revival. When I gave a JPM presentation in my home church two years ago, some of those attending gave written feedback afterwards, saying this was the most important lesson they had learnt that evening.

Recent UK history certainly indicates big challenges in our society today. The writer to the Hebrews indicates that massive shakings will happen in both the heavens and on earth, as a harbinger to people coming to Jesus and thereby 'receiving a kingdom that cannot be shaken'.[9]

Six years on, in 2023, a Gen Z churchgoer called Abigail Buchanan is pondering our present-day context. Reflecting on the recent Asbury revival, she faces the question of whether her generation could be the Church of England's salvation or not. The same question could be asked of the UK Church-at-large. Her view is that young people today are turned off by religion but turned on by spirituality. Also, she thinks, the legacy of the Covid pandemic is that a lot of pain has cathartically come to the surface, making people face the deeper questions of life more openly. Abigail ends up picturing a beach scene to describe our current context, borrowed from an Anglican clergyman friend called Gordon. Frustratingly, it seems, the tide has been going out for a long time in this country, but now it appears our feet might gradually be getting wet again. We may only know for sure in a century's time. In partnership with Abigail, though, I will be watching this space for a high-tide revival.

The tide certainly seems to be coming in at Chroma Church in Leicester this year. Author Ralph Turner,[10] part of the church, recalls the first days of the previous year of 2022 in this way: 'Revival is always accompanied by prayer, so it is no surprise that as preparation for this event, the church at Chroma had spent three days in prayer and fasting, with more than 100 people turning up to pray each evening right at the start of the year.' The revival kicked off at a leaders' meeting on the afternoon of Saturday 8 January 2022. Ralph memorably recalls, 'His presence was so thick in the atmosphere; it was hard to stand. It was impossible to stop worshipping. We were in His presence. There were angels in the room. Time became unimportant.'

In Leicester, the most ethnically diverse city in the region, with fifty per cent non-white residents and various religious backgrounds, people are declaring faith in Jesus in baptism. Some experienced dreams beforehand. 115 people came to know Jesus throughout 2022. At the time of writing, 100 were converted in meetings in the previous two months, with more coming to faith on the streets too. Such is the hunger to see people saved that the following happened: 'At one of our Revival Prayer meetings, we each lifted a chair above our heads and prayed for it. We then extended the number of chairs set out on a Sunday by a considerable amount, believing that the prayed-for chairs would be occupied. God answered.'

One Sunday, fourteen people were baptised: one had nearly died of knife wounds previously, a second had taken drugs at a nightclub eliciting a heart attack, and the third was a girl celebrating her twenty-first birthday who 'told of how God had taken her and her baby from wrong relationships, tarot cards and fortune-telling to coming to Christ a week ago'.

Chroma Church already had existing New Life and Next Steps courses for new believers, but they are presently over-subscribed, causing the courses to be revamped. The worship is described as exceptional, with people basking in Father God's love and stepping out to use spiritual gifts. In October, though, the room was full of lament as participants were led in worship by a Ukrainian couple, poignantly expressing the pain of their nation's hardships. Repentance has been a feature too. In August 2022, at a weekly Tuesday revival prayer meeting, people were called forward to turn away from sin and deal with issues. The queue stretched to the back of the room. Healing-wise, one young lady had a critical heart condition and was consequently uncertain about living and working; she was healed through online prayer and is now fully active, holding down her first job.

A leader who had previously been involved with the mid-1990s'

Toronto Outpouring said the revival was 'like Toronto but more mature'. A missionary woman who had experienced the Pensacola outpouring of 1995 commented that it was almost thirty years since she had seen anything like it. Even a visitor previously involved in revivals in China felt a special presence of the Holy Spirit. If this is not a revival in Leicester, I'm not sure what is…

So, how do we handle these expectations of revival, and reports of them happening?

As a Church, we need to gain a firm handle on God's mission in the world biblically, and thoughtfully consider how it might involve us both individually and within our church communities.

Also, without being unduly cerebral, I suggest we think more deeply about how we define revival and what it might tangibly look like when it comes, coupling this with an expectancy and urgency in praying for such an awakening, whilst not dispensing with weighing prophetic words. Our core yearning should be for Jesus to be made famous across the nations of the earth before every knee ultimately bows to him as Lord.

It is good to realise, too, that successive God-sent revivals have had different colours and flavours. They are far from bland and monochrome. We should be radical enough to consistently flesh out Jesus in everyday life, and to communicate him openly wherever we find ourselves. I would encourage you to read the stories of past revivals, including the Jesus People Movement, to inspire your faith in the Holy Spirit to work powerfully today.

'LORD, I have heard of your fame; I stand in awe of your deeds, O LORD. Renew them in our day, in our time make them known, in wrath remember mercy' (Habakkuk 3:2).

In closing this story of when Jesus met hippies, which began more than fifty years ago, I want to suggest a prayer for UK churches to use today. It is found on the lips of Rachel in Genesis 30:1.

Previously, God had promised to make Abraham's family into a gigantic nation through which the Messiah would come. At this juncture, his grandson Jacob had encountered God at Bethel in a life-changing way.

Subsequently arriving at Paddan Aram, he started working for his long-lost uncle Laban, successively marrying his two daughters – first Leah, and then after waiting seven years, Rachel, the true object of his love.

Leah then has four sons by Jacob; Rachel sadly has none at all. She is barren – a deeply shameful experience in the culture of her day. Her plea comes out of a heart that is both jealous towards her sister Leah and frustrated with her husband, Jacob: 'Give me children, or I'll die!' she yells. In response to this 'come up with the goods' plea, Jacob, her husband, makes clear that her words are effectively a prayer, consequently asking Rachel, 'Am I in the place of God…?' (Genesis 30:2).

Three humanly orchestrated attempts to provide Rachel with a child follow, each with zero success. Rachel's pain multiplies as her older sister, Leah, produces two further sons and a daughter, Dinah. But what is the end of the tale?

'Then God remembered Rachel; he listened to her and opened her womb. She became pregnant and gave birth to a son and said, "God has taken away my disgrace." She named him Joseph, and said, "May the LORD add to me another son"' (Genesis 30:22-24).

One good mark of authentic revival, I would argue, is overworked spiritual midwives. How might Rachel's agonised prayer resonate with us today?

With some noteworthy exceptions, there is not enough new life springing forth in the UK at present. We are certainly not 100 per cent barren, but not as fruitful as we could be. Sometimes, too, we might understandably feel jealous when nations elsewhere see far more new-born Christians than us. These realities should cause us to be utterly desperate to see new life emerging, unless we're too complacent and easy-going, of course. Don't take Rachel's prayer on your lips while a disconnection exists in your heart.

We should also be wary of human pressure to bring something out of the bag ourselves; no one but God can produce life. Jesus said, 'Apart from me you can do nothing' (John 15:5), and he meant it. Nonetheless, we can actively position ourselves for revival through expectancy and prayer. It is also important to appreciate that clever human strategies won't do the trick – three unsuccessful plans were attempted in this Bible story to get Rachel pregnant; the third even used 'mandrakes' (Genesis 30:14), an ancient form of aphrodisiac. We need to keep in mind that a remembering and promise-keeping God never forgets us or his promises to us. He has a great record of creating life *ex nihilo* (out of nothing). Joseph's subsequent life story tells us that his supernatural birth had a huge knock-on effect in Egypt, where God later placed him. Supernatural revival may eventually touch your 'Egypt' and mine.

Lastly, and fascinatingly, one miraculous spiritual birth seems to lead to another – Benjamin was then born after Joseph.[11] Revival makes us greedy for further new life to emerge: when we have seen God break in powerfully once, we have greater faith that he will do so yet again.

So, will there be another revival like the Jesus People Movement? I genuinely don't know but I do believe a heaven-sent revival can, and hopefully will, happen again in my lifetime. Meanwhile, I echo Rachel's yearning prayer: 'Give me children [new-born believers], or I'll die!'

Endnotes

1. When Jesus Strides In, the Echoes Sound Out

1 *Jesus Revolution* was distributed by Lionsgate in the USA from 24 February 2023 onwards and in the UK from 23 June 2023 onwards.

2 David Di Sabatino, *The Jesus People Movement: An Annotated Bibliography and General Resource* (Lake Forest, CA: Jester Media, 2004), pp. 4-5.

3 Author interview with Geoff Bone in person on 6.12.13.

4 Kent Allan Philpott, *Awakenings in America and the Jesus People Movement* (San Rafael, CA: Earthen Vessel Publishing, 2011), p. 120.

5 Greg Laurie, Ellen Vaughn, *Jesus Revolution: How God Transformed an Unlikely Generation and How He Can Do It Again Today* (Grand Rapids, MI: Baker Books, 2018), pp. 23-24.

6 Geoffrey Corry, *Jesus Bubble or Jesus Revolution: The Growth of Jesus Communes in Britain and Ireland* (London: The British Council of Churches Youth Department, 1973). Corry was field officer for the British Council of Churches' youth department, and his published booklet was an interim report for the 62nd meeting of the British Council of Churches.

7 Larry Eskridge, *God's Forever Family: The Jesus People Movement in America* (Oxford: Oxford University Press, 2013), pp. 5 and 7.

8 Kevin John Smith, *The Origins, Nature, and Significance of the Jesus Movement* (Lexington, KY: Emeth Press, 2011), p. 29.

2. This is Your Life, but Not on Television

1 D.E. Hoyt and Friends, *Stop! Hey, What's That Sound?: The 1960's Revolution and Birth of the Jesus People* (Albuquerque, NM: Psalm Press, 2019), pp. 395-398. Reproduced and abridged by kind, written permission of the author, Dave Hoyt.

2 Reproduced by kind, written permission of Sue Palosaari and the *Lonesome Stone* team, and adapted from 'Goin' Back' as originally written by Carole King and Gerry Goffin.

3 Revised Standard Version.

4 Now called Agape UK.

5 Now called London School of Theology.

6 Eskridge, *God's Forever Family: The Jesus People Movement in America*, p. 15.

7 Di Sabatino, *The Jesus People Movement: An Annotated Bibliography and Resource Guide*, p. 10.

8 Di Sabatino, *The Jesus People Movement: An Annotated Bibliography and Resource Guide*, p. 12.

9 Hal Lindsey, Carole C. Carlson, *The Late Great Planet Earth* (Grand Rapids, MI: Zondervan, 1970).

10 Donald E. Miller, *Reinventing American Protestantism: Christianity in the New Millennium* (London: University of California Press, 1997), pp. 1-2.

11 Richard Enroth, 'Where Have All The Jesus People Gone?', *Eternity*, October 1973, pp. 14-17, 28.

12 Di Sabatino, *The Jesus People Movement: An Annotated Bibliography and Resource Guide*, p. 16.

3. The Jesus People Make Their Colourful Marks in Life

1 Arthur Blessitt, Walter Wagner, *Turned on to Jesus* (London: Word Books, 1971).

2 Eskridge, *God's Forever Family: The Jesus People Movement in America*, p. 31, quoting Steve Heefner.

3 Pastor Steve Carr, 'The Jesus Movement and the House Ministries', www.youtube.com (accessed 23.4.23). Reproduced by kind, written permission of the producer, Steve Carr.

4 Hal Lindsey, Carole C. Carlson, *The Late Great Planet Earth* (Grand Rapids, MI: Zondervan, 1970).

5 The 'thousand years' highlighted in Revelation 20:2,3,4,5,7.

6 Views known as Postmillennialism and Amillennialism respectively.

7 Arthur Blessitt, *Arthur Blessitt's Street University: Communicating Your Faith With Confidence* (Nashville, TN: Vision House, 1978).

8 In the UK the Twelve Tribes are based near Honiton, Devon.

9 Acts 17:16-34, especially vv.18 & 28.

4. Welcome to the Swinging Sixties or the Permissive Society

1 David Hilborn, Matt Bird, eds, *God and the Generations: Youth, Age and the Church Today* (Carlisle: Cumbria, Paternoster Press 2002), p. 40.

2 David Pott, 'The Drifting Generation', *Crusade*, March 1967, pp. 16-18, 27-28, quoted from Hilborn, Bird, eds, *God and the Generations: Youth, Age and the Church Today*, p. 2.

3 Maureen Cleave, *London Evening Standard*, 4 March 1966, quoted from Dominic Sandbrook, *White Heat: A History of Britain in the Swinging Sixties* (London: Abacus, 2006), p. 225.

4 The inexpensive shop F. W. Woolworth and Sons Ltd, now no longer in existence.

5 Dominic Sandbrook, *White Heat: A History of Britain in the Swinging Sixties* (London: Abacus, 2006), p. 437.

6 John A.T. Robinson, *Honest to God* (London: SCM Press,1963).

7 Often termed the 'Age of Aquarius', calculated according to the changes of the heavenly constellations.

8 The hotel mysteriously burnt down in 1971.

9 The postmodern theory often termed Deconstructionism.

10 Charles Dickens, *A Tale of Two Cities* (London: Penguin Classics, 2012), p. 1.

11 John 4:25-26, 21 & 23, 42 respectively.

12 Optional locations were Mount Zion in Jerusalem for strict Jews and Mount Gerizim in Samaria for the woman and her fellow mixed-race Samaritans.

5. Liberation is Front and Centre of This Jesus Community

1 Author interview with Joe Barnes by email on 7.8.22.

2 Geoff Bone, 'Liberation Communication', *Buzz*, May 1974, p. 6.

3 Author interview with Richard Hogarth by email on 14.10.21.

4 Author interview with Geoff Bone in person on 6.12.13.

5 Author interview with Geoff Bone in person on 6.12.13.

6 Author interview with Geoff Bone in person on 6.12.13.

7 Author interview with Geoff Bone in person on 6.12.13.

8 Roger Curl, *Three Christian Communities: A Sociological Study* (Hertford College, Oxford: PhD thesis, 1976), p. 25.

9 Curl, *Three Christian Communities: A Sociological Study*, p. 25.

10 Michael Jacob, *Pop Goes Jesus: An investigation of pop religion in Britain and America* (London: Mowbrays, 1972) p. 82.

11 Author interview with Geoff Bone in person on 6.12.13.

12 Author interview with Richard Hogarth by email on 14.10.21.

13 Author interview with Geoff Bone in person on 6.12.13.

14 Author interview with Geoff Bone in person on 6.12.13.

15 Geoff Bone, 'Liberation Communication', *Buzz*, May 1974, p. 6.

16 This is sometimes termed 'Contextualisation' by missiologists.

17 Curl, *Three Christian Communities: A Sociological Study*, p. 25.

18 The Boxalls also got divorced at one stage. In the Bones' case, their marital difficulties were exacerbated by Geoff's accident.

6. Meet the Army Marching on its Spiritual Stomach

1 David Wilkerson, John and Elizabeth Sherrill, *The Cross and the Switchblade* (Lakeland: London, 1967).

2 George G. Chryssides, *Exploring New Religions* (London: Continuum, 1999/2001), p. 151.

3 Simon Cooper, Mike Farrant, *Fire in Our Hearts: the story of the Jesus Fellowship/ Jesus Army*, (Northampton: Multiply Publications, 1991), pp. 86, 89.

4 Matthew 5:14.

5 The Jesus Fellowship Community Trust, 'Jesus Fellowship Redress Scheme', www.jesus.org.uk (accessed 23.3.23).

6 Cooper, Farrant, *Fire in Our Hearts: the story of the Jesus Fellowship/Jesus Army*, p. 50.

7 Cooper, Farrant, *Fire in Our Hearts: the story of the Jesus Fellowship/Jesus Army*, p. 287.

8 Noel Stanton, 'The Jesus Movement takes off', *Jesus Life*, No. 39, First Quarter 1997, p. 3.

9 Nicky Cruz, Jamie Buckingham, *Run Baby Run* (London: Hodder & Stoughton, 2003 Reprint edition).

10 Arthur Blessitt, Walter Wagner, *Turned on to Jesus* (London: Word Books, 1971).

11 Stephen Hunt, 'The Radical Kingdom of the Jesus Fellowship', *Pneuma*, Vol. 20, No.1, Spring 1998, p. 22.

12 Lamb were related to, but not part of, the Jews for Jesus ministry.

13 Cooper, Farrant, *Fire in Our Hearts: the story of the Jesus Fellowship/Jesus Army,* p. 65.

14 William Kay, *Apostolic Networks in Britain: New Ways of Being Church* (Milton Keynes: Paternoster, 2007), p. 152.

7. Throw This Frisbee and He Will Fly Back Quickly

1 Eskridge, *God's Forever Family: The Jesus People Movement in America,* p. 33.

2 David Di Sabatino, *The Life and Death of a Hippie Preacher* DVD (Lake Forest, CA: Jester Media, 2006). Words transcribed from this DVD.

3 *Jesus Revolution* was distributed by Lionsgate in the USA from 24 February 2023 onwards and in the UK from 23 June 2023 onwards.

4 Di Sabatino, *The Jesus People Movement: An Annotated Bibliography and General Resource,* p. 208, n. 14.

5 Lonnie Frisbee, Roger Sachs, *Not by Might, Nor by Power: The Great Commission* (Santa Maria, CA: Freedom Publications, 2016), pp. 4-5.

6 Bill Jackson, *The Quest for the Radical Middle: A History of the Vineyard* (Cape Town, South Africa: Vineyard International Publishing, 1999), p. 74.

7 Kevin Springer, *Power Encounters* (New York, NY: Harper & Row, 1988), p. 12.

8 Carol Wimber, *John Wimber: The Way it Was* (London: Hodder & Stoughton, 1999), p. 162.

9 David Pytches, *Living at the Edge: Recollections and Reflections of a Lifetime* (Bath: Arcadia, 2002), p. 256.

10 Douglas McBain, *Fire Over the Waters* (London: Darton, Longman and Todd, 1997), p. 94.

11 Nigel Wright, 'Weighing up Wimber', *Renewal,* 152, January 1989, p. 22.

12 Frisbee, Sachs, *Not by Might, Nor by Power: The Great Commission,* p. 196.

13 Andrew Atherstone, *Repackaging Christianity: Alpha and the building of a global brand* (London: Hodder & Stoughton, 2022), p. 35.

14 Lonnie Frisbee, Roger Sachs, *Not by Might, Nor by Power: The Jesus Revolution* (Santa Maria, CA: Freedom Publications, 2012), p. 16.

15 Lonnie Frisbee, Roger Sachs, *Not by Might, Nor by Power: Set Free* (Santa Maria, CA: Freedom Publications, 2019), p. 117.

16 Nigel G. Wright, 'The Kansas City prophets: an assessment', *Themelios,* vol. 17, issue 1.

17 Frisbee, Sachs, *Not by Might, Nor by Power: Set Free,* p. 78.

18 David Pytches, ed., *John Wimber: His Influence and Legacy* (Guildford: Eagle, 1998), p. 254.

19 Brett McCracken, *Hipster Christianity: When Church and Cool Collide* (Grand Rapids, MI: Baker Books, 2010), pp. 80-81.

8. Blessitt as He Carries the Cross Through Your Town

1 Eskridge, *God's Forever Family: The Jesus People Movement in America*, p. 56.

2 Edward E. Plowman, *The Jesus Movement* (London: Hodder & Stoughton, 1971), p. 46.

3 Blessitt, Wagner, *Turned on to Jesus*, p. 110.

4 This term is hip-speak for amphetamines.

5 Di Sabatino, *The Jesus People Movement: An Annotated Bibliography and Resource Guide*, p. 79, quoted in Smith, *The Origins, Nature, and Significance of the Jesus Movement*, p. 81.

6 Eskridge, *God's Forever Family: The Jesus People Movement in America*, p. 57.

7 Di Sabatino, *The Jesus People Movement: An Annotated Bibliography and Resource Guide*, p. 10.

8 Apparently, Arthur Blessitt also featured in an article entitled 'The Ultimate Trip' in *The Listener* of 5th August 1971, pp. 171-172, where BBC reporter Dennis Tuohy reflects on his evangelistic wanderings across the USA: quoted from Tony Jasper, *Jesus in a Pop Culture* (Glasgow: Collins/Fontana Books, 1975), p. 97. Tuohy concluded that 'Christianity, which for so long has been identified with conformity and the American Dream, is now being flourished as a revolutionary weapon', quoted from Di Sabatino, *The Jesus People Movement: An Annotated Bibliography and Resource Guide*, p. 66.

9 Arthur Blessitt, *Arthur, A Pilgrim* (Hollywood, CA: Blessitt Publishing, 1985), p. 302.

10 Jacob, *Pop Goes Jesus*, p. 30.

11 Blessitt, *Arthur, A Pilgrim*, p. 305.

12 An artificial slope, created by dumping one and a half million cartloads of earth excavated from Edinburgh's New Town into what was previously Nor Loch (now Princes Street).

13 Ian had previously heard Arthur preach in the USA.

14 Revd Duncan christened me as a baby on 26 July 1953 at Christ Church, Cockfosters.

15 Author interview with Ray Husthwaite by email on 22.12.17.

16 Jacob, *Pop Goes Jesus*, pp. 30 & 33. His evidence for the latter critique is simply that it is a well-known evangelist's practice, and that on the occasions observed, 'All the supplicants seemed to know all of the words.' It is, however, unverified.

17 Blessitt, *Arthur, A Pilgrim*, p. 304.

18 Plowman, *The Jesus Movement*, p. 48.

19 Smith, *The Origins, Nature, and Significance of the Jesus Movement*, p. 86.

20 I am sure this is the tip of the iceberg and that there were many more.

21 Jim King's Gospel Vision website is: www.gospelvision.co.uk. See Chapter 24 for the fuller story of Calvary Chapel.

22 The Heralds Trust website is: www.theheraldstrust.org.

23 Corry, *Jesus Bubble or Jesus Revolution: The Growth of Jesus Communes in Britain and Ireland*, p. 16.

9. A Festival Hits the Capital Before Going Nationwide

1 Celia Bowring, *TURNING THE TIDE? Impacting Culture for Christ* (London: CARE, 2021), p. 10.

2 Highlighted more fully in Chapter 7.

3 John Capon, *...and there was light: story of the nationwide festival of light* (Guildford: Lutterworth Press, 1972), p. 63.

4 In total, thirteen *Kids' Praise!* albums featuring Psalty were released on Maranatha! Music between 1980-91.

5 Author interview with Chuck and Carol Butler by Zoom on 7.7.21.

6 'Two Roads' by Country Faith. Reproduced by kind, written permission of the lyric-writer and band member Chuck Butler. This song appeared on the first Maranatha! Music album, a compilation album called, *The Everlastin' Living Jesus Music Concert* of 1971.

7 Flo Dobbie, *Land Aflame!* (London: Hodder & Stoughton, 1972), pp. 53-54.

8 CARE, 'Our Story So Far', www.youtube.com (accessed 2.5.23). Reproduced by kind, written permission of Celia Bowring.

9 Capon, *...and there was light: story of the nationwide festival of light*, p. 83.

10 Dobbie, *Land Aflame!*, p. 123.

11 Capon, *...and there was light: story of the nationwide festival of light*, p. 83.

12 Blessitt, *Arthur, A Pilgrim*, pp. 303-304.

13 Peter Ward, *Growing Up Evangelical: Youthwork and the Making of a Subculture* (Eugene, OR: Wipf and Stock Publishers, 1996), p. 87.

14 Corry, *Jesus bubble or Jesus revolution: The growth of Jesus Communes in Britain and Ireland,* p.13.

15 Author interview with Lyndon Bowring in person on 17.2.16.

16 Peter Meadows, 'A new charge from the Light brigade', *Buzz*, March 1972, p. 9.

17 Bowring, *TURNING THE TIDE? Impacting Culture for Christ,* p. 22.

18 The highest position it attained was number 31.

19 Peter Meadows, 'Why should the devil have all the good music?', *Buzz*, September 1973, p. 19.

20 The other two declarations were addressed to the media and the churches respectively. See John Capon, *…and there was light: story of the nationwide festival of light,* pp. 76-79.

21 Author interview with Nick Cuthbert by Skype on 21.2.20.

22 Peter Meadows, 'A packed Trafalgar Square', *Buzz*, April 1975, pp. 5-6.

10. Turned Onto Jesus But Turned Off the Bad Trip

1 Editor, Advert, *Renewal,* December 1971/January 1972, p. 23.

2 Vic Ramsey, *They Call it a Fix* (England: New Life Press, 1966), p. 19.

3 Ramsey, *They Call it a Fix.*

4 Tony Jasper, *Jesus in a Pop Culture* (Glasgow: Collins/Fontana Books, 1975), pp. 131-132.

5 Editor, Advert, *Renewal,* December 1971/January 1972, p. 23.

6 Jacob, *Pop Goes Jesus*, p. 82.

7 Editor, Advert, *Buzz,* August 1972, p. 1.

8 Floyd McClung, *Living on the Devil's Doorstep: From Kabul to Amsterdam* (Seattle, WA: YWAM Publishing, 1988).

9 McClung, *Living on the Devil's Doorstep: From Kabul to Amsterdam*, p. 17.

10 McClung, *Living on the Devil's Doorstep: From Kabul to Amsterdam*, p. 73.

11 McClung, *Living on the Devil's Doorstep: From Kabul to Amsterdam*, p. 73.

12 McClung, *Living on the Devil's Doorstep: From Kabul to Amsterdam*, p. 97.

13 Bob Owen, *To Munich with Love* (Chino, CA: Chick Publications, 1972), p. 106.

14 Richard Bustraan, *The Jesus People Movement: A Story of Spiritual Revolution*

among the Hippies (Eugene, OR: Pickwick Publications/Wipf and Stock, 2014), p. 52-53.

15 David Wilkerson, *The Cross and the Switchblade* (London: Lakeland, 1967)

16 Eskridge, *God's Forever Family: The Jesus People Movement in America*, pp. 44-46.

17 Andrew MacDonald, Ed Stetzer, 'The Lasting Legacy of the Jesus People', *Talbot Magazine*, 17 June 2020, p. 7. ('Ablaze' conference for Biola University on 7-9 October 2021).

18 David Wilkerson, *Purple Violet Squish* (Grand Rapids MI: Zondervan Publishing House, 1969).

19 Di Sabatino, *The Jesus People Movement: An Annotated Bibliography and General Resource*, p. 70.

20 Di Sabatino, *The Jesus People Movement: An Annotated Bibliography and General Resource*, p. 70.

21 Bustraan, *The Jesus People Movement: A Story of Spiritual Revolution among the Hippies*, pp. 91-92.

22 David Coomes, *Spre-e '73* (London: Coverdale House Publishers, 1973), p. 51.

23 Frank Wilson, *Counselling the Drug Abuser* (London: Lakeland, Marshall, Morgan & Scott, 1973), and Frank Wilson, *House of New Beginnings* (London: Lakeland, Marshall Morgan & Scott, 1977).

24 Peter Meadows, 'Drug-help centre needs help', *Buzz*, February 1974, p. 9.

25 Kenneth Leech, *Youthquake: The growth of a counter-culture through two decades* (London: Sheldon Press, 1973), p. 161. This extract is from the Trust's *Newscope* newsletter of February 1973, quoted from Leech, p. 228, n. 51.

26 Author interview with Pat Prosser by telephone on 9.8.22.

27 Ron Norman, *No Time to Weep: From Despair to Hope... Addiction to Freedom...* (High Wycombe: MPS Publications, 1989/1994 Revised & Reprinted edition).

11. Norman is as Happy as Larry on the Road

1 David W. Stowe, *No Sympathy for the Devil* (Chapel Hill, NC: University of North Carolina Press, 2011), p. 36.

2 Eskridge, *God's Forever Family: The Jesus People Movement in America*, p. 226.

3 The friends first met on 6 April 1969. 'Norman's Kitchen' is Randy's song that

appeared on his *Born Twice* album, released by Larry's One Way Records in 1971.

4 23 February 1971.

5 Smith, *The Origins, Nature, and Significance of the Jesus Movement*, p. 78, quoted from CCM journalist Steve Rabey as noted on pp. 480-481 under Rabey.

6 Gregory Alan Thornbury, *Why Should the Devil Have All the Good Music? Larry Norman and the Perils of Christian Rock* (New York, NY: Convergent Books, 2018), p. 83.

7 Recorded on his *Stranded in Babylon* album of 1991.

8 One half of the satirical duo Peter Cook and Dudley Moore, popularly called Pete (the deadpan one) and Dud (the buffoon).

9 This performance appeared on the BBC 1 *Greenbelt Live* programme the following year.

10 Allen James Flemming, *Rebel Poet* (USA: Amazon, 2023), p. 196.

11 Thornbury, *Why Should the Devil Have All the Good Music? Larry Norman and the Perils of Christian Rock*, p. 101.

12 Author interview with Ralph Turner by Facebook on 12.5.20.

13 Author interview with Charlie Campbell-Wynter by email on 26.7.20.

14 Mike Rimmer, 'A Legend Quizzed', 27 August 2005. www.crossrhythms. co.uk (accessed 25.7.23). Reproduced by kind, written permission of the CEO Jonathan Bellamy.

15 Marc Allan Powell, *Encyclopedia of Contemporary Christian Music* (Peabody, MA: Hendrickson Publishers, 2002), p. 641, for an alternative explanation.

16 Martin Wroe, 'A Jesus Rock Legend', *Buzz*, September 1984, pages unknown.

17 Les Moir, *Missing Jewel: The Worship Movement That Impacted the Nations* (Eastbourne: David C Cook, 2017), p. 50.

18 Author interview with Rupert Loydell by email on 9.6.20.

19 James Tweed, 'Larry Norman Speaks His Mind', *Christianity*, 2005, pages unknown. www.larrynorman.uk.com (accessed 15.11.15). Reproduced by kind, written permission of the editor, Sam Hailes.

20 Powell, *Encyclopedia of Contemporary Christian Music*, p. 641.

21 The trilogy of albums are as follows: *Only Visiting This Planet* (1972); *So Long Ago the Garden* (1973); and *In Another Land* (1976).

22 Derived from Revelation 13:18.

23 Di Sabatino, *The Jesus People Movement: An Annotated Bibliography and*

General Resource, p. 40, quoted from Michael Jacob, 'Flirting With Pop', *Frontier*, Vol. 17, 1974, pp. 112-115.

24 Author interview with Peter Field by email on 6.8.20.

12. Bow to the Monarch Who United the Kingdom

1 Author interview with Gerard Kelly by email on 11.7.23.

2 Author interviews with Edmund Tustian in person on 4.8.18 and by email on 11.11.20.

3 This is hip-speak for sleeping for the night.

4 Lois Cuthbert, *Sunshine and Shadows* (England: Amazon, 2020), p.102.

5 A mid-60s term, popularised by Mary Quant, speaking of huge cultural changes in fashion and music.

6 Author interview with Nick Cuthbert by Skype on 21.1.20. The following quotations are from this interview, unless indicated otherwise in notes 7-11.

7 Cuthbert, *Sunshine and Shadows,* p.101.

8 Cuthbert, *Sunshine and Shadows,* p.101.

9 Lois was later succeeded by Bob Lloyd.

10 Cuthbert, *Sunshine and Shadows,* p.104.

11 Lois Cuthbert, *Sunshine and Shadows* (England: Amazon, 2020).

12 Author interviews with Andy Scarcliffe by email on 17.6.19 and by Zoom on 9.5.23.

13 One of Arthur's rallies was in the prestigious music venue, Green's Playhouse, before it closed in June 1973.

14 Author interviews with James Givan by email on 26.2.22 and 17.5.23.

15 Author interviews with Andy Scarcliffe by email on 17.6.19 and by Zoom on 9.5.23.

16 Author interview with Hilda Orr by telephone on 5.5.20. For additional information, I received Chris Orr's self-published story, as highlighted in n. 19 below.

17 Luke 9:62.

18 These were published letters written by David 'Moses' Berg ('Mo' for 'Moses'), intended to be read by disciples alongside, and later in place of, the Bible.

19 Chris Orr, *The Ridiculous Life of Chris Orr* (Ireland: Self-published, undated), p. 83. Received from Chris Orr on 12.5.20.

20 Orr, *The Ridiculous Life of Chris Orr*, p. 85

21 Author interviews with Arfon Wyn by email between 23.5.23 and 4.6.23.

13. God Doesn't Lead His Children Down Blind Alleys

1 Their biblical Children of God names were: 'Deborah', 'Aaron', 'Hosea', and 'Faith', respectively.

2 Deborah Davis, Bill Davis, *The Children of God: The Inside Story* (Basingstoke: Marshall Morgan & Scott, 1985), p. 46.

3 Exodus 34:28.

4 Leech, *YOUTHQUAKE: The growth of a counter-culture through two decades*, p. 155, quoted from the *London Evening News* of 7 September 1971 as noted on p. 227 n. 19.

5 Stephen J. Hunt, *A History of the Charismatic Movement in Britain and the United States of America – Book 1: The Pentecostal Transformation of Christianity* (Lampeter: The Edwin Mellen Press, 2009), p. 320.

6 Peter Meadows, 'The Children of God: A New Sect in the Making', *Buzz*, November 1973, p. 15. 'Mo' was the shortened version of 'Moses', later used in his supposed revelations in his *Mo Letters*.

7 J. Edwin Meyer, 'The Jesus People and the Churches', *Renewal*, December 1971/January 1972, pp. 2-8.

8 His real name is Von Driggs.

9 Meyer, 'The Jesus People and the Churches', p. 8.

10 Michael Harper, 'The Jesus People and the Churches', *Renewal*, December 1971/January 1972, pp. 38-39.

11 Harper, 'The Jesus People and the Churches', p. 39.

12 David Hoyt, 'STATEMENT – David Hoyt November 23, 1972': In this document, in my possession, Hoyt openly and repentantly confessed his sorrow about being involved with the COG between May 1971 and June 1972.

13 *Mo Letters* were new 'revelations' from David 'Moses' Berg, initially published to supplement reading the Bible, but which, later, overtook the Bible in importance for the COG.

14 Hoyt and Friends, *Stop! Hey, What's That Sound? The 1960's Revolution and Birth of the Jesus People*, p. 309.

15 An 'Emergency Notice' *Mo Letter* of 12 June 1972, entitled, 'Beelzebub Lord of the Flies'.

16 A historic umbrella body for Bible-believing Christians and churches in the UK.

17 Corry, *Jesus Bubble or Jesus Revolution: The Growth of Jesus Communes in Britain and Ireland*, p. 25.

18 Tony Jasper, *Jesus in a Pop Culture*, p. 97. Previously, BBC Radio One had featured the COG positively on *Speak-Easy* (an hour-long young people's uninhibited discussion programme, interspersed with music, which ran from 1969-1973) and BBC2 television on *Late Night Line Up* (a discussion programme which ran from 1964-1972).

19 Trevor Aspinall, 'The Shocking Truth About the Children of God', *Sunday People*, 24 September 1972, pp. 2-3.

20 Trevor Aspinall, 'The Moment This Girl Was Lured from Her Family', *Sunday People*, 1 October 1972, p. 5.

21 BBC Sounds *Afterlives*: An Overtone production for Radio 4 released on 9 June 2020. www.bbc.com (accessed on 6.6.23).

22 Jacob, *Pop Goes Jesus*, p. 23.

23 Peter Meadows, 'The Children of God: A New Sect in the Making', *Buzz*, November 1973, p. 17.

24 Larry Eskridge, *God's Forever Family: the Jesus People Movement in America*, p. 205.

25 Hebrews 3:3. See also the overshadowing of Moses by Jesus on the mount of transfiguration in Matthew 17:1-13, especially v.5-8.

26 David Breese, *The Marks of a Cult: The Warning Signs of False Teachings* (Eugene, OR: Harvest House Publishers, 1998)

27 Breese, *The Marks of a Cult: The Warning Signs of False Teachings*, pp. 5-6.

14. Experience a Good Spree with Little Retail Therapy

1 Coomes, *Spre-e 73*, p. 10.

2 Peter Meadows, 'SPREE '73', *Buzz*, December 1972, p. 15.

3 Acts 2:13 & 15.

4 Chuck Girard, *Rock & Roll Preacher: From Doo-Wop to Jesus Rock* (USA: World Wide Publishing Group, 2021), p. 199.

5 Girard, *Rock & Roll Preacher: From Doo-Wop to Jesus Rock*, p. 200.

6 Thornbury, *Why Should the Devil Have All the Good Music? Larry Norman and the Perils of Christian Rock*, p. 75.

7 Di Sabatino, *The Jesus People Movement: An Annotated Bibliography and General Resource*, p. 15.

8 Coomes, *Spr-ee 73*, p. 19.

9 Peter Meadows, 'Tell me the old, old story', *Buzz*, January 1973, p. 7.

10 Peter Meadows, 'Spree bounces back', *Buzz*, February 1973, p. 8.

11 Tony Stone, 'Pastor's-eye-view', *Buzz*, March 1973, p. 27.

12 Peter Meadows, 'Why we kept mum', *Buzz*, June 1973, p. 18.

13 Peter Meadows, 'All set for blast-off', *Buzz*, August 1973, p. 9.

14 Watergate: The Democratic Party headquarters were burgled on 17 June 1972, leading to a train of events that revealed President Nixon's cover-up of his illegal misdemeanours, finally leading to his resignation on 9 August 1974.

15 Coomes, *Spre-e 73*, p. 88.

16 Coomes, *Spre-e 73*, respective pages: p. 11; p. 31; pp. 52-3; pp. 72 & 75; pp. 76-77; pp. 89-90.

17 Coomes, *Spre-e 73*, p. 74.

18 Coomes, *Spre-e 73*, pp. 53-54.

19 Coomes, *Spre-e 73*, p. 64.

20 Tony Jasper, *Jesus in a Pop Culture*, p. 94.

21 Ward, *Growing Up Evangelical: Youthwork and the Making of a Subculture*, p. 95.

22 Tony Jasper, *Jesus and the Christian in a Pop Culture* (London: Robert Royce, 1984), p. 134. c.f. Steve Turner, 'The new mindless Christians', *New Musical Express*, 22 September 1973, p. 65, on the cult of personality.

15. If it is Too Hot in the Kitchen, Don't Get Out

1 Sir Richard Hamilton Anstruther-Gough-Calthorpe.

2 Properly known as a fess ermine.

3 Author interview with Gordon Scutt by telephone on 23.4.16 and 20.10.20, and by email on 26.1.21 and 6.5.23.

4 Phil Lawson Johnston, *The Song of the Father's Heart* (Bradford on Avon: Terra Nova Publications, 2004), p. 23.

5 Lawson Johnston, *The Song of the Father's Heart*, p. 24.

6 Lawson Johnston, *The Song of the Father's Heart*, p. 25.

7 Quoted from Phil's 1971 song 'I Am the Vagabond'.

8 Atherstone, *Repackaging Christianity: Alpha and the Building of a Global Brand*, p. 7.

9 Lawson Johnston, *The Song of the Father's Heart*, p. 29: The seven friends comprised: Mark Brooke, Mickey Calthorpe, Mindy Dewar, Sarah Dulley, Phil Lawson Johnston, Annie Rice, Ann Sargent.

10 Lawson Johnston, *The Song of the Father's Heart*, p. 29.

11 Author interview with Chuck and Carol Butler by Zoom on 7.7.21.

12 Author interview with Phil Lawson Johnston by email on 19.4.23 c.f. Atherstone, *Repackaging Christianity: Alpha and the Building of a Global Brand*, p. 8.

13 2 Chronicles 5:12-14.

14 Atherstone, *Repackaging Christianity: Alpha and the Building of a Global Brand*, p. 15.

15 Atherstone, *Repackaging Christianity: Alpha and the Building of a Global Brand*, p. 15.

16 Atherstone, *Repackaging Christianity: Alpha and the Building of a Global Brand*, p. 18.

17 Atherstone, *Repackaging Christianity: Alpha and the Building of a Global Brand*, p. 10.

18 Author interview with Sandy Millar by telephone on 1.9.20.

19 Author interview with Phil Lawson Johnston by email on 19.4.23.

20 Atherstone, *Repackaging Christianity: Alpha and the Building of a Global Brand*, p. 8.

21 Author interview with Ed Pruen by email on 19.4.23.

22 James Atlee, 'Phil Lawson Johnston: One time worship man with Cloud, now solo', www.crossrhythms.co.uk (accessed 19.4.23). Reproduced by kind, written permission of the CEO Jonathan Bellamy.

16. The Extended Family Whose Door is Always Open

1 Sue Palosaari, ed., 'How We Got from There to Here', *Everyman*, Vol. 3, p. 23. Ticket reproduced.

2 Essentially, in American Christian history, a series of evangelistic meetings aimed at reaching unchurched people for Jesus.

3 Sue Palosaari, ed., 'Leaving the Good Life Behind', *Everyman*, Vol. 3, p. 21. Ticket reproduced.

4 Hoyt and Friends, *Stop! Hey, What's That Sound? The 1960's Revolution and Birth of the Jesus People*, p. 347.

5 Russell played a significant part in Jim and Sue's earlier conversion story, as recalled previously in this chapter.

6 Eskridge, *God's Forever Family: The Jesus People Movement in America*, p. 202.

7 Ward, *Growing Up Evangelical: Youthwork and the Making of a Subculture*, p. 97.

8 Author interview with Ray Harris by email on 16.11.16.

9 Author interview with Jacky Hughes by telephone on 17.5.22.

10 Hoyt and Friends, *Stop! Hey, What's That Sound? The 1960's Revolution and Birth of the Jesus People*, p. 492.

11 Margaret subsequently married team member Danny Keating but, after being widowed, later married Phil Talbot.

12 A British TV comedy programme of the day that ran from 1969-1973.

13 Sue Palosaari, ed., 'Scotland Yard Busts the Bus', *Everyman*, Vol. 3, pp. 28-29.

14 Sue Palosaari, ed., 'On the Streets of Soho', *Everyman*, Vol. 2, p. 17.

15 Jim and Sue eventually divorced in 1992.

16 Curl, *Three Christian Communities: A Sociological Study*, p. 75.

17 Corry, *Jesus Bubble or Jesus Revolution: The Growth of Jesus Communes in Britain and Ireland*, p. 28.

18 Stephen Annett, ed., *The Many Ways of Being: A Guide to Spiritual Groups and Growth Centres in Britain* (London: Abacus, 1976), p. 16.

19 Acts 9:2 & 19: 9, 23.

17. God Has a Squad That Motors at Full Throttle

1 John's full name was Kevin John Smith, the name he specifically used as the author of his published PhD thesis, *The Origins, Nature, and Significance of the Jesus Movement*.

2 John Smith, *On the Side of the Angels* (Australia: Strand Publishing, 2015 New, revised edition), p. 135.

3 Smith, *The Origins, Nature, and Significance of the Jesus Movement*, p. 400.

4 John was also widely known as 'Bullfrog'.

5 Smith, *The Origins, Nature, and Significance of the Jesus Movement*, p. 400.

6 Smith, *On the Side of the Angels*, New, revised edition, p. 169.

7 God's Squad, *God's Squad, The First 50 Years* (Australia: God's Squad CMC International, 2022), p. 43.

8 Eskridge, *God's Forever Family: The Jesus People Movement in America*, p. 245,

quoting Smith. John Smith also visited Calvary Chapel as recorded in Eskridge p. 246.

9 Smith, *On the Side of the Angels*, New, revised edition, p. 229.

10 Hoyt and Friends, *Stop! Hey, What's That Sound? The 1960's Revolution and Birth of the Jesus People*, pp. 606-609.

11 God's Squad, *God's Squad, The First 50 Years*, p. 138.

12 This group is still in existence today.

13 God's Squad, *God's Squad, The First 50 Years*, p. 138.

14 'God's Squad, CMC History', www.uk.gscmc.com (accessed on 26.7.23). Reproduced by kind, written permission of Sean Stillman.

15 Sean Stillman, *God's Biker: Motorcycles and Misfit* (London: SPCK, 2020).

16 The original UK God's Squad started life in 1995. However, following re-structuring, the three current chapters were established in December 2010, December 2010, and May 2014 respectively.

17 Smith, *The Origins, Nature, and Significance of the Jesus Movement*, p. 29.

18 Smith, *On the Side of the Angels*, New, revised edition, pp. 173-175.

19 Real name Chris Matthews.

20 Luke 19:1-10.

21 Stillman, *God's Biker: Motorcycles and Misfit*, p. 105.

22 Stillman, *God's Biker: Motorcycles and Misfit*, pp. 5-11.

23 God's Squad, *God's Squad, The First 50 Years* (Australia: God's Squad CMC International, 2022). Available to buy from www.godssquad50.com.

24 Galatians 2:7-8.

25 David Adams, 'Christ at the centre: Australian preacher John Smith's "extraordinary" life', *Sight*, 14 March 2019, www.sightmagazine.com.au (accessed on 2.9.22). Reproduced by kind, written permission of the Editor, David Adams.

18. Make Way for the Two Troubadour Worship Leaders

1 Powell, *Encyclopedia of Contemporary Christian Music*, p. 484.

2 Andrew Walker, *Restoring the Kingdom: The Radical Christianity of the House Church Movement* (Guildford: Eagle, 1998), p. 309.

3 Ward, *Growing Up Evangelical: Youthwork and the Making of a Subculture*, p. 133.

4 Walker, *Restoring the Kingdom: The Radical Christianity of the House Church Movement*, p. 363.

5 www.grahamkendrick.co.uk 'Biography' (accessed on 17.4.23). Reproduced by kind, written permission of the author, Graham Kendrick.

6 Powell, *Encyclopedia of Contemporary Christian Music,* p. 483.

7 Author interviews by Zoom with Graham Kendrick on 1.7.20 and Simon Dennis on 31.7.20 as the source of all the following quotations.

8 The expectation that Jesus will secretly lift believers up from planet Earth before 'the great tribulation' of Revelation 7:14.

9 Kendrick subsequently made many trips to the USA for worship conferences: sometimes teaching, other times serving in the publishing sphere.

10 Author interview with Dave Bilbrough by Zoom on 27.8.20 as the source of all the following quotations in this chapter, except when noted otherwise.

11 www.davebilbrough.com 'About' (accessed on 17.4.23). Reproduced by kind, written permission of the author, Dave Bilbrough.

12 According to Dave, this event was probably on 5 January 1975, but may have been even earlier.

13 This TV programme is undocumented today.

14 Moir, *Missing Jewel: The Worship Movement that Impacted Nations,* p. 66.

15 www.grahamkendrick.co.uk 'Biography' (accessed on 17.4.23). Reproduced by kind, written permission of the author, Graham Kendrick.

16 www.davebilbrough.bandcamp.com (accessed on 17.4.23). Reproduced by kind, written permission of the author, Dave Bilbrough.

17 www.davebilbrough.com 'About' (accessed on 17.4.23). Reproduced by kind, written permission of the author, Dave Bilbrough.

19. The Rolling Stone That Gathered a Lot of Moss

1 Nigel Nelson, 'The rolling stones: Jesus Freaks Put on a Show for Medway', *Evening Post,* 11 June 1973, p. 10.

2 Hoyt and Friends, *Stop! Hey, What's That Sound? The 1960's Revolution and Birth of the Jesus People,* p. 371.

3 Unidentified press report on file, 'Rock Show Orgies but No Nudes.'

4 Then known as William N. Smith.

5 Now called the O2 Academy Brixton.

6 Sue Palosaari, ed., 'Lonesome Stone', *Everyman,* Vol. 1, No. 2, p. 30.

7 Peter Oakes, 'The Cast With an Amazing Past', *Sunday People,* 15 July 1973, p. 10.

8 Author interview with Bill Smith by email on 4.6.22.

9 Peter Oakes, 'The Cast With an Amazing Past', *Sunday People*, 15 July 1973, p. 10.

10 Author interview with Chris Smith by email on 26.6.22.

11 Wythenshawe has a population of 100,000 today.

12 Author interview with Andrew Rushton by email on 17.3.22.

13 Matthew 9:17.

14 12-15 December 1973.

15 Author interview with Norman Amey by email on 27.9.22.

16 15 January 1974 onwards.

17 Author interview with Ant Wren by telephone on 23.10.13.

18 5 February 1974 onwards.

19 Author interview with Max Coates by email on 19.9.16.

20 Author interview with John Tsang by email on 22.4.20. John 3:16 says, 'For God so loved the world that he gave his one and only Son, that whoever believes in him shall not perish but have eternal life.'

21 27 February-15 March 1974.

22 19-23 March 1974.

23 April 1974.

24 6-14 May 1974.

25 Author interview with David Lee by email on 19.6.22.

26 28 May-15 June 1974.

27 Author interview with Colin Marriott by email on 29.9.21.

28 20 June 1974 onwards.

29 Author interview with Christine Lafon (née Ellerton) by email on 15.6.22.

30 24 July-10 August 1974 on publicity, but some people say it was a whole month's run.

31 Author interview with Anna MacDonough by post on 27.7.20.

32 Author interview with Nigel Boney by email on 18.8.22.

20. Jews Given Pole Position in Hearing About Jesus

1 The Hebrew name for Jesus, and the same name as the Old Testament leader Joshua. It means 'Yahweh is salvation'.

2 Kent Philpott, *Memoirs of a Jesus Freak* (San Rafael, CA: Earthen Vessel

Publishing, 2016 2nd Edition), p. 287: quoted from the *Los Angeles Times* of 1985, linked to p. 290 n. 2.

3   Moishe Rosen, *Called to Controversy: The Unlikely Story of Moishe Rosen and the Founding of Jews for Jews* (Nashville, TN: Thomas Nelson, 2012), p. 171.

4   Rosen, *Called to Controversy: The Unlikely Story of Moishe Rosen and the Founding of Jews for Jews*, p. 177.

5   The Hebrew word *Hineni* is usually translated as 'Here I am' in English.

6   Robert S. Elwood, Jr., *ONE WAY: The Jesus Movement and Its Meaning* (Englewood Cliffs, NJ: Prentice-Hall, 1973), p. 58.

7   Rosen, *Called to Controversy: The Unlikely Story of Moishe Rosen and the Founding of Jews for Jews*, p. 190

8   Philpott, *Memoirs of a Jesus Freak*, p. 288: quoted from Ruth Tucker, linked to p. 290 n. 7.

9   Matthew 11:28.

10   Richard Harvey, *But I'm Jewish: A Jew for Jesus Tells His Story* (London: Jews for Jesus/Purple Pomegranate Productions, 1996), p. 20.

11   Harvey, *But I'm Jewish: A Jew for Jesus Tells His Story*, p. 46.

12   Harvey, *But I'm Jewish: A Jew for Jesus Tells His Story*, p. 27.

13   All Nations Christian College, near Ware in Hertfordshire.

14   Initially formed in the UK in 1809.

15   Rosen, *Called to Controversy: The Unlikely Story of Moishe Rosen and the Founding of Jews for Jews*, p. 250.

16   Rosen, *Called to Controversy: The Unlikely Story of Moishe Rosen and the Founding of Jews for Jews*, pp. 254-256.

17   Harvey, *But I'm Jewish: A Jew for Jesus Tells His Story*, pp. 41-42.

18   The four questions asked at the Passover *Seder* meal are as follows: 1. Why is *matzah* (unleavened bread) eaten? 2. Why is *maror* (bitter herbs) eaten? 3. Why is meat eaten that is exclusively roasted? 4. Why is the food dipped twice?

19   Cara Bentley, 'Jews for Jesus Respond to Church of England's Repentance of Antisemitism and Chief Rabbi's Comments about Evangelism', www.premier.org.News/UK (accessed on 23.11.19). Reproduced by kind, written permission of the editor, Sam Hailes.

20   Bodil Skjott, Dan Sered, 'Five Reasons You Don't Want to Evangelise to Jews – and Why You Should', www.lausanne.org (accessed on 26.4.23).

Reproduced by kind, written permission of the senior researcher, Richard Harvey.

21 Inspired by similar ventures launched in Los Angeles in 2019 and New York in 2021.

22 Name changed to protect privacy.

23 Powell, *Encyclopedia of Contemporary Christian Music*, p. 528.

24 Especially the teaching of Chuck Smith and Hal Lindsey.

25 Termed 'Messianic Synagogues' by some.

26 Eskridge, *God's Forever Family: The Jesus People Movement in America*, p. 263.

27 Bentley, 'Jews for Jesus respond to Church of England's Repentance of Antisemitism and Chief Rabbi's Comments about Evangelism', www. premier.org.News/UK (accessed on 23.11.19). Reproduced by kind, written permission of the editor, Sam Hailes.

28 See, for example, Matthew 10:6 & 15:24 and Romans 1:16.

29 A teaching referred to by some as 'Replacement Theology'; alternatively, by others, as 'Fulfilment Theology'.

21. The Church That Comes Together, Stays Together

1 Carol Owens, *Chasing Fireflies in the Twilight* (Newbury Park, CA: SMMI Publishing, 2021), p. 95.

2 Owens, *Chasing Fireflies in the Twilight*, p. 96.

3 Owens, *Chasing Fireflies in the Twilight*, p. 97.

4 Powell, *Encyclopedia of Contemporary Christian Music*, p. 663.

5 Owens, *Chasing Fireflies in the Twilight*, p. 109.

6 Powell, *Encyclopedia of Contemporary Christian Music*, p. 663.

7 Powell, *Encyclopedia of Contemporary Christian Music*, p. 664.

8 Peter Meadows, 'Come Together', *Buzz*, November 1973, p. 21.

9 Moir, *Missing Jewel: The Worship Movement That Impacted the Nations*, p. 46.

10 Owens, *Chasing Fireflies in the Twilight*, p. 134.

11 Moir, *Missing Jewel: The Worship Movement That Impacted the Nations*. p. 47.

12 Author interview with Nick Cuthbert by Skype on 21.1.20.

13 Ward, *Growing up Evangelical: Youthwork and the Making of a Subculture*, p. 99.

14 Peter Meadows, 'All Hugging and Hallelujahs', *Buzz*, August 1974, pp. 10-12.

15 Later, as a married solo artist, known as Jamie Owens-Collins.

16 Karen was initially famed for her 1971 song 'Seek Ye First'.

17 Powell, *Encyclopedia of Contemporary Christian Music*, p. 663.

18 Powell, *Encyclopedia of Contemporary Christian Music*, p. 663.

19 Author interview with Geoff Boland in person on 1.10.20.

20 Moir, *Missing Jewel: The Worship Movement That Impacted the Nations*, p. 46.

21 Owens, *Chasing Fireflies in the Twilight*, p. 122.

22 Ralph Turner, *Gerald Coates: Pioneer* (England: Malcolm Down Publishing, 2015), p. 79.

23 Moir, *Missing Jewel: The Worship Movement That Impacted the Nations*, p. 48.

24 Moir, *Missing Jewel: The Worship Movement That Impacted the Nations*, p. 51.

25 Author interview with Phil Lawson Johnston by email on 5.2.21.

26 Owens, *Chasing Fireflies in the Twilight*, p. 136.

22. You Can Trust Deo Gloria to Make Jesus Famous

1 The Great Depression began in the USA in 1929, and in the UK in 1930.

2 Richard Massey, *No Ordinary Trust: A History of the Deo Gloria Trust (To God Be the glory)*, (London: Deo Gloria Trust, 2015), p. 3.

3 Massey, *No Ordinary Trust: A History of the Deo Gloria Trust (To God Be the Glory)*, p. 3.

4 Massey, *No Ordinary Trust: A History of the Deo Gloria Trust (To God Be the Glory)*, p. 5.

5 Named 'Samson' and 'Micaiah' respectively by the Children of God.

6 Author interview with Chris Tozer by Facebook on 28.4.22.

7 Children of God – Chapter 13; Jesus Family – Chapter 16 and their rock-musical *Lonesome Stone* – Chapter 19; Greenbelt Festival – Chapter 25.

8 Formally called the Unification Church.

9 Deprogramming aimed to forcibly delete the impact of brainwashing.

10 Information Network Focus On Religious Movements. Cults subsequently became known as 'New Religious Movements' (NRMs), particularly in academic circles.

11 Author interview with Phil South by email on 8.6.20.

12 Author interview with Christine Lafon (née Ellerton) by email on 15.6.22.

13 MV *Logos* was run by Operation Mobilisation (OM).

14 Author interview with Peter Holmes by telephone on 14.5.20.

15 Author interview with Kent Philpott by email on 15.4.23.

16 The first occasion, a trip of six weeks' duration, is recounted in Philpott, *Memoirs of a Jesus Freak*, 2nd Edition, pp. 153-154.

17 Hoyt and Friends, *Stop! Hey, What's That Sound? The 1960's Revolution and Birth of the Jesus People*, p. 329.

18 Author interview with Mike Damrow by email on 22.2.22.

19 Author interview with Karin Bienge by Facebook on 18.5.20.

20 Author interview with Matt Spransy by Zoom on 20.7.22.

21 Author interview with Susan Wilson Carter by Facebook on 26.7.23.

22 Author interview with Sean Steinke by Facebook on 26.7.23.

23 Massey, *No Ordinary Trust: A History of the Deo Gloria Trust (To God Be the Glory)*, pp. 13-15.

24 Massey, *No Ordinary Trust: A History of the Deo Gloria Trust (To God Be the Glory)*, p. 19. The Bible verse quoted is Matthew 25:23.

25 Acts 16:11-40, especially v. 15 and v. 40 regarding Lydia's house.

23. When Jesus Says GO, Get Your Skates on Quickly

1 Revelation 19:9.

2 Eskridge, *God's Forever Family: The Jesus People Movement in America*, p. 120.

3 Bustraan, *The Jesus People Movement: A Story of Spiritual Revolution Among the Hippies*. p. 82.

4 Matthew 28:18-20.

5 See www.ywammendocino.org for 'The Story of the Lord's Land' under 'History' (accessed 21.7.23).

6 Author interview with Alex Elsaesser by email on 6.11.19.

7 Author interview with Harry Hewat by email on 18.11.19.

8 Marc S. Allan, *What Happened to You? Hippies, Gospel Outreach and the Jesus People Revival* (Enumclaw, WA: Redemption Press, 2016), p. 253.

9 Author interview with Brian Martin by email on 29.3.21.

10 Allan, *What Happened to You? Hippies, Gospel Outreach and the Jesus People Revival*, p. 254.

11 Editor, 'Special Report', *Radiance*, December 1984/January 1985, p. 18.

12 Author interview with Brian Martin by email on 29.3.21.

13 Editor, 'Special Report', *Radiance*, December 1984/January 1985, p. 18.

14 Author interview with Alex Elsaesser by email on 10.2.20.

15 For further details see their website: https://betel.uk/what-we-do/about-us/

24. The Tragedy of Calvary That Launches a Happy Chapel

1 Chris Walker, 'Packing them in with the Sound of the Gospel – as well as Pinball', *Telegraph & Argus*, 3 June 1974, p. 1.

2 Chuck Smith, Tal Brooke, *Harvest* (Eastbourne: Kingsway Publications, 1987), p. 31.

3 Smith, Brooke, *Harvest*, p. 39.

4 Girard, *Rock & Roll Preacher: From Doo-Wop to Jesus Rock*, p. 134.

5 According to the Smith's daughter Janette, as directly recalled by her and recorded in Chuck Girard, *Rock & Roll Preacher: From Doo-Wop to Jesus Rock*, p. 134.

6 *Jesus Revolution* was distributed by Lionsgate in the USA from 24 February 2023 onwards and in the UK from 23 June 2023 onwards.

7 Bustraan, *The Jesus People Movement: A Story of Spiritual Revolution Among the Hippies*, p. 84, n. 150.

8 Chuck Smith, Hugh Steven, *The Reproducers* (Ventura, CA: Gospel Light Publications, 1972), p. 97. www.calvarycca.org (accessed 22.6.23).

9 Smith, Brooke, *Harvest*, p. 49.

10 Pete Greig, *Dirty Glory* (London: Hodder & Stoughton, 2018), p. 192.

11 D. Martyn Lloyd-Jones, *Revival: Can We Make It Happen?* (Basingstoke: Marshall Pickering, 1986): This book features material from a preaching series in 1959 to celebrate the centenary of the 1859 revival.

12 Author interview with Brian Broderson by Zoom on 7.1.21.

13 Keith Gibbins, *Church on the Way: The First 25 years* (Leeds: Duffield Printers, 2003) p. 97.

14 Gibbins, *Church on the Way: The First 25 years*, p. 14.

15 Author interview with Richard Cimino by email on 21.12.20.

16 Author interview with Brian Broderson by Zoom on 7.1.21.

17 Author interview with Phil Vickery by Zoom on 12.1.21.

18 Tony Cummings, 'Creation Fest: Devon's Annual Festival', 21 April 2005. www.crossrhythms.co.uk (accessed on 25.11.20). Reproduced by kind, written permission of the CEO, Jonathan Bellamy.

19 Tony Cummings, 'Creation Fest: Cornwall's Free Festival, 10 years and Still Going Strong', 27 July 2012. www.crossrhythms.co.uk (accessed on 10.1.20). Reproduced by kind, written permission of the CEO, Jonathan Bellamy.

20 Tony Cummings, 'Creation Fest', 11 August 2006, www.crossrhythms.co.uk

(accessed on 10.1.20). Reproduced by kind, written permission of the CEO, Jonathan Bellamy.

21 Donald E. Miller, *Reinventing American Protestantism: Christianity in the New Millennium* (London: University of California Press, 1997).

22 Chuck Smith, *Charisma v Charismania* (Irvine, CA: Harvest House Publishers, 1983).

23 Author interview with Jim Hillier by email on 16.12.20.

24 Is verse-by-verse teaching the sole way the Bible should be communicated (as under Chuck Smith's previous leadership), or are there other legitimate methods?

25. Not Built on a Brown-field Site But on Greenbelt

1 Paul Northup, *Turning Thirty* (London: Greenbelt Festivals, 2004), p. 3.

2 Author interview with Steve Shaw by email on 28.5.20. Attachment: Eulogy to James Holloway, given by Steve Shaw at his Thanksgiving Service, following his death on 18 October 2019.

3 Author interview with Susan Carter (now Odie) by Facebook on 12.6.20. Sue eventually ended up living in the Jesus Family commune and being in the cast of *Lonesome Stone*.

4 Northup, *Turning Thirty*, p. 5.

5 Northup, *Turning Thirty*, p. 5.

6 Stewart Henderson, *Since the Beginning: Greenbelt* (Ipswich: Greenbelt Publications,1984), p. 1.

7 Henderson, *Since the Beginning: Greenbelt*, p. 8.

8 Moir, *Missing Jewel: The Worship Movement That Impacted the Nations*, p. 47.

9 Editor, Advert for Greenbelt, *Buzz*, August 1974, p. 22.

10 Peter Meadows, 'Greenbelt has a guaranteed audience', *Buzz*, August 1974, p. 8.

11 Steve Turner, 'New Mindless Christianity', *Buzz*, December 1973, pp. 18-19, 30.

12 Jasper, *Jesus and the Christian in a Pop Culture*, p. 139, summarising the perspective of Greenbelt coordinator Jonathan Cooke from *Strait* magazine.

13 Three hundred times until the finale in 1896.

14 Ward, *Growing Up Evangelical: Youthwork and the Making of a Subculture*, p. 100.

15 Richard P. B. Wallis, 'The Greenbelt Festival: A case study of communication and evangelical Christianity'. Dissertation for the degree of B.A. (Hons) Communication Studies at Sunderland Polytechnic in 1983. Website mislaid (accessed 21.5.20).

16 Martin Evans, 'James Holloway – the builder of Greenbelt's foundations', p. 2. www.greenbelt.org.uk (accessed 29.10.20). Reproduced by kind permission of stakeholder and commercial coordinator, Hannah Burns.

17 Hans Rookmaker, *Art Needs No Justification* (Vancouver, Canada: Regent College Publishing, 2010).

18 Moir, *Missing Jewel: The Worship Movement That Impacted the Nations*, p. 86.

19 Lindsay Tuffin, 'Greenbelt gets angry', *Buzz,* October 1978, pp. 4-7.

20 Progressive Christianity is a fairly recent development and is quite complex. To learn about its five core values, see www.progressivechristianity.org under the headings 'About', then 'The Core Values of Progressive Christianity'.

21 Ward, *Growing Up Evangelical: Youthwork and the Making of a Subculture*, p. 99.

22 Ward, *Growing Up Evangelical: Youthwork and the Making of a Subculture*, p. 102.

23 Editor, 'Guinness slams Greenbelt', *Buzz,* October 1986, p. 15.

24 Derek Walker, 'Greenbelt at 50', *Christianity,* August 2023, p. 51. Reproduced by kind, written permission of the editor, Sam Hailes.

26. A New Wineskin is Crafted in the Vineyard

1 Girard, *Rock & Roll Preacher: From Doo-Wop to Jesus Rock*, p. 228.

2 Jackson, *The Quest for the Radical Middle: A History of the Vineyard*, p. 82.

3 Lester Ruth, Lim Swee Hong, *A History of Contemporary Praise & Worship: Understanding the Ideas That Reshaped the Protestant Church* (Grand Rapids MI: Baker Academic, 2021), p. 104.

4 Carol Wimber, *John Wimber: The Way it Was* (London: Hodder and Stoughton, 1999), p. 145.

5 Wimber, *John Wimber: The Way it Was*, p. 156.

6 Church Growth was an approach to world mission that emphasised reaching people with the gospel in culturally appropriate ways. Its ideas were first outlined by Donald McGavran in his influential *The Bridges of God* volume in 1955, becoming more prevalent from the 1970s onwards.

7 Stephen Hunt, 'The Anglican Wimberites', *Pneuma*, Vol. 17, No. 1, Spring 1995, p. 107.

8 Pytches, *John Wimber: His Influence and Legacy*, p. 146.

9 The term 'Third Wave' was popularised by missiologist Peter Wagner: the first wave being the Pentecostal revival of the 1900s, the second wave being the charismatic renewal of the 1960s, the third being evangelical Christians vitally experiencing the Holy Spirit whilst retaining their denominational distinctives (ostensibly uniting, for example, Pentecostals and conservatives together).

10 Andrew Atherstone, 'John Wimber's European Impact', *Global Pentecostal and Charismatic Studies*, Vol. 41; p. 220.

11 Penny is John Wimber's sister.

12 Jackson, *The Quest for the Radical Middle: A History of the Vineyard*, p. 259.

13 Pytches, *John Wimber: His Influence and Legacy*, p. 88.

14 St Albans Vineyard, for example, planted eight churches, as far north as Thornaby, Stockton-on-Tees, south as Southampton, east as Canterbury, and west as Dunstable.

15 John Wimber's end-times approach was deeply influenced by George Eldon Ladd's eschatology, especially as taught in his influential book, *The Presence of the Future: The Eschatology of Biblical Realism* (London: SPCK, 1974), a revised and updated version of his previous *Jesus and the Kingdom* (New York: Harper & Row, 1964).

16 Pytches, *John Wimber: His Influence and Legacy*, p. 276.

17 Pytches, *John Wimber: His Influence and Legacy*, p. 318.

18 Pytches, *John Wimber: His Influence and Legacy*, p. 315.

19 John Wimber, *Power Evangelism: Signs and Wonders Today* (London: Hodder & Stoughton, 1985).

20 Pytches, *John Wimber: His Influence and Legacy*, p. 152.

21 Pytches, *John Wimber: His Influence and Legacy* pp. 265 and 267 respectively.

22 Clive Price, 'The Wonder of Wimber', *Christianity*, January 1998, p. 7. Regarding Terry Virgo see also Pytches, *John Wimber: His Influence and Legacy*, p. 242.

23 See www.biblesociety.org.uk under 'Resources'; and www.novouk.org. discovery-bible-study.

27. These Amplifiers Buzz with the Rhythms of the Cross

1 Derrick Phillips, *Pilgrims Rock! The True Story of the First Christian Rock Group* (England: Amazon, 2018).

2 Author interview with Geoff Shearn and Peter Meadows by Zoom on 9.8.21.

3 Peter Meadows, 'A Special Investigation: THE TRUTH ABOUT THE JESUS PEOPLE', *Buzz*, June 1972, p. 7.

4 Derek Walker, 'The Rise and Fall of Christian Music', *Christianity*, December 2019, pp. 48-53.

5 Editor, Feedback, Two letters under the heading, 'Missing History?', by Derrick Phillips and Pete Honour, *Christianity*, January 2020, pp. 6-7.

6 The two other albums released were *Saved* in 1980 and *Shot of Love* in 1981.

7 Kerry Cole, *Gotta Die to Live* (Plymouth: Rose and Gate Publishing, 2020), p. VI.

8 Cole, *Gotta Die to Live*, p. IX.

9 Cole, *Gotta Die to Live*, p. 50.

10 Cole, *Gotta Die to Live*, p. 125.

11 Cole, *Gotta Die to Live*, p. 133.

12 Cole, *Gotta Die to Live*, p. 169.

13 Regional Director for GOD TV from 2005-2010, and then a Trustee from 2015 to the present day.

28. Inhabiting the Big Story of God's Lasting Friendship

1 I fully realise this contention raises huge questions, such as the apparent harshness of God. In the Old Testament he seems to command genocide for the Canaanite nations (Deuteronomy 7; Joshua 10:28 etc.), and Ananias experienced instant death for his sin of lying (Acts 5:1-11) in the New Testament. My desire is not to trivialise such important questions, but there is not space in this chapter to address them properly. I do believe the ways of a just God are right (Genesis 18:25), despite my personal wrestling. Regarding the issue of genocide, for example, there are helpful books such as: Paul Copan, Matthew Flannagan, *Did God Really Command Genocide?* (Grand Rapids, MI: Baker Books, 2014).

2 By King Jehoshaphat (2 Chronicles 20:7); the prophet Isaiah (Isaiah 41:8); and church leader James (James 2:23).

3 Matthew 26:23; Luke 22:21; John 13:10-11.

29. Your Older Men and Women Will Dream Revival Dreams

1 Eugene H. Peterson, *A Long Obedience in the Same Direction* (Downers Grove, IL: Inter-Varsity Press, 2000).

2 Philippians 1:23.

3 James Goll, 'It's Time For a New Jesus People Movement to Emerge!', www.charismamag.com (accessed 28.10.19). Reproduced by kind, written permission of the author, James Goll.

4 James Goll, '20 Prophetic Points for 2020', www.godencounters.com (accessed 13.1.20). Reproduced by kind, written permission of the author, James Goll.

5 A Calvary Chapel musician, who also played with the bands Selah and Good News.

6 Author interview with Steve Backlund by email on 23.12.19.

7 Jason Mandryk, 'Beyond Asbury: 6 other places where revival is happening now', *Christianity*, 13 March 2023, www.premierchristianity.com (accessed 17.3.23). Reproduced by kind, written permission of the editor, Sam Hailes.

8 Girard, *Rock & Roll Preacher: From Doo-wop to Jesus Rock*, pp. 167-174.

9 Girard, *Rock & Roll Preacher: From Doo-Wop to Jesus Rock,* pp. 171-172.

10 Author interview with anonymous author by email on 21.1.20.

11 Now called 'City Church'.

12 Wayne Drain, 'Can a New Jesus Movement Rise From a Pandemic?', www.waynedrain.com (accessed 14/11/2022). Reproduced by kind, written permission of the author, Wayne Drain.

13 Hoyt and Friends, *Stop! Hey, What's That Sound? The 1960's Revolution and the Birth of the Jesus People* (Albuquerque, NM: Psalm Press, 2019).

14 Philpott, *Awakenings in America and the Jesus People Movement*, pp. 76-121.

15 Philpott, *Awakenings in America and the Jesus People Movement*, p. 121.

16 Author interviews with Kent Philpott by email on 28.10.22 and 9.11.22.

17 *Jesus Revolution* was distributed by Lionsgate in the USA from 24 February 2023 onwards and in the UK from 23 June 2023 onwards.

18 Laurie, Vaughn, *Jesus Revolution: How God Transformed an Unlikely Generation and How He Can Do It Again Today,* p. 112.

19 Laurie, Vaughn, *Jesus Revolution: How God Transformed an Unlikely Generation and How He Can Do It Again Today, p.* 226.

20 Laurie, Vaughn, *Jesus Revolution: How God Transformed an Unlikely Generation and How He Can Do It Again Today, p.* 244.

21 Laurie, Vaughn, *Jesus Revolution: How God Transformed an Unlikely Generation and How He Can Do It Again Today*, p. 250.

30. Your Younger Men and Women Will See Revival Visions

1 Alan Scott, 'The Water is Rising', www.youtube.com (accessed 5.2.23): preached at the Dwelling Place in Anaheim on 31.7.22 from Matthew 13:24-30, 36-43.

2 Jeannie Law, '60,000 Christians gather in Orlando, for "Jesus Movement" of this generation', www.christianpost.com (accessed 10.11.19). Reproduced by kind, written permission of the managing editor, Melissa Barnhart. The quotations following are taken from this article.

3 1 Corinthians 1:10-15 & 3:3-9. The apostle particularly focuses the attention of believers on God's role being primary in 3:7-8.

4 *Superspreader: The Rise of # LetUsWorship*. Directed by Josh Franer and released in the USA on 19 September 2022.

5 Jennifer Miskov, *Ignite Azusa: Positioning for a New Jesus Revolution* (Redding, CA: Silver to Gold, 2016).

6 *Jesus Revolution* was distributed by Lionsgate in the USA from 24 February 2023 onwards and in the UK from 23 June 2023 onwards.

7 Tim Wyatt, 'Gen Z's first revival? What really happened at Asbury University', *Christianity*, www.premierchristianity.com (accessed on 28.3.23). Reproduced by kind, written permission of the editor, Sam Hailes.

8 Tim Wyatt, 'Gen Z's first revival? What really happened at Asbury University', *Christianity*, www.premierchristianity.com (accessed on 28.3.23), p. 2. Reproduced by kind, written permission of the editor, Sam Hailes.

9 Tim Wyatt, 'Gen Z's first revival? What really happened at Asbury University', *Christianity*, www.premierchristianity.com (accessed on 28.3.23), p. 2. Reproduced by kind, written permission of the editor, Sam Hailes.

10 Author interview with Gerard Kelly by email on 11.7.23.

11 Andy Butcher, 'John Fischer: The pioneering Jesus Music singer-song-writer and CCM's dark horse', *Cross Rhythms*, www.crossrhythms.co.uk (accessed 16.12.22). Reproduced by kind, written permission of the CEO, Jonathan Bellamy.

12 John Fischer, Facebook post of 13.12.22. Reproduced by kind, written permission of the author, John Fischer.

31. The Holy Spirit Poured Out on Everyone in the Last Days

1 J. Edwin Orr, *The Second Evangelical Awakening in Britain* (London: Marshall, Morgan & Scott, 1953 Reprint), p. 57.

2 Sam Storms, '10 Things You Should Know About the Welsh Revival of 1904-06', www.samstorms.org (accessed 24.4.23). Reproduced by kind, written permission of the author, Sam Storms.

3 Stanley C. Griffin, *A Forgotten Revival* (Bromley: Day One Publications, 1992).

4 Griffin, *A Forgotten Revival*, p. 17.

5 Mark Stibbe, *Revival* (Crowborough: Monarch Books, 1998), p. 75.

6 Duncan Campbell, *God's Answer: Revival Sermons* (Edinburgh: The Faith Mission, 1960), pp. 72, 88-90.

7 R. T. Kendall, '8 Observations on the Hebrides Revival', *Christianity*, www.premierchristianity.com (accessed 16.12.22). Reproduced by kind, written permission of the editor, Sam Hailes.

8 Author interview with John Groves by email on 15.8.17, reproduced by kind permission of the author.

9 Hebrews 12:25-29 (quoting verse 28 here).

10 Ralph Turner, 'Revival in Leicester', www.mountain50.blogspot.com (accessed 5.2.23). Reproduced by kind, written permission of the author, Ralph Turner. All the following quotations are taken from his blogs.

11 Tragically, of course, Rachel died while giving birth to Benjamin: Genesis 35:16-18.

Acknowledgements

Early in life, I was encouraged to write 'Thank You' letters, a habit I have never shelved, so here goes…

Thanks, my Father-God, and the local hospital's 'Jigsaw' oncology team for restoring me to health through prayer and chemotherapy, to complete this legacy project.

I am grateful to my farming parents – legends of generosity – who taught me how to sow seeds, my dad sadly not seeing the fruit of this one. My amazing mum, however, happily did.

As for my wife Rosie, 'supportive' would be a British understatement; I just love doing life with you, my patient, ever-curious encourager. Our two lads Phil and Tom have regularly spurred me on, occasionally when the going was tough, for which I am extremely grateful.

Four scholars paved the way for me. Thanks to Larry Eskridge and Richard Bustraan in the USA, Kevin John Smith in Australia (d. 2019), and Pete Ward in the UK. Larry, you especially deserve a gold medal! I have also been inspired by my author-friends, Max Coates, Tony Goodman, Tony Horsfall, John Houghton, Dave Hoyt, Chris Mabey, Sam Storms and Ralph Turner.

My first interview, over a decade ago, was with Geoff Bone, who recently moved home to heaven. My gratitude goes to him and at least thirty subsequent interviewees mentioned in my Endnotes section, all of whom gave their time and energy so freely. You know who you are…

In terms of production, I want to honour my encouraging publisher Malcolm Down, creative director Sarah Grace, cover designer Esther Kotecha, eagle-eyed editor Lydia Jenkins, and patient proofreader Louise

Stenhouse for serving this venture so brilliantly. What a team. Tim Miller, you kindly served me in the computer arena at the eleventh-hour.

Two people particularly deserve huge credit. My younger son Tom for being alongside me as my insightful 'Associate Editor' for four months, and my long-term friend Debby Jones for proofreading so cheerfully.

I am blessed with good friends, and gladly express my profound thanks to the select squad of reviewers who took the time both to read the manuscript and endorse my book. You all encouraged me at a crucial stage in the journey.

Thanks to those from the Jesus Family days for strengthening my hand, especially Susan Cowper, Mike Damrow, Dave Hoyt and Carol Trott across the 'pond' and others here in the UK. A special mention goes to the 'Hardwick Gathering 2017' clan. Christian Beese was a one-year-old believer when he became my spiritual dad in 1973. Still a great friend today, I will never forget you and your family.

During the writing process, my church family at GodFirst Church in Christchurch, Dorset have strengthened my hand immensely. Special thanks to our enthusiastic leaders Duncan and Jo, Morné and Leanne, also to Josh (see Chapter 1) and Meghan, who Rosie and I happily coach.

Like the writer to the Hebrews, highlighting heroes of faith in chapter eleven and verse thirty-two, space dictates that I may have omitted someone, for which I send my heartfelt apologies.

Penultimately, I take final responsibility for *When Jesus Met Hippies*, and thank you, the reader, for buying this book, in the hope you are inspired by reading it. If you spot any factual errors, please do let me know through my website contact form, and I will attempt to eventually correct them.

As for my gracious rescuer, Jesus:

'Lord, to whom shall I go? You have the words of eternal life. I believe and know that you are the Holy One of God' (John 6:68-69, personalised).

Find Out More

To find out more about my speaking and writing ministry, please do visit my Jesus People Revival UK website.

It contains masses of fascinating visuals, a Jesus People timeline, presentations, articles, my personal backstory, potential touring plans and so on...

If you are a serious JPM researcher, there is also a sizeable Comprehensive Bibliography available. And for the less ambitious, there is a Selected Bibliography of a further twenty-two books to read.

Additionally, please contact me personally using the contact form on the site. I look forward to connecting with you!

Blessings,

Andrew

www.jesuspeoplerevivaluk.com